Informing Design

INFORMING
Design

Edited by

Joan Dickinson
Radford University

John P. Marsden
Mount Mercy College

Fairchild Books   New York

Executive Editor: Olga T. Kontzias
Acquisitions Editor: Joseph Miranda
Senior Development Editor: Jennifer Crane
Development Editor: Sylvia L. Weber
Associate Art Director: Erin Fitzsimmons
Production Director: Ginger Hillman
Production Editors: Andrew Fargnoli and Elizabeth Marotta
Copy Editor: Joanne Slike
Cover Design: Erin Fitzsimmons
Cover Art: © CNAC/MNAM/Dist. Rèunion des Musèes Nationaux/Art Resource
Text Design: Felice Tebbe

Library of Congress Catalog Card Number: 2007938029
ISBN: 978-1-56367-563-8
GST R 133004424
Printed in the United States of America

TP 09

Brief Contents

Extended Contents

Preface

Physicians don't prescribe penicillin because they
like the color pink. They prescribe it because it has
well-documented capabilities for fighting bacterial
infection. The understanding of how penicillin works,
and the effects it has under different conditions, comes
from pain-staking research. Why can practitioners still
be found prescribing architectural form, space plans,
furniture, colors, and materials based on their personal
preferences, rather than empirical data.
(Becker, 1999, p. 56)

Knowledge is the truth that has been obtained
from research.   (Kopec, 2006, p. 9)

For the past 10 years, we have been teaching a version of a design theory and research course in interior design and architecture programs at a variety of universities. These universities have ranged from teaching colleges where the focus has been on undergraduate education and teaching excellence to research institutions that emphasize the advanced degree and scholarship. Regardless of the university type, we have observed the lack of understanding regarding the term *research* at the undergraduate and graduate level. When students begin the design theory and research course, they are often confused and perplexed as to why they are enrolled in such a class.

This comes as no surprise, particularly since the design professions over the last few years have been bombarded with home and garden television (Waxman & Clemons, 2007). These television shows, which the majority of students watch, often portray interior design as a trade rather than a profession. And unfortunately, many of the solutions on the shows are based on a "flair" for design rather than a systematic process of inquiry.

The term *research* is also used incorrectly in secondary and higher education. Elementary, middle school, and high school teachers use "research" to describe anything from retrieving a book from the library to browsing on the Internet. Design professors in higher education often define research as a casual walk through a building, the creation of sketches, or any activity that involves information gathering. In a recent study, Wang (2003) critically assessed current architectural research by reviewing 253 papers from four Association of Collegiate Schools of Architecture (ACSA) conferences. He found that more than half of the published papers were subjective speculations that lacked robustness. Based on a study with 65 faculty members in interior design programs throughout the country, we found that nearly a third described research simply as information gathering (Marsden, Dickinson, & Anthony, 2007).

In addition, many practitioners are not aware of research that is produced by the academy, which is what the editors of this volume experienced in the industry. Joan Dickinson remembers designing a child care center while working at an interior design firm. Although the ideas were innovative and unique, at no time during the design process did the designers look to the body of knowledge in the area of design for children, child development, or theories of daycare centers or cared to inform their design decisions. In fact, the designers were not aware of the *Journal of Interior Design* or *Environment and Behavior* (only a few of the many journals available to the practicing designer). Joan did not become aware of these journals until she started her advanced degrees.

As suggested in the first epigraph of this preface, the designers at Joan's firm essentially specified color, texture, and three-dimensional form and space based on their preferences. This is unfortunate considering there are numerous research studies published in a variety of journals that could help inform the decision making of practicing designers.

Practitioners who are aware of research must also assess the validity of the information that is presented. When John Marsden was working on a retirement housing facility at an architecture firm, the designers reviewed the projects that were highlighted in trade journals and books or at conferences as award winning. Like most practitioners, they assumed that these projects were "best-practice" examples and applied lessons learned from award-winning designs to future projects. However, the evaluation process for award competitions, like design juries in architecture and interior design programs, is highly subjective and unpredictable (Anthony, 1991; Nasar, 1999). When John pursued an advanced degree, he began to review the numerous design guides that are also available for practitioners focusing on senior living. Yet these books of design guidance mostly consist of hypotheses grounded in the literature or the professional and personal experiences of expert scholars and practitioners. He began to realize that empirical research is often needed to validate or modify hypotheses to prevent ineffective ones from guiding standard practice (Marsden, 2005).

In this book, we are suggesting a pedagogy in which design decision making is informed by more than speculative hunches, preferences, and intuition. Hasell and King (in press) proposed that design decision making can be guided by different forms of knowledge that increase in validity and rigor. Building upon their work, we are proposing that design decision making can be informed by (a) gathering information from soft sources such as manufacturer product searches and reading best-practice design guidelines from books, the Internet, or trade magazines; (b) collecting data through programming, which may include the gathering of information as defined in (a) and the collection of information through tools such as questionnaires, focus groups, and interviews for a specific project; (c) applying published findings from empirical research studies in journal articles to design solutions; and (d) actually conducting a research investigation that yields findings that are applicable to the design problem at hand as well as other projects and can be disseminated to advance the field.

In both (a) and (c), the practitioner and student are consumers of information gathering and/or empirical research. Accordingly, they must be able to assess the credibility and quality of the information; distinguish between information that is based on empirical research, best practices, or opinion; and apply the findings of others. A vital step toward achieving that goal can occur in undergraduate education if students are provided with an introduction to the research process and are taught how to conduct literature reviews and incorporate credible findings into their work. In (b) and (d), the practitioner and student are either conductors of programming data collection or empirical research. A solid foundation in research methods is critical in both instances. It is important to note that as a student and/or practicing designer, you will not conduct empirical research every time you start a project. Research studies can take months or years to complete, while the fields of interior design and architecture are fast-paced and solutions must be generated quickly. This is why practitioners often collect data through programming for a specific project only.

This book consists of a collection of contributed chapters, with leaders in both design practice and education sharing their expert knowledge with a building type in the specialty areas. This book begins with two introductory chapters. In Chapter 1, we define the term *research*, discuss the research process, define programming, and explain the difference between research and programming. The purpose of this first chapter is to ensure that students understand that programming is systematic information gathering that is conducted extensively in interior design and architecture practice. Research is systematic discovery that is generalizable. Practitioners should read research studies as part of the programming process. Yet in order for practitioners to read published research, it is imperative that they understand what constitutes research. In Chapter 2, we discuss data collection methods and research terminology that is often seen in published journal articles so design students have the background information necessary to read published investigations and use findings to inform design or to conduct research that can also inform design. Chapters 4 through 10 each address one building type within the design specialty areas of corporate, retail, learning environments, hospitality, and healthcare, while Chapter 3 focuses on sustainability as an overall philosophy for approaching design. The authors provide general background information about a specialty area and more specific examples of how one building type in that specialty area was informed through a variety of sources in student work and/or design projects.

Chapters 3 through 10 are organized along a continuum of validity with beginning chapters providing examples of less rigorous forms of informed design. For example, Chapter 3 shows examples of student work that are mostly informed by soft sources or what are the least rigorous forms of knowledge. Chapters 4 and 5 illustrate examples of practitioner work that are informed through programming data collection methods specific to a project. Chapters 6, 7, and 8 demonstrate how students and practitioners can use empirical research studies to inform design. And Chapters 9 and 10 provide the most rigorous examples of informed design in which students conduct research advancing the body of knowledge. The final chapters are most closely associated with *evidence-based design*, a term that has permeated interior design and architecture, particularly in the healthcare realm. Evidence-based design stems from evidence-based medicine, which is dedicated to administering the best care to patients using conscientious, explicit, and judicious use of current evidence in making decisions (CEBM, 2007; Hamilton, 2004). Refer to Chapter 10 for a more detailed description of evidence-based design. Although later chapters illustrate increased authority in design decision making, this is not to suggest that earlier chapters are not of value. All of the chapters illustrate how students or practitioners used more than speculation, intuition, or hunches to inform their design decision making.

It is important to note that this book is not a textbook on research methods or programming. There are a number of other texts that cover research methods (e.g., Groat & Wang, 2002; Sommer & Sommer, 2002) and programming (e.g., Cherry, 1999) more comprehensively and in more detail. Nor is this a book that provides an overview of best-practice design guidelines for the specialty areas in design. Refer to Kopec (2006) for an overview of the specialty areas.

Research is not a new topic in the design fields, and in 1983, Chenoweth and Chidister identified the need for "research-based information to support landscape architecture" (p. 98). In 1992, Guerin and Fowles recognized the call for research studies that justified the profession and documented the effectiveness of interior design. In the mid-1990s, Dickson and White wrote a number of articles that examined how practicing designers did not value graduate education where research is the focus and did not use published research studies during the design process. And in 2007, a substantial portion of the *Journal of Interior Design* was devoted to where and how research should be incorporated into the interior design curriculum (see Guerin, Kroelinger, and Rabun). The discussion of research has not only permeated landscape architecture and interior design, but a number of architects have written opinion pieces stressing the need for research to inform design and have noted that designers have "largely ignored" empirical research (Fisher, 2004, p. 1; LaGro, 1999).

Nearly a decade into the millennium, designers are still confused about research and its value and use. Design decisions are complicated and if not completed correctly can have life-altering consequences. We have a responsibility to educate future generations that design is an applied art and science; and as an applied discipline, it imposes on us a responsibility to understand how people interact and behave in their surroundings. This understanding must come through an inquiry-led process that involves habitually reading current literature during the programming process so that design can be based on up-to-date research findings and other sources. We hope to provide students with the background necessary so they may become more fluent and comfortable with informed design.

BIBLIOGRAPHY

Anthony, K. (1991). *Design juries on trial: The renaissance of the design studio.* New York: Van Nostrand Reinhold.

Becker, F. (1999, Winter). Good medicine. *Perspective,* 56–62.

Centre for Evidence-Based Medicine (CEBM) (2007). Introduction to evidence-based medicine. *Centre for Evidence-Based Medicine.* Retrieved on September 16, 2007, from http://www.cebm.net

Chenoweth, R., & Chidister, M. (1983). Attitudes toward research in landscape architecture: A study of the discipline. *Landscape Journal, 2*(2), 98–113.

Cherry, E. (1999). *Programming for design.* New York: John Wiley & Sons.

Dickson, A. W., & White, A. C. (1993). Are we speaking the same language? Practitioners' perceptions of research and the state of the profession. *Journal of Interior Design, 19*(1), 3–10.

Fisher, T. (2004, Fall). Architects behaving badly: Ignoring environmental behavior research. *Harvard Design Magazine,* 1–3.

Fowles, D. L. (1992). Interior design education in the year 2000: A challenge to change. *Journal of Interior Design Education and Research, 17*(2), 17–24.

Groat, L., & Wang, D. (2002). *Architectural research methods.* New York: John Wiley & Sons.

Guerin, D. A. (1992). Issues facing interior design education in the twenty-first century. *Journal of Interior Design Education and Research, 17*(2), 9–16.

Guerin, D. A. (2007). Defining graduate education in interior design. *Journal of Interior Design, 33*(2), 11–14.

Hamilton, D. K. (2004). Four levels of evidence-based practice. *The American Institute of Architects.* Available from http://www.aia.org

Hasell, M. J., & King, J. (in press). Social dimensions of the interiors of tall buildings. In A. D. Seidel & T. Heath (Eds.). *Social effects on building environment.* London: Chapman and Hall.

Kopec, D. (2006). *Environmental psychology for design*. New York: Fairchild Books.

Kroelinger, M. D. (2007). Defining graduate education in interior design. *Journal of Interior Design, 33*(2), 15–17.

LaGro, J. A. (1999). Research capacity: A matter of semantics. *Landscape Journal, 18*(2), 51–58.

Marsden, J. P. (2005). *Humanistic design of assisted living*. Baltimore: The Johns Hopkins University Press.

Marsden, J. P., Dickinson, J. I., & Anthony, L. (2007). Empirical design research: Faculty definitions, perceptions and values. *Proceedings of the 44th Annual International Conference of the Interior Design Educators Council (IDEC),* 233–240, Austin, TX.

Nasar, J. L. (1999). *Design by competition: Making design competitions work*. New York: Cambridge University Press.

Rabun, J. H. (2007). Defining graduate education in interior design. *Journal of Interior Design, 33*(2), 19–21.

Sommer, R., & Sommer, B. (2002). *A practical guide to behavioral research*. New York: Oxford University Press.

Wang, D. (2003). Categories of ACSA conference papers: A critical evaluation of architectural research in light of social science methodological frameworks. *Journal of Architectural Education, 56*(4), 50–56.

Waxman, L. K., & Clemmons, S. (2007). Student perceptions: Debunking television's portrayal of interior design. *Journal of Interior Design, 32*(2), v–xi.

Acknowledgments

A project of this magnitude could never have been accomplished without the help of several people. We especially thank the authors who contributed to the individual chapters. Without their expertise, this book could not have been published. We are also indebted to the staff at Fairchild Books for the dedication and encouragement they exhibited to make this book a reality. Specifically, Joe Miranda and Olga Kontzias expressed initial interest in the conceptual plan for the book, and Sylvia Weber provided outstanding editing revisions and kept us on track during the entire process. A special thanks to those three for their support and enthusiasm for this project. We would also like to acknowledge and thank the reviewers selected by Fairchild Books: Theodore J. Drab, Oklahoma State University; Denise A. Guerin, University of Minnesota; Migette Kaup, Kansas State University; Bridget May, Marymount University; Margaret Portillo, University of Florida; and Allison Carll White, University of Kentucky. The reviewers gave useful feedback and insight on the content and organization of the book. Their help was invaluable and the final book is due to their commitment to the profession.

Individually, we would like to thank each other. John's previous experiences in writing books were invaluable to Joan as a first-time author of a book manuscript. His editing advice and research knowledge provided helpful input during the writing process. John considers Joan a wonderful collaborator. They have conducted studies and taught together, copresented papers at conferences, copublished articles and have now coedited a book. Joan took the lead with this manuscript and her work ethic, openness to ideas, and dedication to building a body of knowledge for the design professions are greatly appreciated.

Last, our gratitude goes to our parents and individual families—Dave, Maddie, and Sam for Joan and Margaret and Will for John—who endured the amount of time we spent working with chapter authors, writing, editing, and assembling the manuscript. Their support and patience are greatly appreciated.

Informing Design

1   What Is Research and What Is Programming?
Understanding the Difference

Joan Dickinson and John P. Marsden

> Designers and planners must become more attached to
> the tradition of scholarship and learning. We cannot solve the
> problems that face us by employing raw creative genius with
> the hope of producing innovations.   (Rodiek, 1995, p. 5)

Abstract

In this chapter, we discuss and define research and describe why the research process is important to the interior design and architecture professions. In particular, we spend time discussing how research differs from information gathering. We also define design programming and explain how the programming process benefits the design profession as well. In the last part of the chapter, we examine both the similarities and differences between research and programming.

Introduction

There is a tension between the terms *research* and *design* within the interior design and architecture professions. Design is viewed as expressive, free, energetic, imaginative, and creative, which is certainly what we strive for in the studio environment. In fact, we have even heard the term *glamorous* used to describe the design professions. When the term *research* is mentioned, yawns can be observed throughout the audience. Research is seen as dry, boring, and regimented (Dickson & White, 1993). Groat and Wang (2002), in their interview with an undergraduate architectural student, suggest that design is "off the page" from facts (p. 99), while research is often seen as a fact-based activity. In the minds of students, a connection between research and design is hard to discern. Yet the link between the two is critical:

- Research demands accurate observation and description (Sommer & Sommer, 2002; Touliatos & Compton, 1988). So does design.
- Research involves gathering, analyzing, and interpreting data (Leedy & Ormrod, 2005; Touliatos & Compton, 1988). So does design.
- Research informs decisions and problem solving and expands knowledge (Groat & Wang, 2002; Sommer & Sommer, 2002; Touliatos & Compton, 1988), which is needed in design (Becker, 1999; Guerin & Thompson, 2004; LaGro, 1999).
- Research helps solve problems (Zeisel, 1981; Zeisel, 2006). So does design.
- Research is discovery (Becker, 1999; Boyer, 1990; Dickinson, Marsden, & Read, 2007; Groat & Wang, 2002; Guerin & Thompson, 2004). Design can also be discovery when it moves the field forward.

What Is Research?

Often there is confusion over the true definition of research, and the term seems to be overused (LaGro, 1999; Marsden, 2005). To illustrate, when students are collecting information from soft sources (e.g., trade magazines or the Internet), we have found ourselves calling this research

(LaGro, 1999). Although collecting information is *a part* of the research process, it does not encompass the entire meaning of research (Dickson & White, 1993; Fraenkel & Wallen, 1996; Fraenkel & Wallen, 2006; LaGro, 1999; Leedy & Ormond, 2005). Let's look at some definitions:

- "Research is careful inquiry or examination to *discover* new information or relationships and to expand and to verify existing knowledge" (Rummel, 1964, p. 2).
- "Research is defined as a systematic way of asking questions, or a careful inquiry or examination to *discover* new information or relationships and to expand and to verify existing knowledge" (Touliatos & Compton, 1988, p. 7).
- "Research is a careful, systematic, patient study and investigation in some field of knowledge, undertaken to *discover* or establish facts or principles" (Fraenkel & Wallen, 1996, p. 9; Fraenkel & Wallen, 2006; Guralnik, 1978, p. 1208).
- "Research is careful, patient, and methodical inquiry done according to certain rules" (Sommer & Sommer, 2002, p. 1).
- "Research is systematic inquiry directed toward the *creation* of knowledge" (Groat & Wang, 2002, p. 7).
- "Research is a systematic process of collecting, analyzing, and interpreting information (data) in order to . . . communicate what we *discover* to the larger scientific community" (Leedy & Ormrod, 2005, p. 2).
- "Research, according to researchers, is a systematic *discovery* of knowledge or a systematic inquiry" (Guerin & Dohr, 2007, p. 4).
- "Research . . . can be described as the generation of new knowledge which has application for a wide general domain" (Wang, 2007, p. 34).

First, it is important to note that the definitions cited here range from 1964 to 2007 and have not changed over the course of 40 years. Second, the definitions are written from different fields of knowledge. For example, Robert Sommer (2002) is a well-known educator in the field of psychology. Fraenkel and Wallen (1996; 2006) write from an educational perspective. Touliatos and Compton's book *Research Methods in Human Ecology* caters to the field of human sciences and home economics (1988), while Groat and Wang (2002) are both educators in architecture, and Guerin and Dohr (2007) are interior design educators. Despite these differing backgrounds, the definitions have much in common, including the following:

- Research demands accurate observation and description. Researchers can utilize quantitative and numerical measuring devices or qualitative descriptions and/or observations. Regardless, the most accurate method of observing a particular problem is employed (Touliatos & Compton, 1988).
- Research involves the quest to answer unsolved problems (Guerin & Dohr, 2007; Leedy & Ormrod, 2005). The goal of research ultimately is to advance the field or profession and to contribute to the body of knowledge. The objective is to discover new information, or to verify existing information, or to assimilate information in new ways that extend or expand knowledge in a field, even if this creation of knowledge occurs in small increments (Groat & Wang, 2002; Guerin & Thompson, 2004; Marsden, 2005; Touliatos & Compton, 1988). This part of the definition is critical and is a key characteristic (Boyer, 1990) that separates research from information gathering and design programming.
- Research is replicable. Thus, research must be carefully recorded and reported (Touliatos & Compton, 1988).
- Research involves defining a problem (Zeisel, 1981; Zeisel, 2006). Defining this problem usually occurs by reviewing the literature in the particular area of study. This enables the

researcher to fully understand what has already been investigated pertaining to the problem of interest (Leedy & Ormrod, 2005; Touliatos & Compton, 1988).

- Research involves the systematic collection and analysis of data and dissemination of information (Leedy & Ormrod, 2005; Touliatos & Compton, 1988).

Research and Information Gathering

Research is not just information gathering (Dickinson et al., 2007; Dickson & White, 1993; LaGro, 1999; Leedy & Ormrod, 2005; Marsden, 2005). To illustrate, Joan's daughter came home from school and had to complete a project on the Greek and Roman gods. She spent the next few days searching for facts from the library and the Internet. Even though her teacher sent the students to the library to do "research," this was not the end result. Joan's daughter was essentially involved in information gathering (Leedy & Ormrod, 2005). She found information pertaining to the Greek and Roman gods and was able to use this information for her project. She certainly became more knowledgeable on the subject matter, but she did not participate in conducting the full process of research. Remember, a key part of the definition of research is to expand the body of knowledge or discovery that moves a field forward (Boyer, 1990). Did Joan's daughter's information gathering meet this part of the definition? Although Joan's daughter may have learned new facts on the subject matter, she did not move forward the study of Roman and Greek gods.

This is an important distinction. Often in the design studio, we tell our students that we will be participating in the "research phase of design" when students are expected to collect information on a particular client or product. We should call it what it is: information gathering. To illustrate, consider designing a space for children.

Without a doubt, you would want facts and data on behaviors of children, sizes appropriate for children, developmental information, and products geared toward children. You would again be involved in information collection or gathering. Information gathering is an important prerequisite to research and an important part of the design process that supports informed design. But on its own, information gathering does not build a profession, and to suggest that information gathering is research is to give research too narrow a definition (LaGro, 1999).

Research is not just fact compilation (Leedy & Ormrod, 2005). Imagine you were required to write a "research" paper on a particular designer or architect, such as Frank Lloyd Wright. As part of writing this paper, you would be involved in collecting data and assembling these data into a cohesive and organized written document. Indeed, you have participated in some of the research process: You may have collected data from various sources such as books, the Internet, journal articles, and magazines articles. You spent time analyzing and organizing these data. But you essentially repeated and regurgitated what had already been written about Frank Lloyd Wright, and more than likely the "research" paper did not require discovery of new information, which is a hallmark of the research process (Kinkead, 2003). This is not to suggest that this type of paper is not beneficial to the student. Rather, the point is that we are still found at the university calling this a "research" paper when the student has essentially participated in fact assembly or more involved information gathering. Unfortunately, the term *research* is still loosely used in the design profession and is employed to describe a search on the Internet, a walk-through of a building, a search for products, or frankly any activity that involves information gathering (LaGro, 1999; Marsden, 2005). According to Boyer (1990), "the scholarship of discovery is the closest to what is meant when academics speak of research" (p. 17), and "discovery of new knowledge is absolutely crucial" (p. 18). More importantly, the growing trend in the profession, particularly in healthcare, is for design solutions to be informed by research, thus the term *evidence-based design* (Hamilton, 2004; Roth, 1999). In order to better understand research, in the next section we define the research process using the example of a pilot study of three interior design programs.

The Research Process

The research process requires four steps: definition of the problem and reading of the literature, data collection, data analysis, and interpretation and implications.

Definition of the Problem and Reading of the Literature

The first part of the research process involves defining the problem (Leedy & Ormrod, 2005; Zeisel, 1981; Zeisel, 2006). Let's look at an example. For the past few years, we have been teaching a design theory and research course to juniors and seniors in an interior design program. In teaching this class, we have observed that undergraduate interior design students are often confused about the definition of research. As we previously discussed, most students think of research as finding information on a specific topic through books, the Internet, or articles (Dickinson et al., 2007). We found through reading the literature that interior design practitioners are also confused about research and, like students, think of research as information gathering (Dickson & White, 1993). This is problematic because many practitioners base design decisions solely on personal preference and/or past experience without utilizing research findings to support and defend their design solutions (Becker, 1999; Fisher, 2004; Guerin & Thompson, 2004; Hamilton, 2004). Why is this happening? Are current practitioners not learning the value of research during their undergraduate education? Clearly a problem exists. The question becomes, what do interior design undergraduate students know about research?

Reading the literature, gathering information, and observing led us to a real design problem that could be researched and gave us precedent. Reading the literature and observing allowed us to define a research problem and also allowed us to determine what research had already been completed on the subject matter. This is often the first step in the research process: defining the problem (Zeisel, 1981; Zeisel, 2006). We continued to read the literature and further refined our problem or research purpose: to examine interior design undergraduate student attitudes, perceptions, definitions, and values toward research. (See Dickinson et al., 2007, for a thorough description of this research study.)

Data Collection

The next step in the research process is data collection (Leedy & Ormrod, 2005). Data can be collected in a number of ways (e.g., observations, mapping, questionnaires, interviews, and archival research), and we will provide an overview of data collection methods in Chapter 2. For this particular study, we opted to use a questionnaire to collect data. Keeping in mind the purpose of our study, we developed a questionnaire that consisted of both open-ended and closed-ended questions (Table 1.1). It is important to note that our questionnaire was reviewed by several outside readers in order to increase the reliability and accuracy of the instrument. Remember that research demands accurate observation and description and careful, systematic inquiry (Groat & Wang, 2002; Sommer & Sommer, 2002; Touliatos & Compton, 1988).

The questionnaire was administered to third- and fourth-year students in three different interior design programs. Each interior design

Table 1.1. Survey Instrument: Sample Questions

Type of Question	Examples
One open-ended question (remember that the purpose of our study was to determine how students define research)	1. In the space below, please define the term "research."
Closed-ended questions based on a Likert Scale where 1= Strongly Agree; 2 = Agree; 3 = Unsure; 4 = Disagree; and 5 = Strongly Disagree Questions 1 through 11 examine students' value of research in interior design practice, which relates back to the purpose of our study.	1. I believe that research findings can provide useful information to interior design practitioners. 2. The results of research **are used** extensively in interior design practice. 3. The results of research **should be used** extensively in interior design practice. 4. In my opinion, the results of research are of little help in solving design problems in interior design practice. 5. I think the research findings published in the *Journal of Interior Design* are relevant to interior design practice. 6. An interior designer's ability to **understand** research is a big help in gaining employment in private practice. 7. An interior designer's ability to **conduct** research is a big help in gaining employment in private practice. 8. Research related to interior design should be conducted primarily by interior design practitioners. 9. Research related to interior design should be conducted primarily by interior design educators. 10. Research related to interior design should be conducted primarily by specialists in other fields. 11. When I graduate from undergraduate school, it is doubtful I will ever do research in interior design practice.
Questions 12 through 21 examine the importance of research during the undergraduate experience. Again, closed-ended questions were used for this part of the questionnaire.	12. The research studies I have read for my interior design studio projects have provided me with useful information. 13. The research studies I have read for my interior design studio projects have been easy to understand. 14. The research studies I have read for my interior design studio projects have been easy to find. 15. I think research information is very useful for justifying design solutions. 16. I think interior design **undergraduate** students should know how to use research results in design studio projects. 17. I think a course should be taught to interior design **undergraduate** students on how to evaluate the research findings of others. 18. I think a course should be taught to interior design **undergraduate** students on how to conduct research about an interior design issue. 19. I think interior design **graduate** students should know how to use research results in design studio projects. 20. I think a course should be taught to interior design **graduate** students on how to evaluate the research findings of others. 21. I think a course should be taught to interior design **graduate** students on how to conduct research about an interior design issue.

Table 1.1. Survey Instrument: Sample Questions (*continued*)

Type of Question	Examples
The last part of the questionnaire consisted of additional questions on the definition of research. Closed-ended questions were used.	22. Research is gathering factual data that pertain to design problems about different building types and users for the purpose of solving an interior problem.
	23. Research is studying trends.
	24. Research is studying technology.
	25. Research is reading books or articles about famous designers and their built works.
	26. Research is looking at images of interior design projects in trade magazines or on the Internet in order to generate ideas for design projects.
	27. Research is investigating alternative solutions to design problems during the design process.
	28. Research is evaluating the success of a building after occupancy.
	29. Research is advancing or creating new knowledge about interior design.

program was housed in a university that had a strong tradition of research. Two programs were in a College of Human Sciences/Resources, and the last program was located in an architecturally based school. This provided us with a well-balanced differentiation of programs for comparison. The students completed the questionnaire during class time. In looking back to our definitions of research, we see that Leedy & Ormond define it as "a systematic process of collecting . . . data." This essentially means the process is organized and logical and consists of certain steps or a plan (Groat & Wang, 2002; Leedy & Ormrod, 2005; Sommer & Sommer, 2002). Thus far our steps have included defining the problem and stating the purpose of our research study, conducting a literature review, examining data collection methods and determining the best approach for our study, generating a data collection instrument that is consistent with the purpose of our study, and having external review of the instrument to ensure accuracy and collecting data in a consistent, planned manner (for a detailed description of the sampling technique, statistical outcomes, and findings, please see Dickinson et al., 2007).

Data Analysis

Once the data were collected, we analyzed the results. Interestingly enough, we found that although the undergraduate students from the three programs valued research as part of the design process (e.g., when asked, "I believe that research findings can provide useful information to interior design practitioners," 73 percent [n = 65] of the students from the three universities strongly agreed), they did not have an understanding of the true meaning of research. Students view research as gathering existing knowledge, demonstrating that the link between research and discovery is missing from these three programs. We also discovered that the students are not "good consumers of research" (Guerin & Thompson, 2004; Hasell & Scott, 1996). Their open-ended definitions reveal an overreliance on soft sources of information such as the Internet, magazines, and books. Furthermore, the majority of students expressed difficulty in finding relevant research studies for their studio projects. Then, we learned that many of the students expressed reluctance in taking coursework pertaining to research. This result reinforces the studio and design emphasis often experienced in interior design programs (Burnett, 2004; CIDA Accreditation Manual, 2008). Last, the majority of the students from the three universities did not believe that interior design educators should be conducting research, (e.g., when asked, "Research related to Interior Design should be conducted primarily by Interior Design educators," 42 students disagreed, 20 students agreed, and 18 students were unsure), which illustrates that students do not understand the role of a faculty member as part of a research university (Dickinson et al., 2007).

Interpretation and Implications

Remember that a key component of research involves *discovery and expanding the body of knowledge*. From the findings above, interior design educators learned that undergraduate students do not have a clear understanding of research. These results are important and lead to discovery that will help interior design undergraduate programs. As a field, if we want to bridge the gap between education and practice, the results from this study suggest that it is imperative that undergraduates are exposed to the research process. By providing undergraduate students with an awareness and understanding of research, educators have the power to change how the profession as a whole views the link between research and design. Although it is not possible to draw definitive conclusions based on the sample size, this one small study expands knowledge in the field of interior design education and suggests that starting from the freshman year, the interior design curriculum needs to encompass experiences that illustrate to students the value research brings to the profession. The knowledge is relevant to interior design educators and was disseminated through a peer-reviewed journal article.

Based on the definitions and example provided above, it should be clear that research is much more than the retrieval of information. This is certainly a part of the research process. But the key to research is the expansion of existing knowledge (i.e., discovering new information) or verifying existing information (Boyer, 1990).

What Is Programming?

Programming is one of the first steps in the design process, and it is often referred to as the "information gathering phase" of design (Ballast, 2006; Duerk, 1993). In fact, the best way to distinguish programming from research is as follows: *research* is the systematic pursuit of new knowledge, while programming is the systematic search for information (Pena, Parshall, & Kelly, 1987). Although programming includes components of the research process, programming does not complete the entire cycle of research. Programming involves gathering, organizing, and interpreting information that is relevant to the project (Ballast, 1993; Ballast, 2006; Duerk, 1993). Information may be gathered from soft sources such as manufacturer product searches and best-practice guidelines from books, the Internet, and trade magazines, or with tools such as questionnaires, interviews, and observations, which yield information about a specific project. This gathering of information is then summarized in a bound document termed a *program* (White, 1972). The idea is that before you can design a project, you must take the time to understand client needs and how the client functions in the space (Cherry, 1999; Eakins, 2005; Kopec, 2006).

Good programming is a must. Suppose we asked you to take out some tracing paper and design a prototypical memory care unit. Could you do this? More than likely you would have great difficulty. First, you may not be aware of what a memory care unit is. Thus, you would have trouble determining the space requirements, adjacency needs, equipment or furnishing necessities, or functional issues. If you were able to produce some type of design, more than likely the client would require numerous changes because of your lack of understanding of basic requirements for a memory care unit.

Interior designers and architects design for people who are different from us all the time. In this example, you are designing for individuals who have dementia. You could design for children, the seriously ill, older adults, people with different cultural backgrounds, the physically or mentally disabled, or people from a different socioeconomic status. Before we put the pencil to the paper, however, we take the time to understand our clients (Ballast, 2006; Cherry, 1999; Eakins, 2005). Therefore, before you would ever design a memory care unit you would do the following:

1. *Learn about dementia.* You would spend quite a bit of time reading about the symptoms of dementia and might observe individuals who have some form of dementia. You would understand the behavioral problems that are often associated with cognitive declines that are indicative of dementia-related illnesses.

2. *Understand the functional requirements for this type of facility.* What types of spaces, equipment, furnishings, finishes, and staff are required in this facility? What are the staff responsibilities? Through this analysis, you would learn that a memory care unit is a separate entity in a nursing home or assisted living facility that is designed for individuals who are diagnosed with some form of dementia such as Alzheimer's disease. These are individuals who essentially suffer from progressive cognitive declines.

3. *Understand safety issues.* What building and fire codes apply to this type of facility? Are there other code requirements (e.g., if the facility is Medicaid certified, then you would have to become intimately familiar with the code requirements issued by the state Department of Public Health for the state where the facility was located)? Do resident symptoms lead to safety problems?

4. *Learn the adjacency requirements* (Cherry, 1999). What spaces need to be next to one another? What staff needs to be adjacent to certain areas? How is communication handled in the facility?

5. *Complete a site evaluation* (Cherry, 1999). Is the project new construction or the renovation of an existing building? You would spend time understanding building constraints or opportunities such as site context and characteristics, views, and topography (Cherry, 1999).

This is just a partial list, but it clearly illustrates the importance of gathering information prior to designing a space: thus, programming. Designing a space that is just aesthetically pleasing is not enough. The facility must also function for the users of the space, and designers must consider how the interior environment influences people (Kopec, 2006; Sommer, 1969).

Definitions of Programming

The literature includes numerous definitions of *programming*. Here are a few examples:

- Programming is a written, organized document that provides background information that is relevant to the specific project (White, 1972).
- Programming is determining, examining, and analyzing the problems, while design is solving or synthesizing the problem. Programming is problem seeking and defines the problem. Design is problem solving (Pena et al., 1987). *Analysis* and *synthesis* are two terms often heard when describing programming and design. *Analysis* implies dissecting, taking apart, and identifying problems or programming, while *synthesis* implies putting back together or generating design solutions that consider all parts in a new whole or design (Cherry, 1999).
- "Programming is the gathering, organizing, analyzing, interpreting, and presenting of information that is relevant to a design project" (Duerk, 1993, p. 9).
- Programming identifies the needs and values of the client for the project and is a "plan of action for defining and achieving desired results and goals" for a project (Scott-Webber, 1998, p. 2). Thus, programming not only determines the existing state or restraints for a design project (i.e., building codes, site analysis, client needs), it also evaluates the future goals for the design project (Duerk, 1993).
- "Programming is the . . . decision-making process that defines the problem to be solved by design" (Cherry, 1999, p. 3).
- "Programming is an intensive and comprehensive study of the client's needs. Programming is intended to generate requirements a design will meet" (Eakins, 2005, p. 63).

Benefits and Importance of Programming

As artists, we are under social pressure to be creative. As scientists, we are also under pressure to be creative, but in a more disciplined, organized way (Pena et al., 1987). Thus, the quality of the programming document has everything to do with the quality of the designed space (Sanoff, 1977). The idea is that every design solution is based on the information that is compiled, organized, and analyzed in the programming document. Two quotations come to mind: Winston Churchill said, "We shape our buildings, and afterwards our buildings shape us"; and George Nelson said, "Study life not just design." Both of these quotations illustrate the importance of the programming process: understand whom it is you are designing for and understand explicitly their requirements, behaviors, and functional needs. Programming has numerous benefits:

- Avoiding preconceived ideas (Ballast, 1993; Ballast, 2006). Programming allows the designer to base decisions on facts rather than opinion, assumptions, or experience. To illustrate, many nursing homes or assisted living facilities are designed with a "pale" color scheme of peach, sea-foam green, and baby blue. Why has this color scheme been chosen? Perhaps this is based on the preconceived idea that this color scheme is desirable to older individuals and their families. In fact, designers who know about age-related changes to the eye, would never specify a scheme lacking in color contrast for the older individuals who occupy these facilities. Because the lens of the eye yellows with age, an older individual would have an incredibly difficult time distinguishing between the baby blue and sea-foam green. Programming would allow the designer to be familiar with normal aging along with comprehending the population who typically live in a nursing home and what ailments they might suffer from.

Figure 1.1. Overall view of Pruitt-Igoe designed by Minoru Yamaski.

- Allowing the designer to understand client values and goals (Ballast, 1993; Ballast, 2006; Duerk, 1993), which increases client involvement from the start of the project (Cherry, 1999). The interior designer may know more about "design," but clients know more about their functional requirements, goals, and values.

- Encouraging accuracy and creativity in design solutions (Ballast, 1993; Ballast, 2006; Cherry, 1999). A good programming document essentially describes how the space should perform based on client needs. This allows the designer to generate solutions based on the performance criteria (Cherry, 1999).

- Increasing the marketability of the design firm (Duerk, 1993).

Why Programming Is a Must: A Classic Example

Pruitt-Igoe was a public housing facility that was designed and built in the 1960s in St. Louis by Minoru Yamasaki (Newman, 1997; The Origins of Architectural Research, 2005). The facility was 11 stories high and consisted of approximately 3,000 units that primarily appealed to single-parent families on welfare (Figure 1.1).

Figure 1.2. Conceptual sketch of the communal areas.

Figure 1.3. Exterior.

Pruitt-Igoe was designed by one of the United States eminent architects and was hailed as a wonderful example of modernism. The building won a design award from the American Institute of Architects. The architect's concept consisted of creating common areas on the first floor and every third floor. Communal corridors, laundry facilities, and storage areas were designed to foster a sense of community among the residents (Newman, 1997; The Origins of Architectural Research, 2005). See Figure 1.2.

Figure 1.4. Demolished Pruitt-Igoe.

Was the building a success? Less than 20 years later, the building was demolished. The common grounds and communal areas became unsafe. They were covered with garbage and were vandalized. Women were afraid to do their laundry and were afraid to use the public stairwells (Newman, 1996). See Figures 1.3 and 1.4.

Yet the individual apartments were very well kept. The residents of this high-rise housing community would only maintain and identify with areas that were demarcated as their own (Newman, 1997). Pruitt-

Igoe is a classic example of a building that was highly valued by the architect's peers, but the people who lived in this facility were miserable. The design ultimately was a disaster, as witnessed by its short life span. What went wrong? The architect did not completely understand whom he was designing for. This was a public housing facility; thus, there was no sense of ownership in the public or communal areas. There was no hired staff to care for the public grounds, which led to vandalism (Newman, 1996; Newman, 1997). Design programming would have allowed the architect to spend time with single-family parents on welfare to determine their needs and values. The following quotations help to clarify.

> The resulting building may even be regarded as architecture by the architect's own peers or the popular press if the architect's own values are strong enough to instill a meaningful order on the resulting design, but it will not be architecture in the eyes of those whose values have been misrepresented (Author Unknown).

> Those of us who are concerned with buildings tend to forget too easily that the life and soul of a place depend not simply on the physical environment but on the pattern of events which we experience there (Alexander, 1979).

> [E]nvironmental behavior research shows an architectural discipline that has been overeager to impose its aesthetic ideologies and utopian visions on others, particularly the most vulnerable among us (Fisher, 2004, p.2).

As designers, we should never forget that interior space is used by people who have aspirations, goals, and values that are critical to the success of the environment (Cherry, 1999). As Cherry and Sommer ask, "Whose values were being expressed?" (1999, p. 7; 1969).

More importantly, Pruitt-Igoe could have benefited from research in the area of low-income housing. To illustrate, Oscar Newman developed the concept of defensible space over 30 years ago (Newman, 1996). Newman recognized that the size of public housing was positively correlated with crime rate. In other words, larger public housing complexes with no sense of identity or control had higher levels of crime, while smaller units with clearly demarcated areas and a sense of ownership had lower rates of crime. Since programming involves systematic information gathering, part of this should include thoroughly understanding the literature and research on the area of interest. If the field of design had been more informed about the user group and research on low-income housing, perhaps the disastrous effects of Pruitt-Igoe would not have occurred.

Research versus Programming

So, how do research and programming differ, and how are they the same? Table 1.2 provides a comparison between the two.

Programming and research have some similarities. The programming process allows the designer to better understand the client prior to designing. Thus, the designer may rely on published research studies while programming, and this information may become part of the programming document (i.e., the background section). But unless the programming document moves the field of interior design forward, it cannot be considered "research" (see Table 1.2). Another difference is that research can be generalized to the larger public, while programming is site specific (Guerin & Dohr, 2007; Guerin & Thompson, 2004). If you were programming for a child care center, more than likely the programming document would be written for a specific facility such as Rainbow Riders located in Blacksburg, Virginia. Essentially, programming would document client problems and needs explicit to Rainbow Riders. Another child care facility could not use the Rainbow

Table 1.2. Research and Programming: Similarities and Differences

Research	Programming
Systematic process of discovery	**Systematic process of information gathering**
Involves a planned, organized, methodical process of steps; is a systematic investigation	Involves a planned, organized, methodical process of steps; is the systematic retrieval of information (Pena et al., 1987).
Defining a problem	**Identifying problems**
Studying a problem or area of interest. Our ultimate goal is to advance the field or to move the field forward (Dickinson et al., 2007).	Attempting to define the problem(s), with the goal of thoroughly understanding client needs so that we may generate design solutions that help solve client problem(s). The research that we conduct is used as a means to solve design problems. Thus, research is not defined as scientific inquiry. Rather, we are gathering existing knowledge (Dickson & White, 1993; Dickson & White, 1995).
Data collection and dissemination	**Data collection and documentation** are disseminated to the client and the programming document is not typically viewed through a public forum.
Because the ultimate goal is discovery, disseminating the information is very important. Many research studies are published in journal articles, books, or other public sources of information	
Accurate observation and description	**Accurate observation and description**
Because research must be replicable, the way in which data are collected must be accurate and precise. Research is written so that anyone can repeat the study if need be. "The scientific method (or empirical research) relies on repetition efforts" (Cherry, 1999, p. 37).	"[P]rogramming seeks to identify the uniqueness of a project" (Cherry, 1999, p. 37).
Typical sections, for example, in a journal article. The first section is the **Introduction**, which rationalizes the importance of the investigation (i.e., why are we conducting this research?).	**Typical sections** in programming document. The first section is the **Project Statement** (also known as the **Mission** or **Priority Statement**), which describes the client, location, and site, overall mission, and services provided for the project. It essentially gives a brief overview of the project and states why we are doing the work (Cherry, 1999; Duerk, 1993).
Usually has a **Literature Review** or **Background Section**, which cites any previous research that has been conducted on the area of interest and typically cites gaps in the literature that justify the importance of the study. In other words, the goal of the literature review is to evaluate the current state of knowledge.	Usually has a **Literature Review** or **Background Section**, which is typically broader in context and includes any background information that is relevant to designing the project. This section becomes a statement of the existing state and can include physical conditions such as site, geography, and climate parameters; code constraints; and a client profile (Duerk, 1993).
Data Collection describes in great detail how the data were collected, through an explanation of the sample, instrument, and procedure in the **Methods** section. This detailed explanation allows the study to be repeated if necessary (remember that research is replicable) (Cherry, 1999; Touliatos & Compton, 1988) and generalized.	**Data Collection** is described.

Riders program, since its needs and problems would be different. For a research study, you would want your findings to be generalized beyond Rainbow Riders. To illustrate, suppose you were interested in how color affected cooperative play behavior among children. You might design an experiment in which children would play under a red-wall condition versus a blue-wall condition. You would define or operationalize "cooperative play behavior." In other words, what does this phrase mean and how will you measure this behavior? You would collect and analyze your data. Ultimately, you want your findings to be generalized beyond Rainbow Riders so that other child care centers may use this information when designing their facilities.

Summary

In this chapter, we discussed the differences between programming and research. After reading this chapter, you should fully understand that research involves much more than information gathering. Research is discovery that can be generalized, while programming is information gathering pertaining to a specific project. Both are invaluable to the design professions. Programming allows designers to intimately understand their clients, while research moves the design professions forward.

BIBLIOGRAPHY

Alexander, C. (1979). *The timeless way of building.* New York: Oxford University Press.

Ballast, D. K. (1993). *Interior design reference manual.* Belmont, CA: Professional Publications.

Ballast, D. K. (2006). *Interior design reference manual: A guide to the NCIDQ exam* (3rd ed.). Belmont, CA: Professional Publications.

Becker, F. (1999, Winter). Good medicine. *Perspective,* 57–62.

Boyer, E. L. (1990). *Scholarship reconsidered: Priorities of the professoriate.* New York: The Carnegie Foundation for the Advancement of Teaching.

Burnett, L. (2004, August). Get real. *Contract, 24.*

Cherry, E. (1999). *Programming for design.* New York: John Wiley & Sons.

CIDA Accreditation Manual. (2008). *Council for Interior Design Accreditation (CIDA).* Retrieved from http://www.accredit-id.org

Dickinson, J. I., Marsden, J. P., & Read, M. A. (2007). Empirical design research: Student definitions, perceptions, and values. *Journal of Interior Design, 32*(2), 1–12.

Dickson, A. W., & White, A. C. (1993). Are we speaking the same language? Practitioners' perceptions of research and the state of the profession. *Journal of Interior Design, 19*(1), 3–10.

Duerk, D. P. (1993). *Architectural programming information management for design.* New York: John Wiley & Sons.

Eakins, P. (2005). *Writing for interior design.* New York: Fairchild Books.

Fisher, T. (2004, Fall). Architects behaving badly: Ignoring environmental behavior research. *Harvard Design Magazine,* 1–3.

Fraenkel, J. R., & Wallen, N. E. (1996). *How to design and evaluate research in education* (3rd ed.). New York: McGraw-Hill.

Fraenkel, J. R., & Wallen, N. E. (2006). *How to design and evaluate research in education* (6th ed.). New York: McGraw-Hill.

Groat, L., & Wang, D. (2002). *Architectural research methods.* New York: John Wiley & Sons.

Guerin, D. A., & Dohr, J. (2007). Research 101: Part 1—Research-based practice. *InformeDesign.* Retrieved from http://www.informedesign.umn.edu

Guerin, D. A., & Thompson, J. A. (2004). Interior design education in the 21st century: An educational transformation. *Journal of Interior Design, 30*(1), 1–12.

Guralnik, D. B. (Ed.). (1978). *Webster's new world dictionary of the American language* (2nd college ed.). New York: The World Publishing Co.

Hamilton, D. K. (2004). Four levels of evidence-based practice. *The American Institute of Architects.* Retrieved from http://www.aia.org

Hasell, M. J., & Scott, S. C. (1996). Interior design visionaries' explorations of emerging trends. *Journal of Interior Design, 22*(2), 1–14.

Kinkead, J. (2003). Learning through inquiry: An overview of undergraduate research. *New Directions for Teaching and Learning, 93,* 5–17.

Kopec, D. (2006). *Environmental psychology for design.* New York: Fairchild Books.

LaGro, J. A. (1999). Research capacity: A matter of semantics. *Landscape Journal, 18*(2), 51–58.

Leedy, P. D., & Ormrod, J. E. (2005). *Practical research planning and design* (8th ed.). Upper Saddle River, NJ: Prentice Hall.

Marsden, J. P. (2005). *Humanistic design of assisted living.* Baltimore: Johns Hopkins University Press.

Newman, O. (1996). Creating defensible space. *U.S. Department of Housing & Urban Development.* Retrieved from http://www.huduser.org

Newman, O. (1997, May/June). Defensible space. *NHI Shelterforce Online.* Retrieved from http://www.nhi.org/online/issues/93/defense.html

The Origins of Architectural Research (2005). Retrieved from http://home.worldcom.ch/~negenter/021ArResOrigE.htm

Pena, W., Parshall, S., & Kelly, K. (1987). *Problem seeking: An architectural programming primer (3rd ed.).* Washington, DC: AIA Press.

Rodiek, J. E. (1995). Editorial. *Landscape and Urban Planning, 32,* 1–2.

Roth, S. (1999). The state of design research. *Design Issues, 15*(2),18–26.

Rummel, J. F. (1964). *An introduction to research procedures in education* (2nd ed.). New York: Harper & Row.

Sanoff, H. (1977). *Architectural problems and purposes. Architectural design as a basic problem-solving process.* New York: John Wiley & Sons.

Scott-Webber, L. (1998). *Programming a problem solving approach for users of interior spaces.* Houston: Dame Publications.

Sommer, R. (1969). *Personal space: The behavioral basis of design.* Upper Saddle River, NJ: Prentice Hall.

Sommer, R., & Sommer, B. (2002). *A practical guide to behavioral research.* New York: Oxford University Press.

Touliatos, J., & Compton, N. H. (1988). *Research methods in human ecology/home economics.* Ames, Iowa: Iowa State University Press.

Wang, D. (2007). Diagramming design research. *Journal of Interior Design, 33*(1), 33–42.

White, E. (1972). *Introduction to architectural programming.* Arizona: Architectural Media, Ltd.

Zeisel, J. (1981). *Inquiry by design.* New York: Cambridge University Press.

Zeisel, J. (2006). *Inquiry by design: Environment/behavior/neuroscience in architecture, interiors, landscape, and planning.* New York: W. W. Norton & Company.

2   Research and Programming Processes

Joan Dickinson

Abstract

This chapter addresses the research and programming processes, with an emphasis on the research process. The chapter is not intended to replace more comprehensive texts on research methods and programming. The chapter begins with the research process and addresses problem definition, the literature review, variables, sampling, research design, and data collection tools. One goal is to provide students and practitioners with an overview that will help them to better comprehend research terminology and understand the findings from published investigations. A second goal is to provide a starting point for students and practitioners who might be conductors of research. Two research examples are presented to illustrate the research terminology in a practical application. The chapter ends with a discussion of the programming process, including problem definition, the literature review to establish the constraints and parameters for the project, and some of the same data collection tools associated with the research process. The research and programming processes are compared so that readers can see how the steps differ from those for research.

Introduction

An understanding of research terminology is important to the design student, hence future practitioner, for several reasons. First, architecture and interior design have become increasingly complex fields where designers are making decisions that directly influence the health and safety of people (Guerin & Thompson, 2004). Gaining a knowledge base in research will allow future designers to make sense of published investigations in which findings have value to the design professions (Guerin & Dohr, 2007; Guerin & Thompson, 2004). Second, a savvy clientele in an information society require that the designer stay current and informed (Fisher, 2004; Guerin & Dohr, 2007). With the availability of databases such as InformeDesign (www.informedesign.umn.edu), clients may expect designers to know this information (Fisher, 2004). Reading published research not only allows the practicing professional to become a consumer of research (Hasell & Scott, 1996), but it may also give practitioners and students ideas on their own methods of inquiry. Third, the term *evidence-based design*, as discussed in the preface, has become popular in both architecture and design, particularly in the specialty area of healthcare, where the surrounding environment can influence the number of days in acute care, the amount of pain medication, patient well-being, and staff efficiency (Hamilton, 2004; Ulrich, 1984; Ulrich, Quan, Zimring, Joseph, & Choudhary, 2004). As the term evidence-based design increases in popularity, clients may expect interior designers to better justify and rationalize their design decision making. Fourth, many of the data collection techniques that are discussed in this chapter can be used for research and/or programming purposes. For the student who eventually practices in a design firm that is heavily involved in programming, this chapter provides an overview of ways in which information can be collected (see Chapters 4 and 5 for design examples informed by programming data collection). For the student who becomes a consumer of research by reading published investigations, this chapter will familiarize the reader with terminology that is often found in hard sources of information (see Chapters 6, 7, and 8 for examples informed by journal articles). For the student who may become a conductor of research, this chapter will provide a starting point for research design and data collection (see Chapters 9 and 10). Last, an overview of both the research and programming processes is given so that students can better understand how the two differ in terms of the steps and procedures followed.

The Research Process

Defining the Problem

For the research process, defining the problem essentially sets the stage for the investigation that will be conducted. It is the focus of the research study. Defining the problem can come from numerous sources. Casual observations, information gathering, data collection, and keeping current with the literature all lead to identification of problems that might be worth studying in the field of interior design. Reading the literature leads to recognition of design problems; but once the problem is defined, all related literature must be reviewed to ensure that the problem is thoroughly understood.

Research problems tend to be specific in nature. For example, in a study conducted by Shin, Maxwell, & Eshelman (2004), mothers who had given birth in the previous six months were interviewed to determine factors in a labor, delivery, recovery, and postpartum (LDRP) unit/birthing center that would contribute to hominess during the birthing experience. Even though a number of problems could occur in the LDRP, such as difficulties in wayfinding, patient safety, and the spread of infections, to name a few, this study focused only on the problem of hominess.

To provide another example, in a study by Dickinson, Shroyer, and Elias (2000), residential carpet was examined to determine how this floor covering influenced gait (i.e., walking) among older individuals. Even though there are other factors that could affect gait such as footwear, normal aging, and health issues, the focus of this research study was on a particular issue, illustrating the specific nature of research problems.

The Literature Review

Basically, a *literature review* is a "survey of various sources" (Groat & Wang, 2002, p. 45). For the research process, a review of the literature is critical for a number of reasons. First, the researcher may read the literature to identify a research problem (Groat & Wang, 2002). Knowing the literature in one's field generates ideas that may merit future study. Critical reading allows the researcher to identify gaps in the literature and leads to research problems or questions that are worth investigating. Second, the literature review may focus or narrow the research problem or questions (Groat & Wang, 2002). Research is typically based on a legacy of previous work (Walliman, 2006). Thus, it is the investigator's responsibility to understand the context of that work. Last, the ultimate goal of research is to advance the body of knowledge. In order to achieve this goal, the researcher must know the literature or the current state of knowledge in order to expand it (Groat & Wang, 2002). "A researcher must be informed about the existing literature his or her research needs to draw from, because the outcome of the research will expand that body of literature" (Groat & Wang, 2002, p. 46). Thus for research purposes, the review of literature involves the systematic identification, location, and analysis of documents containing information related to the research problem. Essentially, the designer or researcher analyzes the documents to determine how they contribute to the new investigation.

To summarize, the literature review for the research process can be used for the following purposes: (1) to identify the problem or to determine the research questions, (2) to focus the purpose of the research, and (3) to understand the context for the research study so the findings can expand that context or knowledge (Groat & Wang, 2002).

When conducting a literature review, it is important to note the dates of publications and content of the information. Utilizing current references is preferred (Sommer & Sommer, 2002) unless the study is classic or pioneering work. Next, it is essential to determine whether the information is fact, opinion, or research. For example, information from trade magazines may classify as opinion or fact. But these articles are not typically research-based. Journal articles are often referred to as *primary, original,* or *hard sources* (Sommer & Sommer, 2002), because they are publishing the original research investigation. Additionally, journal articles are often peer reviewed, a step that makes the publication process more rigorous. *Secondary* or *soft sources* include books, magazine articles, and articles from the Internet. These sources often provide summary information or general ideas on a topic. They may also reference the primary source and often describe the work of others (Fraenkel & Wallen, 2006). When beginning a literature review, designers should start with secondary sources, as this type of information will provide an overview related to the problem and will lead to additional primary sources.

It is important to note that the distinction between secondary and primary sources can vary depending on the type of research strategy used. To illustrate, Chapter 3 explores the connection between sustainability and historic preservation. For research that investigates the past, a primary source can be the "words of a witness or the first recorders of the event" (Groat & Wang, 2002, p. 60). Regardless, it is important to read a variety of sources such as journal articles (typically research based), books, and articles from magazines (Sommer & Sommer, 2002) when conducting a literature review.

Benefits of the Literature Review

The literature review is valuable for the research process for the following reasons:

- Offers information that can lead to design problems that are worth researching.
- Offers information from experienced designers and researchers.
- Can provide research-based information that can be used for evidence-based design solutions (Guerin & Thompson, 2004).
- Can inspire ideas for research studies.
- Provides a framework for a research problem. The literature review allows the researcher to determine the gaps in the area of interest, which ultimately provides stronger rationalization for the research investigation.
- Develops a knowledge of related research articles that enables the investigator to define the frontiers of the field and to place the research question in perspective.
- The study of related literature and research helps investigators learn which methodologies have proved useful and which seem less promising for their area of interest.
- Places researchers in a better position to interpret the significance of the results of their study and avoids unintentional replication of previous studies.

Difficulties in Conducting the Literature Review

The researcher should be aware of the following difficulties that might occur during the literature review:

- When reviewing the literature, the researcher and/or designer can find conflicting information.
- Information may not always be easy to find.

- For the reader, it is important to distinguish among research, opinion, or fact—distinctions that may be difficult. To illustrate, information and research issued by the Carpet and Rug Institute may be somewhat biased or slanted in a positive way toward carpet use as a floor covering option. For a designer, it is important to judge the degree of accuracy of the document (Walliman, 2006).
- Reading and collecting the literature is time-consuming.

Steps of the Literature Review

Prior to the beginning of the literature review, the problem must be somewhat defined. Let's look at an example for a research study cited earlier. If you were interested in how carpet affects gait among older individuals, you would search for information related to gait and carpet. Typically, you would begin your search with secondary sources that might discuss the problems associated with gait among older individuals. This general or summary information would eventually lead you to primary sources. In this case, you would be most interested in previous investigations that examined flooring in relationship to gait. This would allow you to understand the background pertaining to your study of interest. Furthermore, you would better know the gaps in the literature related to your specific research problem and how your study would fill those gaps. Thus, the steps in the literature review include the following:

1. Defining the research problem
2. Reviewing relevant secondary sources
3. Reviewing primary sources and making notations of the findings from these studies in relationship to your research problem

What is important to note about these steps is how they are tied back to the specifics of the research problem. The more clearly stated the research problem is, the easier the literature review will be to conduct. The literature review is typically placed after the introduction of a research study. For a research study, the literature review is not just a compilation of facts. Rather, the literature review is a coherent argument that clarifies the relationship between the proposed study and previous work completed on the topic. Ultimately, the literature review allows the reader to say, "Yes, this is exactly the study that needs to be done."

Research Methods

Data collection involves how the information will be gathered and from whom. Data can be collected through observations, questionnaires, interviews, and focus groups, to name a few. Data can be collected from people, documents, or the actual space. Essentially, the designer must decide, based on the problem, which is best to answer the questions. For example, if you were conducting research on four-year-old children to determine whether the design (e.g., color and space) of the preschool supported cooperative play, should the children respond or should the parents respond? Should you survey the parents, children, or child care workers? Should you observe the children while they play? In this case, you will have to determine how you will collect the data. If you decided to observe the children, then the children would become your sample. Keep in mind that data can be collected in more than one way. In the example above, you might decide to observe the children and interview both parents and staff. Regardless, based on your research problem, you will need to decide who or what will form your population and sample.

Populations and Sampling

For a research study, the *population* is the entire group of people or events you are studying (Guerin & Dohr, 2007; Howell, 1987; Pagano, 1994; Touliatos & Compton, 1988). To illustrate, suppose you were interested in examining stress management scores for college freshman design students in the United States; then the collection of all college freshman design students would form your population. Other examples of populations are high school seniors in the state of Virginia or individuals over the age of 65 in the United States. Our population in the example above could be all preschool children aged four in Radford, Virginia. The size of the population can range from very small to an infinitely large number that may be impossible to study (Howell, 1987). Instead, investigators typically rely on sampling techniques when collecting data.

A *sample* is a subset of the population and the group about whom information is obtained. The larger group to whom one hopes to apply the results is the population (Fraenkel & Wallen, 2006; Sommer & Sommer, 2002). Using the example above, freshman college design students in one particular state could form your sample or subset. A single member of the sample is termed a *subject* (Guerin & Dohr, 2007).

Probability Sampling Methods.   When determining the type of sample, one of the most important characteristics is whether to use probability or nonprobability sampling. In *probability* or *random sampling*, each and every member of the population has an equal chance of being selected (e.g., selecting every tenth person in the phonebook) (Howell, 1987; Pagano, 1994; Zeisel, 2006). With random sampling, the results can be generalized to the population because the sample is representative of the population (Guerin & Dohr, 2007). Suppose you were interested in determining how interior design faculty who are members of the Interior Design Educators Council (IDEC) feel about incorporating sustainability in their studio courses. You have obtained a list of all IDEC members and placed these names in a hat. From the hat, you have drawn 100 names. This is an example of random sampling because each IDEC member had an equal chance of being selected.

There are times when the sample populations of certain subgroups are kept in the same proportion as the proportion of the subgroups in the whole population; this is termed a *stratified random sample* (Sommer & Sommer, 2002; Touliatos & Compton, 1988). For example, if you discover that your population has 60 percent women and 40 percent men, you might want to keep that same strata or proportion. The last random sampling technique is *cluster random sampling*. Instead of using individuals, this type of sampling uses clusters of individuals. To return to our previous example, if we were studying how the environment affected cooperative play behavior among four-year-old preschool children, we could randomly select preschools (i.e., clusters) located in our target population area (i.e., Radford, Virginia).

Nonprobability Sampling Methods.   It is important to note that probability sampling (i.e., a random sample) is more desirable because of the ability to generalize to the population. Since every member in the population has an equal chance of being selected, there is less sampling bias (Sommer & Sommer, 2002). Yet, in the design fields, random sampling is often difficult to achieve, and many investigations rely on nonprobability sampling techniques. A *convenience sample* is a group of individuals who are available for study (e.g., an instructor using his or her class for data collection) (Guerin & Dohr, 2007; Sommer & Sommer, 2002; Touliatos & Compton, 1988). The disadvantage is that one cannot generalize the findings to the population, yet these individuals are often easy and convenient to study or collect data from.

In a *purposive sample*, another form of nonprobability sampling, we use personal judgment to select the sample. This is different from convenience sampling in that researchers are not studying only subjects who are available. Instead, the investigator is using judgment to select a sample that will provide the needed data (Sommer & Sommer, 2002; Touliatos & Compton, 1988). As stated earlier, we conducted a study that examined the influence of carpet on the gait of healthy, older individuals. In this study, we used a purposive sampling technique to ensure that our subjects were indeed healthy. Subjects were excluded from the research study if they were (1) using assistive devices for standing (e.g., canes or walkers), (2) diagnosed with vestibular problems, (3) diagnosed with Parkinson's disease or other neurological disorders, (4) diagnosed with ear infections at the time of the study, (5) diagnosed with severe orthopedic problems (e.g., osteoporosis, previous hip or spine fractures, severe stooped posture; individuals who were experiencing mild to moderate arthritis were not excluded), and (6) experiencing problems with dizziness (Dickinson, Shroyer, & Elias, 2000). This exclusion criteria helped to ensure that any changes we observed in gait were due to the flooring rather than aging or health issues.

In many of the examples we have provided, people have served as the sample. Keep in mind that the sample may not always consist of individuals. To illustrate, perhaps you are interested in the amount of times sustainability is mentioned in trade magazines from 1990 until 2009. In this case, the trade magazines would ultimately serve as your sample, and you would be involved in a research strategy called *content analysis*. In this case, a document serves as the sample.

Variables

Variables are characteristics or properties in a research question, problem, (i.e., typically what you are interested in studying) or hypothesis (Guerin & Dohr, 2007; Sommer & Sommer, 2002). Here is an example of a research question: How will residential carpet influence gait among healthy, older adults? Residential carpet and gait are the variables and healthy, older adults are the sample. These variables can also be stated in a *hypothesis*, which is an educated guess, testable statement (Sommer & Sommer, 2002), or prediction (Walliman, 2006). For example, we might hypothesize that healthy, older adults will walk more slowly on vinyl tile than carpet because a fear of falling may be higher when walking on a hard, shiny floor surface than when on a soft, compliant surface. Variables are basically any characteristic that varies (Fraenkel & Wallen, 1996; Sommer & Sommer, 2002) such as weight, running speed, gait speed, age, and educational level. In our LDRP example, interior features and hominess would be the variables and women who had given birth in the last six months would be the sample.

Independent Variable.   The variable that is manipulated or changed is the *independent variable* (Sommer & Sommer, 2002; Walliman, 2006). In the above example, residential carpet is the independent variable. Other terms used to describe the independent variable include the experimental variable or the predictor variable (Sommer & Sommer, 2002).

Dependent Variable.   The *dependent* or *outcome variable* is the variable that will be affected by the independent variable (Sommer & Sommer, 2002; Walliman, 2006). In our example, gait is the dependent variable.

Extraneous Variable.   Independent variables that might influence the results of the study (could affect changes in the dependent variable and typically need to be controlled) are termed *extraneous variables* (Fraenkel & Wallen, 1996). In our example, footwear would be an extraneous variable. If we had not controlled for health issues through our purposive sampling technique, these would have also been extraneous variables that could have influenced the results of the study.

Discrete or Categorical Variable.   Variables that take on a limited number of values such as sex, eye color, or high school class are called *discrete* or *categorical variables* (Fraenkel & Wallen, 1996; Howell, 1987; Pagano, 1987). These variables do not differ in amount or degree. Rather, they are qualitatively not the same. To illustrate, religious preference or political party are categorical variables. You are either a registered Democrat or a registered Republican. In the previous example on how carpet influenced gait, we could have examined the categorical variable of sex to determine whether men walk differently from women.

Continuous Variable.   Variables that in theory have an unlimited number of values such as weight, height, gait speed, and age are said to be *continuous variables* (Pagano, 1987).

Variables form the research questions, problem, or hypothesis. In our previous example with four-year-old children, we might be interested in determining how different ceiling heights and color combinations influence cooperative play behavior. Color and ceiling heights are independent variables. Yet color is categorical in nature, while ceiling height would be considered a continuous variable. Cooperative play behavior is our dependent variable. Whether this would be considered categorical or continuous would depend on how we operationalized (i.e., defined) this variable.

Data Collection Tools

In this section, we examine data collection tools that are commonly used in the design profession and that are illustrated in the chapters of this book. We do not cover every single type of data collection technique available to the interior designer and/or researcher. As we explain these data collection tools, it is also important to be aware that there is some overlap between research design (discussed later in this chapter) and data collection. Surveys are a type of research design; yet the tools used for surveying can include questionnaires, face-to-face interviews, or telephone interviews, which are all ways to collect data.

Observations.   Observations involve watching people and their behavior as they use the built environment (Guerin & Dohr, 2007; Sommer & Sommer, 2002; Zeisel, 2006) to understand how the environment affects human behavior. In many cases, we are interested in observing how the physical space either supports or hinders the intended activities (Zeisel, 2006). Observations can be casual (as in the early stages of research) or systematic, in which categories of information are recorded consistently on a checklist (Sommer & Sommer, 2002). The natural setting is the direct source of data, and the researcher is the key instrument. In other words, the setting in which you are observing is the source of information or data that you will collect. It is also important to note that observations as a data collection method can be used in a number of circumstances: (1) observing the results of an experiment as in a research study; (2) observing the reactions to people in answering questions during an interview, which could happen in a research study or programming; or (3) essentially recording conditions, events, or activities through observing versus asking, both of which could apply to a research investigation or programming (Fraenkel & Wallen, 1996; Walliman, 2006). In all situations, direct observation requires the researcher to draw inferences about the environment or people.

Prior to starting your observations, you need a foreshadowed problem (Walliman, 2006). This foreshadowed problem can be gleaned from reading the literature or from causally observing to determine a problem or narrow a focus that you are interested in (Guerin & Dohr, 2007). We began by conducting some casual observations at a local nursing home/dementia care unit. As we observed, we discovered that exiting behavior by the residents was a huge problem in this particular dementia care unit, and the residents would attempt to exit (escape) constantly throughout the day. This was problematic, as the majority of the residents were diagnosed with Alzheimer's disease and needed 24-hour care for their safety. The problem was so intense that a number of residents escaped from the unit. As we continued to observe, we realized that the interior environment was a factor in the exiting behavior. Casual observations can often lead to the start of a research plan and may be the starting point for defining the research problem. Observations may also be reinforced by the literature or theory in the area of interest (Guerin & Dohr, 2007; Zeisel, 2006). For example, exiting behavior by individuals who have Alzheimer's disease is mentioned frequently in the literature (Brawley, 2006). Casual observing and reading led to a "foreshadowed problem" worth studying. Zeisel (2006) refers to the foreshadowed problem as follows: who (whom will you observe or the actors), doing what (what activities will you observe), in what context, where (the physical setting), and with whom? The foreshadowed problem is an important first step before conducting systematic, formalized observations. As mentioned by Zeisel, observing behavior can seem like an easy form of data collection. Yet the observer can omit important details and descriptions if the observations are not focused.

Factors to Consider When Observing.   When conducting formal observations, pay attention to the following factors, all of which can influence what you will see: time of your observations, participant versus complete observer, and recording behavior.

The time of your observations makes a difference in people's behavior. Will you observe at night? Will you observe during the day? What time of the day or night? Will you observe during the week or on weekends? For the observations in the dementia care unit, we observed from 2:00 p.m. until 4:00 p.m. everyday. After talking with the staff and conducting preliminary observations, we discovered that this was when residents were most active. Many of the residents napped after lunch (1:00 p.m. until 3:00 p.m.), while wandering and exit-seeking behavior were commonly seen from 2:00 p.m. to 4:00 p.m. Keep in mind that you may have to conduct observations in the evening or at night to get an accurate picture of what is happening in the environment. For example, if you were observing a hotel lobby to better understand traffic patterns, you would have to observe on the weekends, since many hotel check-ins and checkouts occur during this time.

The difference between a *participant observer* and *complete observer* is an important distinction. A participant observer, or full participant, actually becomes part of the group (Fraenkel & Wallen, 2006; Guerin & Dohr, 2007; Sommer & Sommer, 2002; Walliman, 2006; Zeisel, 2006). In the dementia care unit example, you could disguise yourself as a staff member or as an older individual and become a part of the group. You can become totally immersed in the group and not tell your group members, or you can become immersed in the group and divulge that you are conducting research (Fraenkel & Wallen, 2006; Walliman, 2006). The complete observer does not become involved in the activities of the group (Fraenkel & Wallen, 1996; Walliman, 2006). As a complete observer, you can be a hidden observer behind a two-way mirror. This type of observation method works well for groups that would be influenced by your presence, such as small children. You can also be a disguised observer. I disguised myself as a nurse in the research that was conducted in the dementia care unit, but I was *not* immersed in the group. I sat in the nurse's station, and the nurses on duty were fully aware that I was observing resident behavior.

Recording behavior is another factor to consider and there are several ways to do it. When conducting open-ended observations, you should make a record of all behavior that deals with the foreshadowed problem that you have identified. The key, however, is to *know* the problem up front. This way you will know what to look for when observing (Walliman, 2006).

Behavioral mapping typically involves a floor plan where the behavior is mapped (Guerin & Dohr, 2007). Often people's locations and movements in a particular area are recorded (Sommer & Sommer, 2002). For example, if you were interested in circulation patterns in a hotel lobby, or if you wanted to see if people really made use of the hotel lobby space, this type of recording method would allow you to map where people travel. Additionally, you could use annotated notes to record where people stop and why. This form of mapping would allow the researcher to determine where people circulate, how they spend their time, and what they do in a hotel lobby. To do behavioral mapping, you need the following: (1) the map, (2) a decision about the behavior you will record, and (3) the specific times and days you will observe (Sommer & Sommer, 2002). See Figures 2.1 and 2.2.

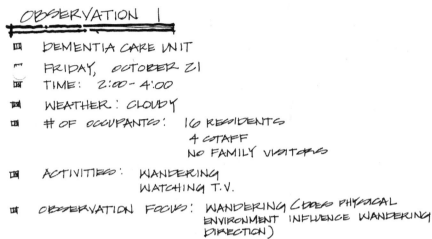

OBSERVATION I

- DEMENTIA CARE UNIT
- FRIDAY, OCTOBER 21
- TIME: 2:00 - 4:00
- WEATHER: CLOUDY
- # OF OCCUPANTS: 16 RESIDENTS
  4 STAFF
  NO FAMILY VISITORS

- ACTIVITIES: WANDERING
  WATCHING T.V.

- OBSERVATION FOCUS: WANDERING (DOES PHYSICAL
  ENVIRONMENT INFLUENCE WANDERING
  DIRECTION)

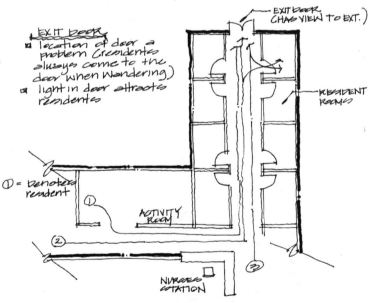

EXIT DOOR
- location of door a
  problem (residents
  always come to the
  door when wandering)
- light in door attracts
  residents

EXIT DOOR
(HAS VIEW TO EXT.)

RESIDENT
ROOMS

① = Denotes
    resident

ACTIVITY
ROOM

NURSES
STATION

Figure 2.1. Behavioral mapping floor plan.

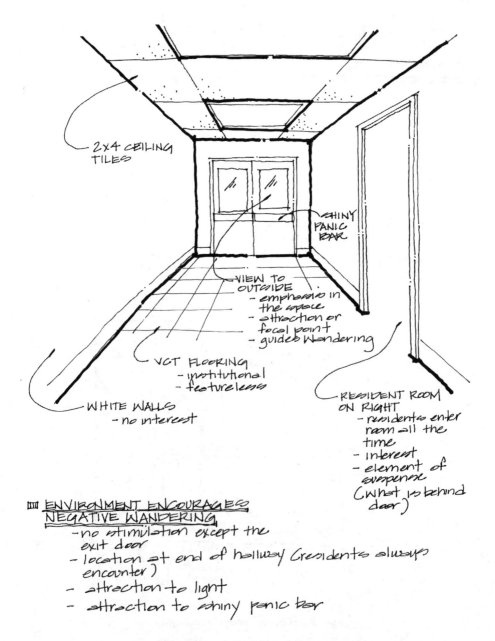

2X4 CEILING
TILES

SHINY
PANIC
BAR

VIEW TO
OUTSIDE
- emphasis in
  the space
- attraction or
  focal point
- guides wandering

VCT FLOORING
- institutional
- featureless

WHITE WALLS
- no interest

RESIDENT ROOM
ON RIGHT
- residents enter
  room all the
  time
- interest
- element of
  suspense
(what is behind
door)

▥ ENVIRONMENT ENCOURAGES
   NEGATIVE WANDERING
   - no stimulation except the
     exit door
   - location at end of hallway (residents always
     encounter)
   - attraction to light
   - attraction to shiny panic bar

Figure 2.2. Behavioral mapping perspective sketch.

Advantages of Observations.   As a data collection method, observation offers the following advantages:

- Observations provide a more complete picture and a more holistic impression because you are describing in as much detail what you see (Fraenkel & Wallen, 1996).
- Observations bridge the gap between what people say and do. Imagine you are designing an office space and the staff has requested a formal conference room. You could actually observe to see what kind of conferencing currently takes place. As you observe, you might find that communication among employees is often impromptu. Employers tend to stand in the hallways and brainstorm. You may observe, in fact, that formal conferencing does not take place. This might lead to small brainstorming areas (e.g., open seating areas along the corridors, or niches in the wall) instead of a formal, enclosed conference space that frankly no one would use.
- Observations as a data collection method work well for special populations. Small children and individuals who are mentally ill, for example, may be unable to complete a questionnaire.

Disadvantages of Observations.   However, there are drawbacks to observations, including the following:

- Observations are time consuming and time can be wasted waiting for the behavior to happen (Walliman, 2006).
- The observer could jump to the wrong conclusions. This is why observations should be backed by precedent (the literature) and can also be backed by surveys.
- The individuals whom you are observing can change their behavior. This is especially true of small children. If you enter a preschool and try to observe, the children could be very

impressed by your presence, and their behavior could change. Using two-way mirrors or disguises could alleviate this problem.

Questionnaires.   *Questionnaires* involve the systematic collection of information using standardized questions (i.e., asking questions) (Fraenkel & Wallen, 1996) and could be concerned with a population and the environment it occupies. Questionnaires can also be used to collect attitudinal information from a particular population or sample. As discussed in Chapter 1, a questionnaire was used to collect information about interior design students' perceptions of research. The information can be obtained through face-to-face interviews, telephone interviews, focus groups, mailed questionnaires, Web-based questionnaires, or self-administered written questionnaires (Zeisel, 2006). Some researchers have also used visuals to understand how people experience their physical environment. Freehand maps, drawings, photographs, or games are all forms of visual responses to questions (Zeisel, 2006). For example, Lynch (1960) asked residents to sketch maps of their city; Cooper Marcus (1995) requested homeowners to draw a sketch that reflected feelings about their current home. In other instances, visuals such as models have represented proposed or existing environments and provided subjects with a range of alternatives in a format that they could easily understand.

Questionnaires can be used for the following purposes:

- User needs or studies such as those questionnaires used for programming documents. For example, when starting a project, a designer often collects information and typically spends time understanding client needs and problems. A survey might be used in the form of a questionnaire to collect data such as adjacency information, space requirements, employee data (number of employees, position), and equipment or storage requirements. All of this information is used to help solve the design problems and to help the designer better understand the project/client.

- Questionnaires can be used for post-occupancy evaluations. In this situation, as designers, we are trying to better understand whether our design solution met client needs.
- Questionnaires can be used for empirical research.
- Questionnaires can be used to explain and describe information about a population (e.g., demographics).
- Questionnaires can be used to explain and describe people's attitudes, thoughts, feelings, knowledge, and beliefs (see Dickinson, Marsden, & Read, 2007 and Dickson & White, 1993).

Advantages of Questionnaires.   Some advantages of using questionnaires are as follows:

- The key advantage to self-administered questionnaires is the ability to gather a large amount of information in a short amount of time.
- Questionnaires can be relatively inexpensive and quick to administer (Walliman, 2006), especially if administered online.
- Questionnaires can be anonymous, which may allow the researcher to ask sensitive questions and receive truthful answers (Walliman, 2006).
- Researcher bias or personal influence may be eliminated (Walliman, 2006).

Disadvantages of Questionnaires.   Some disadvantages of using questionnaires follow:

- People are generally resistant to filling out a form, a situation that can lead to a low-return rate (Walliman, 2006). If the return rate is low, you have to wonder whether those who answered the questions are significantly different from those who did not.

- The sample could exaggerate needs, which is why wording of questions is so important. Questionnaires can take quite a bit of time to prepare (Walliman, 2006).
- Face-to-face interaction can be missing if the survey is conducted using a written or Web-based questionnaire; thus, further probing of the question is not possible (Walliman, 2006).
- Not everyone can fill out a questionnaire (Walliman, 2006); the illiterate or blind, for example, would be excluded. In addition, you cannot be sure that the person who filled out the questionnaire is the one you targeted.
- Confusion over questions can occur. If the questionnaire is not well-written, misunderstandings can occur in the interpretation of the question.

Post-Occupancy Evaluations.   *Post-occupancy evaluations* involve collecting data after the design project has been installed. Analyzing as-built drawings or conducting interviews with building occupants to understand how the building has performed are examples of post-occupancy evaluations (POEs) (Groat & Wang, 2002). As discussed by Duerk (1993), there are two reasons for POEs: (1) to test how well a building design met the client needs as spelled out in the programming document and (2) to evaluate an existing building as a model for the design process, which is more common for a research investigation. The POE can answer questions such as, "What about the building or design supported the designer's intentions?" or "What about the building or design influenced client behavior in a way that was not intended?" (Zeisel, 2006).

There are many designers who would argue that the POE is part of the design process, which would include the following steps: programming, to conceptual development, to design development, to construction documentation and administration, to construction and move-in, and from move-in to a post-occupancy evaluation (Duerk, 1993). For research purposes, the POE can be used as a form of data collection. In Chapter 1, we discussed the work of Oscar Newman and his research involving defensible space, which included the review of over 100 different housing projects. As mentioned previously, this work was instrumental in providing information on sense of ownership, safety, and security in public-housing complexes. Chapter 10 provides an example of post-occupancy evaluations being used to inform design decision making.

Interviews. The interview differs from the standardized questionnaire in that the questions are asked face-to-face rather than in a written format. As described in Sommer and Sommer (2002), the *interview* is a "conversation with a purpose" (p. 112). Because of this face-face interaction, there are numerous advantages. First, the face-to-face interaction may seem more personal and can allow for additional probing or clarification on questions (Walliman, 2006). Furthermore, gaining cooperation from the respondents can be effective in this type of data collection method (Fraenkel & Wallen, 2006). Immediate response is possible with face-to-face interviews, and vulnerable populations such as the elderly, illiterate, and blind can be included. When interviewing, you may also observe how individuals react to a particular question or make note of personal appearance and overall health attributes (Sommer & Sommer, 2002).

As with all data collection methods, there are also disadvantages to interviewing. Face-to-face interviewing can be time-consuming, and your subjects may exaggerate their needs. Certain populations such as infants, the mentally ill, or people with Alzheimer's disease either cannot be interviewed or may have great difficulty in answering questions. The designer or researcher who is conducting the interview must have the necessary social skills, and if not careful, this individual could sway answers through certain body language (Walliman, 2006).

Interviews may also be conducted over the telephone. Telephone interviewing may provide increased efficiency and a larger sample size.

To illustrate, many universities use telephone interviewing to determine students' attitudes regarding various services provided (Sommer & Sommer, 2002).

Focus Groups.   *Focus groups* involve interviewing groups of people (typically six to ten) and can be used for both programming purposes and empirical research. When focus groups are used for data collection, typically a particular theme or topic becomes the focus, with a trained moderator who leads the discussion (Sommer & Sommer, 2002; Walliman, 2006). Focus groups can be used when collecting information related to consumer behavior or in understanding why people think in a particular way. It is important to note that focus groups are not a discussion, a brainstorming session, or a problem-solving meeting (Franekel & Wallen, 2006). Rather, focus groups are an interview that takes place with participants seated together responding to the questions in a group format.

Focus groups are often used when measuring consumer behavior and consumption patterns. Chapter 5 illustrates how focus groups were used to collect information about consumer shopping patterns and how these behaviors influenced store design. Another familiar example would be in political campaigns where focus group sessions would explore voter issues.

Focus groups typically last one to two hours to fully explore the topic. The moderator must have training as a skilled interviewer and usually starts the session with opening questions that give every participant an opportunity to speak. These opening questions are used to build rapport among the group and to make participants feel comfortable. The goal of the moderator is to gain participation from all members of the group and to lead the questioning in a neutral manner. The moderator is also responsible for keeping the group on track with the necessary questions and preventing any one person from monopolizing the conversation (Sommer & Sommer, 2002). In addition to the moderator, there may be an observer or recorder who is taking notes during the session, or the focus group may be videotaped as long as all participants give full consent.

Research Design

In this next section, we discuss various strategies that can be utilized when conducting a research study. Not every research strategy is covered. Rather, we explain the research designs that are utilized in this book. First, research may be completed during a single point in time (i.e., *cross-sectional research*) or it may involve measuring a group of individuals over a longer period of time (i.e., *longitudinal research*). To illustrate, we might study the color preferences of a single group of older adults at ages 65, 75, and 85 to understand how vision may change with age and influence color perception. In this case, we would be involved in longitudinal research, which can be challenging because of the time commitment and the possibility of attrition.

Research conducted with different groups of people on a single occasion is cross-sectional in nature (Sommer & Sommer, 2002). Instead of collecting information from the same group of older adults over a 20-year span, we could have compared the color preferences of different groups of 65-, 75-, and 85-year-olds.

In this section, we cover both quantitative and qualitative forms of research. *Quantitative research* involves investigations in which the researcher tries to explain phenomena through controlled data collection and analysis (Fraenkel & Wallen, 2006). In *qualitative research*, the investigator is interested in naturally occurring phenomena. Typically, qualitative research involves a more holistic approach to the problem studied, and the data usually cannot be measured or counted. The data is usually in words rather than in numbers (Walliman, 2006). Research that is quantitative in nature tends to provide the researcher with quantities or numbers to be analyzed (Fraenkel & Wallen, 2006).

Quantitative Research Strategies

Experimental Design.   *Experimental design* differs from other forms of research in the level of control that is exhibited in the study (Guerin & Dohr, 2007; Walliman, 2006). In its truest sense, the researcher tries to isolate all extraneous variables that might influence the results of the study—for example, experiments in a laboratory setting (Walliman, 2006). Additionally, in experimental design, the researcher is directly involved in manipulating the independent variable in an attempt to prove cause-and-effect relationships (Guerin & Dohr, 2007; Fraenkel & Wallen, 2006). In the study where we examined the effects of carpet on the gait of healthy, older individuals, we controlled and changed the independent variable (i.e., flooring), which is a hallmark feature of experimental design. Our subjects walked on a vinyl tile floor and also walked on a residential carpet with pad that we specifically chose for the study (see Dickinson et al., 2000). We also tried to control extraneous variables that might influence the dependent variable (i.e., gait). Yet, in the design professions, true experiments are often difficult to conduct. Control of all extraneous variables and randomization (another characteristic of true experiments) is sometimes not possible. There are several ways in which extraneous variables can be controlled. First, subject variables can be held constant. As we mentioned earlier, our subjects were operationalized (i.e., defined) as healthy older individuals. Thus, we controlled for health factors that might influence gait measures. Second, extraneous variables can be eliminated. In our study, fatigue could have been a factor. By making our gait course short in length and providing the subjects with frequent breaks, we were able to eliminate this extraneous variable. Third, the setting can be controlled. Measuring subjects on the same day, at the same time, and in the same room can help eliminate threats to internal validity (Sommer & Sommer, 2002).

Experimental design is the only research strategy that gives the investigator a cause-and-effect relationship between variables and allows the investigator to understand or determine the cause of why something happened. It is also the only research methodology that involves manipulation of the independent variable. We will see how students were consumers of experimental design in Chapter 8.

Causal Comparative.   *Causal comparative* research involves the comparison of groups. To illustrate, suppose you were interested in whether family structure affects maturity levels of children. You might compare group one, which consists of two-parent families with a six-year old boy, to group two, which consists of one-parent families with a six-year old boy. In this situation, the researcher can control for age, gender, and family structure. The investigator has not manipulated the independent variable as we saw in experimental design. Rather, the groups were selected based on the independent variables of age, gender, and family structure, and these two groups are essentially reacting to something that has already occurred.

Correlational Research.   In *correlational research*, the focus is on the association between variables. The investigator does not manipulate variables in this research design. The purpose of correlational research is either to predict relationships or to explain existing relationships that might help us better understand human behavior (Fraenkel & Wallen, 2006). A classic example of correlation is the relationship between smoking and lung cancer. When the initial studies appeared, they were based on an association between these two variables. But at the time, many individuals believed that lung cancer had other mitigating factors such as genetic predisposition, lifestyle issues, and environmental exposure (e.g., living in a smoggy area). It was not until experimental studies were conducted on animals that the surgeon general issued warnings on smoking. This example illustrates that correlational research often precedes experimental design in order to first clarify that a relationship does exist among the variables (Fraenkel & Wallen, 2006).

Correlation can also be used to make predictions. Eshelman and Evans (2002) examined environmental predictors of place attachment and self-esteem among residents living in a retirement community. The variable that is used to make the prediction is termed the *predictor variable,* while the variable about which the prediction is made is termed the *criterion variable* (Fraenkel & Wallen, 2006). In their research study, Eshelman and Evans examined two independent variables (or predictors): function and aesthetics of the space, which were clearly defined. The dependent variables (or criteria) were self-esteem and place attachment. The results indicated that personalization (e.g., easy to accommodate possessions, home appears lived in, and display spaces) was the most important predictor of self-esteem and place attachment. It is important to note that personalization was included as part of the definition of the function and aesthetics of the space.

Survey Design.   *Survey design* differs from the other methods discussed in that there is no manipulation of variables, as seen in experimental design; there is no formulation of groups, as discussed in causal comparative studies; and we are not looking for relationships or predictions, as observed in correlational design. When utilizing survey design, information is collected from people to describe characteristics of the group or attitudes, opinions, or beliefs of the group (Fraenkel & Wallen, 2006). Surveys are meant to describe, explain, or evaluate. As we discussed previously, surveys involve asking questions, and data can be collected through written questionnaires; face-to-face interviews; telephone interviews; focus groups; or visuals such as drawings, photographs, models, or maps.

With a survey methodology, it is important to determine the purpose of the research first. In other words, you must have a thorough understanding of the design problem or what it is that you want to study (Fraenkel & Wallen, 1996). This comes through a literature review. Next, you must decide a survey design: cross-sectional versus longitudinal.

When designing the survey instrument, you must be cognizant of wording, sentence structure, and whether you will use open-ended or closed-ended questions. The structure of the survey instrument is critical to the success of your research study. In Chapter 1 we discussed a study in which we surveyed undergraduate students to compare their (1) perceived value of research in interior design practice, (2) perceptions of who should conduct research, (3) attitudes toward research in interior design education, and (4) definitions of research. When devising the questionnaire, we were aware of the purpose of the study, and the questions on our survey instrument were organized and ordered accordingly. (See Figure 2.3.)

As mentioned earlier, one of the key problems with survey design is response rate, particularly when written, mailed questionnaires or Web-based questionnaires are used. In order to increase your response rate, you want to ensure that you keep your questions simple and specific. The graphics and directions on your survey are also important, since you will not be there to answer questions.

Content Analysis.   Guerin and Dohr (2007) discuss *content analysis* as a method or strategy to use when conducting a research study. In some research methods books, content analysis is placed under the heading of qualitative research (see Fraenkel & Wallen, 2006). In others, content analysis is treated as a separate chapter and is discussed in a quantitative format (see Sommer & Sommer, 2002). We have placed content analysis under the heading of research design because this is a strategy that can be utilized when conducting an investigation. In content analysis, the researcher is systematically evaluating printed or spoken material. The material can come from magazines, newspapers, publications, recorded interviews, letters, television, and advertising. The key to content analysis is quantification. In other words, the researcher is interested in utilizing numbers to explain the data, which is why we have placed this strategy under the heading of quantitative research (Sommer & Sommer, 2002).

This first part of the questionnaire provides directions for the participants. It is imperative that the questionnaire be clear and concise. Next, you will notice that subjects are assured that their responses will be kept confidential, a promise that relates to ethical issues for research studies.

Notice how this heading relates back to the purpose of the study.

An example of an open-ended question for an empirical study that is more qualitative in nature.

Heading relates back to purpose of the study.

Example of instructions given to the participants so there is no confusion as to how the questions should be answered.

Example of a question using a Likert scale that is quantitative in nature.

UNDERGRADUATE STUDENT ATTITUDES TOWARD RESEARCH

You are invited to participate in a research study that examines undergraduate Interior Design students' perceptions regarding "research" conducted by Joan Dickinson Ph.D., John Marsden, Ph.D., and Marilyn Read, Ph.D. Your responses will be kept completely confidential. We ask no identifying information on the questionnaire. It is very important that you complete the entire questionnaire. Once you have answered a question, please do not go back to revise your answer. We are interested in your first instinctual response. Thank you for your willingness to participate.

DEFINITION OF RESEARCH

In the space below, please define the term *research*:

ATTITUDES TOWARD RESEARCH IN INTERIOR DESIGN PRACTICE

For the questions below, we are asking for your attitudes toward research as they relate to interior design practice. Please circle your answer below. Note the following: 1 = Strongly Agree; 2 = Agree; 3 = Unsure; 4 = Disagree; and 5 = Strongly Disagree

1. I believe research findings can provide useful information to Interior Design practitioners.

   1   Strongly Agree
   2   Agree
   3   Unsure
   4   Disagree
   5   Strongly Disagree

2. The results of research are used extensively in Interior Design practice.

   1   Strongly Agree
   2   Agree
   3   Unsure
   4   Disagree
   5   Strongly Disagree

Figure 2.3. Extracts from a questionnaire for a research study.

To provide an example, Eckman, Clemons, and Oliver (2001) used content analysis to examine the classification of articles, research methods, patterns of authorship, and funding sources of the *Journal of Interior Design* from 1975 to 1997. For this research study, Eckman et al. (2001) clearly operationalized their major themes. Classification of articles was defined as research, theory development, or editorial, and each definition was given in the published research investigation, which is a key factor when completing content analysis. Chapter 9 provides an example of informed design based on visual content analysis.

Qualitative Research Strategies

In qualitative research, we are often concerned with a holistic approach (Fraenkel & Wallen, 2006; Groat & Wang, 2002), and in many cases, we are interested in describing the "why" behind a research problem in as much detail as possible. A major theme of qualitative research is that the investigator will describe the quality of the problem versus the quantity. There are several components of qualitative research strategies. First, the natural setting serves as the source of data collection (Groat & Wang, 2002). In qualitative research, the investigator does not manipulate any variables. Nor is the environment changed in any manner. Rather, the problem is studied within the context of the natural setting. Second, many forms of qualitative research employ several modes of data collection (e.g., observations, open-ended interviews, and diaries) and often include prolonged contact in the field or situation (Groat & Wang, 2002). Third, qualitative research can be more open-ended in nature, and the data is often described in words instead of numbers.

Let's look at an example. Joan became interested in the meaningful use of time among nursing home residents diagnosed with dementia. After reading the literature and conducting casual observations in numerous nursing homes across the United States, she noticed the lack of "purposeful activity" (Kuhn, Kasayka, & Lechner, 2002, p. 291) among

March 11, 2006, 2:00 p.m.
All of the residents are in the activity room. There are no scheduled activities, and the residents sit and do nothing. The TV is on, but no one watches. There is country music playing in the background, but no one listens.

Resident 1 begins to push the trash barrel around the activity room to the exit door. This resident and many others exhibit a repetitive motion. Rubbing hands together is a common symptom as well as rubbing their hand along the handrail in the hallway. The handrail is not used for support; rather, it is used more for the textural quality that is derived from the hand touching a different, three-dimensional material (wood handrail that projects from the drywall).

Resident 2 is rubbing the piping on the chair. This resident seems to be interested in the 3-dimensional quality and is specifically pulling the piping from the chair fabric.

2:45 p.m.
Resident 1 is interested in the panic bar of the exit door and other shiny objects (door hardware in particular). She rubs her hand along this textural and reflective change.

3:30 p.m.
Majority of residents are still in activity room. Sitting and staring into space or sleeping are common ways to pass the time. I talked with the head nurse. She also mentions the fascination with texture and with rubbing hands over different textures. For example, she explains how residents will rub their hands over signage that has a tactile quality to it.

Based on my thoughts thus far, residents seem to be attracted to 3-D qualities (3-dimensional change, but can be subtle change). They are also interested in repetitive motion, particularly motion that involves rubbing. There is nothing to do in this facility. So the residents find interest in objects that are shiny and reflective since they offer something unique and different in a bland, medical setting.

Figure 2.4. Example of open-ended observations for qualitative forms of research.

residents and began to question the quality of life in the nursing home setting. She began her qualitative investigation by conducting open-ended observations in a local nursing home for an extended time frame.

As you read Figure 2.4, you will notice several aspects about this beginning investigation that hold true for qualitative strategies. The nursing home served as the natural setting and became an important part of the observation recording. As Joan observed, she noticed that residents were interested in reflective and three-dimensional qualities in the context of the setting (e.g., door hardware and light switches) that often occupied their time. Her observations were recorded through the use of descriptive words and sketches and support the existing literature, which states that residents often have nothing to do. Yet the open-ended nature of the observations allowed Joan to explore areas of resident behavior that may not have been captured through quantitative forms of research (e.g., resident rubbing motion and repetitive quality of their motions). She was also able to talk with the staff on an impromptu basis to gain more insight into the behaviors she was interested in.

Research Ethics

In this section, we examine ethical issues involved in conducting research investigations. When working with human subjects, it is important to consider the following questions: (1) Will any physical or psychological harm come to anyone as a result of my research? and (2) Will the participants be at any risk, no matter how minimal? If minimal risk is involved, the investigator must establish a clear and fair agreement up front with the subjects prior to their participation in the actual research study. In other words, you must let your subjects know up front of the risks, and then respect their decision to decline if they so desire. When we conducted the study that examined how carpet influenced gait among older individuals, a consent form was signed by each participant that clearly stated the risks involved.

As a researcher, you are also bound to keep information confidential unless otherwise agreed upon. No one should have access to the data except those involved in the research study, and subjects should be assigned numbers if applicable. When reporting results, the subjects' numbers are reported rather than their names.

Many universities and governmental agencies have Institutional Review Boards (IRBs) that deal with human subject issues. When we conducted the study that examined how carpet influenced gait among older individuals, we submitted the necessary paperwork (e.g., a thorough description of the study, consent form, how data was handled to ensure confidentiality) to the IRB for approval prior to the start of our study. This internal review process ensured that our study and the protocol used provided the necessary protection for our subjects and also dealt with liability issues for the investigators (Figure 2.5).

Quality of Research

In addition to dealing with human subjects issues, it is also important, prior to the start of the investigation, to consider factors that influence the quality of the research study and how the research methodology can be improved. In this next part, we discuss reliability and validity, two characteristics of an investigation that relate to its quality.

Reliability

Reliability examines the consistency of the measurement data or the scores obtained (Fraenkel & Wallen, 1996). To illustrate, consider a test to measure typing ability. If the test is reliable, an individual who obtains a high score on this test the first time should score high again when taking the test for a second time. When conducting our study that examined how older individuals walked on carpet versus vinyl tile, we videotaped each individual when walking. This allowed us to review the tapes after the data was collected. Using an instrument we developed to evaluate the gait, two independent investigators scored each subject. These scores were compared and an inter-rater reliability measure was provided. Inter-rater reliability measures agreement between the two investigators (Sommer & Sommer, 2002). A high agreement score means that the instrument is a reliable measuring device.

You are invited to participate in a study examining the effect of selected commercial-grade carpet on the balance of older adults to be conducted by Joan Dickinson, Assistant Professor. We hope to learn how commercial carpeting affects balance control. You were selected as a possible participant because you have met the criteria required to participate in that you are over the age of 60 and meet the definition of healthy, community-dwelling older adult. If you decide to participate, we, Joan Dickinson and Associates, will require 20 to 30 minutes of your time. You will be individually escorted to the balance machine, where you will be equipped with a safety harness. You will be assisted onto the balance machine. Once your feet are in place, the safety harness will be connected. You will be instructed to stand upright and to direct your gaze straight ahead. For most of the assessment, you will stand quietly on the balance platform. For one assessment, the platform will move slightly to tilt the toes up and down.

The testing procedures are not designed to make you lose your balance. One of the procedures requires you to close your eyes, and one will have the forceplate you stand on move forward and backward slightly. You can move your feet between measurements and use the grab bars to maintain your balance between tasks. Individual measurements last 20 seconds. The total testing period should last 20 to 30 minutes.

The risks involved with this research are minimal. Prior to using the balance machine, you will be equipped with a safety harness. If you should lose your balance, the safety harness will catch you. It may feel awkward to wear the safety harness, and you may not need it, but it is a necessary safety precaution. You might feel tired after standing.

There is no compensation for participation in this study beyond receiving the results. In the event of physical injury resulting from the research procedures described, neither [name of institution] University, the Principal Investigator, nor her staff are able to offer financial compensation or absorb the cost of medical treatment.

Any information obtained in connection with this study and that can be identified with you will remain confidential. You will be given a subject identification number. You will not be identified by name. Only the Principal Investigator and graduate assistant will have access to the files. Any publications or conference presentations will use subject identification numbers. Your name will not be used. If at any time during the study you feel you can no longer participate, you may withdraw at any time without penalty. You may also withdraw any data which has been collected about yourself. Your decision whether or not to participate will not jeopardize your future relations with [name of institution] University.

If you have any questions we invite you to ask them now. If you have any questions later, you may contact [contact information]. You will be provided with a copy of this form to keep.

HAVING READ THE INFORMATION PROVIDED, YOU MUST DECIDE WHETHER OR NOT YOU WISH TO PARTICIPATE. YOUR SIGNATURE INDICATES YOUR WILLINGNESS TO PARTICIPATE. THE CONSENT FORM MUST BE SIGNED PRIOR TO ANY TESTING PROCEDURES.

_____   _____
Participant's signature   Date

Figure 2.5. Example of informed consent form.

Notice how this first part of the informed consent letter given to the subjects of this research study explains exactly the testing procedure.

These paragraphs explain the risks of the research and protect the research investigator and university from liability.

This paragraph explains subject confidentiality.

Validity

Validity refers to the appropriateness, correctness, or usefulness of an instrument for your particular research study. In other words, is the instrument valid in terms of measuring the type of data you would like to collect, and will you be able to make the necessary inferences once the data are analyzed (Fraenkel & Wallen, 2006)? *Internal validity* examines how valid it is to conclude that the independent variable is responsible for the changes measured in the dependent variable (Kirk, 1995; Touliatos & Compton, 1988). Control of extraneous variables will increase the internal validity of the study.

External validity is concerned with the generalization of the results to the population (Touliatos & Compton, 1988). When probability sampling techniques are used, external validity is stronger (Kirk, 1995). Studies that use non-random sampling techniques may lack external validity (Howell, 1987).

Analysis and Interpretation

The last part of the research process involves analyzing the data. Data can be analyzed using both descriptive statistics and inferential statistics. *Descriptive statistics* are used to describe the data and include frequencies, percentages, measures of central tendency (e.g., the mean, median, and mode), and measures of variability (e.g., the range and standard deviation) (Guerin & Dohr, 2007; Howell, 1987; Pagano, 1994).

Inferential statistics are used to infer characteristics from the sample to the population within a margin of error. This type of statistical analysis can be used to establish causal relationships between variables (Guerin & Dohr, 2007; Howell, 1987; Pagano, 1994).

In the end, data must be analyzed to gain results concerning the problem. Moreover, the results must be analyzed and related back to the literature cited in the literature review section. Remember that the goal of the research study is to expand the body of knowledge. Thus, the interpretation of the findings must reinforce how the literature was moved forward. Once the data are analyzed and interpreted, typically new problems arise that merit study. This is why the research process is cyclical.

Research Example One: Falls, Gait, and Carpet

In this next section, we walk through a research study and examine the terminology we have learned in this chapter thus far. In this investigation, how gait is affected by carpet versus vinyl tile is the focus. Below is the introduction to the research study. Notice how this introduction is written to justify why the research is important and thoroughly cites the literature. Also notice how the introduction is organized from the general (e.g., demographics on falling) to the specific (e.g., relationship between falling and the interior environment).

Studies show that falls are a serious problem and are one of the leading causes of death for older adults. Approximately one-third of individuals aged 65 years and older who live at home sustain one or more falls each year. The risk of falling not only increases with age but also reaches a prevalence of 50 percent in persons over the age of 85. Unfortunately, these figures are considered low estimates of the problem, since most falls experienced by senior citizens are not reported.

When a fall occurs, the older adult is much more likely to suffer from injury including bone fractures, sprains, and dislocations, with hip fractures having the greatest impact on an individual (NCIPC, 2007). Yet physical injury is only part of the problem. Falls can result in decreased functioning, disability, and a reduced quality of life and account for up to one-third of all nursing home admissions. Decreased confidence and fear of falling can lead to further functional decline, depression, feelings of helplessness, and social isolation. In fact, falls are the most common cause of morbidity and mortality among the elderly, and falls kill more people than any other type of home injury (Gibson, 1998; Gray-Miceli, 1997).

Falling can occur as a result of normal age-related changes, certain medications, balance and gait disorders, chronic disease, and environmental design hazards (e.g., slippery floor surfaces, high-pile carpets, steep stairs, clutter, and inadequate lighting) (Connell & Wolf, 1997; Hausdorff, Edelberg, Mitchell, Goldberger, & Wei, 1997; Schoenfelder & Why, 1997; Shroyer, Elias, Hutton, & Curry, 1997; Wilson, 1998). In particular, many falls experienced by the older adult occur when a change in body position is required such as walking on different floor surfaces (Hausdorff et al., 1997; Maki, 1997; Woolley, Czaja, & Drury, 1997). Many of these factors can be modified, and studies suggest that falling may be reduced by multifactorial intervention programs (Pynoos, Rose, Rubenstein, Choi, & Sabata, 2006; Tse, 2005). Yet much of the fall-related research has focused on how the aging process affects gait. The problem with this clinical focus is that little thought has been given to the built environment. Considering that one-third of all falls experienced by the older adult are caused by environmental design hazards, a research focus that examines how floor surface impacts gait is needed (Shroyer et al., 1997; see Dickinson et al., 2000 for a detailed description of this study).

Remember that the researcher must know the literature in order to expand it (Groat & Wang, 2002). Notice how primary and secondary sources are cited and how the last section justifies the need for this investigation. Next, the purpose of the study is stated and the methods of the research study are thoroughly described.

The purpose of this research was to determine whether residential carpet and pad affected gait among healthy, community-dwelling older adults.

The research team gave a 20- to 25-minute presentation explaining the purpose of the research study to various senior citizen organizations located in West Texas. Upon completing the presentation, the research team asked for volunteers. Those individuals who expressed interest in participating completed a medical information sheet that provided the research team with a detailed medical history. A total of 39 subjects volunteered to participate. From the 39 interested subjects, a purposive sampling technique was used in order to ensure that potential subjects met certain criteria. Subjects were excluded from the research study if they were (1) using assistive devices for standing (e.g., canes or walkers), (2) diagnosed with vestibular problems, (3) diagnosed with Parkinson's disease or other neurological disorders, (4) diagnosed with ear infections at the time of the study, (5) diagnosed with severe orthopedic problems (e.g., osteoporosis, previous hip or spine fractures, severe stooped posture; individuals who were experiencing mild to moderate arthritis were not excluded), and (6) experiencing problems with dizziness.

After the research team examined the information provided on the medical information sheet, three subjects were excluded from the research study. These three subjects had numerous medical conditions (e.g., multiple sclerosis, glaucoma, and use of assistive devices) that would have affected their gait performance. The remaining 36 subjects were contacted by phone to schedule a time and date for data collection. Of the 36 subjects, 29 agreed to be tested. Four subjects did not arrive for their scheduled time; thus, the total sample size for this investigation was 25 subjects.

In this study, a purposive sampling technique was used (i.e., non-random sampling) to ensure that the sample represented a group of healthy older individuals who did not have preexisting conditions that might affect their gait. This sampling technique helped to control extraneous variables that might influence the dependent variable, thus increasing the internal validity of the investigation. Remember that control is a feature of experimental design.

> Subjects were measured on carpet and vinyl tile. The carpet used for the gait course was a 36-ounce, 1/8-inch gauge, 100 percent nylon, solid color (neutral gray), 1/2-inch pile height, cut-pile carpet. This specification represented the most common carpet specified for residential use during the 1998 year (RBI International Carpet Consultants, 1997). Because the purpose of this research was to determine if selected residential carpeting affected gait among older adults, the goal was to simulate an actual residential carpet installation. In order to achieve this simulation, padding was adhered to the back of the carpet. A rebonded polyurethane pad, 6-pound density, 7/16 inch thick, was recommended for use with this carpet (Carpet Cushion Council, 1997). The vinyl tile used for this investigation (i.e., a vinyl composition tile, 12 inches by 12 inches, 1/8-inch gauge, and light mauve in color) was an existing floor material installed at the testing site, the Neurology Research and Education Center located in West Texas.

This section above describes the independent variables for the research study. In this case, the researcher manipulated flooring and used carpet for one test condition and vinyl tile flooring for the second test condition. The choice of carpet and pad is justified and illustrates the importance of the literature in providing current (at the time of the investigation), rationalized decisions.

A gait evaluation scale was developed by the authors. Sitting to standing, standing to sitting, manner of turning, gait speed, number of steps, change in gait speed, single-leg timed stance, and weaving were measured. These variables were chosen due to their practical applications—in other words, sitting to standing, standing to sitting, and turning are types of activities that are encountered by the older adult in everyday life. The single-leg timed stance was used because this has been shown to be a predictive measure of falling in older adults. Gait speed was defined as the duration of the subject's gait and was measured using a stopwatch. Number of steps was defined as the number of steps taken while walking the gait course. Counting of steps started when the subject took the first step and stopped at the start of the first turn.

In order to increase the reliability of the gait scale, the subjects were videotaped while walking the gait course. In addition, prior to completing the research study, a trial experiment was conducted in order to give the research team training prior to commencement of the investigation, and in order to make any necessary revisions to the gait scale. Finally, two members of the research team scored the qualitative aspects of the scale independently.

The section above describes the dependent variables or measurement variables. In this experiment, we were interested in examining how the independent variables (carpet versus vinyl tile) influenced the change in the dependent variables (e.g., gait speed, number of steps), a hallmark of experimental design. Also notice how the reliability of the instrument is mentioned. Several items from the instrument were pulled from well-established scales with high reliability. Next, the subjects were videotaped in order to reexamine their walking patterns on the test conditions, and the tapes were reviewed by two independent reviewers.

Research Example Two: Older Adults' and Family
Members' Perceptions of Assisted Living

In this study, another example is presented to highlight other ways of collecting information from people. The introduction to the research that follows defines the problem and identifies the purpose. (See Marsden, 2005, for a detailed description of the research.)

> Many older Americans would like to age in their own homes. When this is not feasible, frail older adults must consider alternatives. Moving in with family is not a desirable option for more than two-thirds of older Americans (AARP, 2000). Relocating to a nursing home is not only an unwelcome choice but also a dreaded one. Assisted living, a relatively new industry, is promoted as a favorable alternative to traditional long-term care, largely due to its resident-centered philosophy and residential environment. However, it is unclear whether assisted-living buildings are perceived favorably by older adults and family members. The purpose of this research is to examine older adults and family members' perceptions of assisted-living building exteriors and interior spaces including entries, living rooms, and dining rooms.

In the next section, the methodology for the research is described. Specifically, a face-to-face interview format was used to facilitate data collection from older adults, and responses were structured through a multiple sorting task to engage older adults and minimize the monotony associated with most surveys. A convenience sampling technique was used because a sampling frame does not exist for all older adults who reside in assisted-living buildings and all family members of older adults.

A series of small studies were conducted by Marsden (2005) that employed a method, called the picture preference procedure

(Kaplan & Kaplan, 1989). In this procedure, participants view pictures of existing or simulated environments and indicate how much they like or dislike each picture using a five-point rating scale. The task is easy and even enjoyable for most people. Although photographs of environments are not the same as "being there," studies have demonstrated that responses to photographs of environments correlate highly with responses to actual environments (Stamps, 1990).

The *picture preference procedure* was adapted for the studies that focused on assisted living. All of the studies used color photographs of existing exteriors or interior spaces of assisted-living buildings. Exterior scenes typically focused on either main entries or an expanse of the building near the main entry. Photographs were taken from a main parking lot or street under sunny conditions with the vegetation in bloom. Interior scenes focused on entries or foyers, common living rooms, and common dining rooms and included the entire space from a major access point. All scenes, whether they focused on the exterior shell or interior rooms, comprised buildings that were freestanding, three stories or less, and in good condition.

A face-to-face format was used for all of the studies. Directions were read aloud, and responses were recorded by the investigator. The actual interview procedure consisted of two distinct parts: a rating scale and open-ended questions. For the first portion, participants were told that they would be looking at photographs of retirement housing whose cost and location were the same. Participants were asked to imagine they were helping a close friend or relative to select a housing arrangement and were instructed to sort photographs into piles marked with bold, large type, based on a five-point rating scale. The second part of the interview asked participants to explain, in an open-ended format, why they rated certain scenes favorably or unfavorably. More than 500 participants, consisting of older adults and family members, evaluated more than 60 different assisted-living buildings in Alabama, Florida, Massachusetts, and Michigan across several studies.

This research shows an example of survey design in which subjects responded to visuals in the form of photographs using a multiple sorting task in a face-to-face interview format.

The Programming Process

In this last section of the chapter, we explain the programming process and examine how the steps taken for programming are either different or similar to the research process.

Defining the Problem

In programming, we are identifying client needs, values, and problems that can be solved through design. As we discussed earlier, research problems tend to be specific. In programming, defining the problems tends to be broader in nature. Let's go back to our example of the labor, delivery, recovery, and postpartum unit or birthing center. If you were completing a programming document for an LDRP unit located in Roanoke, Virginia, you would be interested in identifying issues such as wayfinding, creating a healing, nurturing, and homelike environment for soon-to-be mothers, safety of infants and patients, privacy, family visitation, amenities for laboring mothers, staff needs, and the spread of infections (e.g., hand washing) to name a few. These types of problems need to be identified so that design may be used to solve them. In programming, typically the identification of problems comes directly from the client through interviews, questionnaires, or site visits.

Yet, an understanding of the programming problems can be informed by staying current with the literature as well. To illustrate, Ulrich et al. (2004) identified 600 research investigations that examined how "hospital design can impact clinical outcomes" (p. 2). This published investigation would be an excellent article for interior designers to read in order to understand common problems that influence hospital design and to eventually implement evidence-based design solutions. As stated in Chapter 1, however, programming is site and client specific. In this example, the problems identified for the LDRP in Roanoke may be different from other LDRP units across the country.

The Existing State

As discussed in Duerk's book (1993), the existing state consists of the constraints and parameters for the project that must be taken into consideration before implementing design solutions. The existing state can consist of a background section, depending on how the design firm organizes its programming documents. For programming, the background section, or what is sometimes referred to as a literature review, is typically broader in context than the literature review for a research project and includes any background information that is relevant to designing the project. The background section becomes a record of the existing state and can include physical conditions such as site, geography, and climate parameters; code constraints; and a client profile (Duerk, 1993). For the designer, reading the literature provides familiarity with the field or topic area and, most importantly, allows the designer to base decisions on research findings and fact versus opinion or past experience. Thus, for programming, the literature review can be used for the following: (1) to glean facts and ideas for a project, (2) to learn about relevant background information related to a specific project, (3) to justify design solutions, and (4) to offer design strategies and solutions that create a foundation of current information from which to design.

What is important to note here is that the background section or literature review for programming is much broader in context than a literature review for a research study. In our birthing center example, the research study was focused on the mother's perceptions of hominess. Thus, the literature review would focus exclusively on the variables for the study. For programming purposes, the background section would be broader and would include the specific code requirements for the LDRP in Roanoke, Virginia; an analysis of the site including views to and from the site, climate, landscaping, the existing neighborhood or zoning requirements; a client profile, which would document the needs, activities, and work flow of the client; and a broad review of literature that relates to design issues for birthing centers. This literature could include design solutions or best-practice guidelines on lighting, space requirements, wayfinding, or finishes for LDRPs. As stated by Duerk (1993), "The constraints imposed by the existing state become the external set of forces that shape the design" (p. 13).

The Future State

In addition to documenting existing constraints, the programming process also provides sections that deal with the future mission and goals of the project along with performance criteria (Cherry, 1999; Duerk, 1993). In this part of programming, the client values and objectives about the future design of the particular company are taken into consideration. In programming there is often a section that documents the mission of the company, and the company goals and objectives are listed. The goals of the project are the desired result or purpose of the project, while the objectives examine how these goals will be achieved. Essentially, the goals state the future—they are what we want to achieve for the project. The objective is a statement about how the building must perform in order to achieve the goal. The goals tend to be more general, while the objectives tend to be more specific. Yet the objective must be general enough to support several design solutions.

Whether we are dealing with the existing or future state, like the research process, the programming process involves data collection, and typically this data collection occurs from the client of the project. Data are most commonly collected through questionnaires, face-to-face interviews, site visits, and focus groups. In Table 2.1, we provide a comparison of the research process and programming process.

Summary and Recommended Readings

How to Design and Evaluate Research in Education by Fraenkel and Wallen (2006)

Architectural Research Methods by Groat and Wang (2002)

A Practical Guide to Behavioral Research by Sommer and Sommer (2002)

Inquiry by Design by Zeisel (2006)

InformeDesign "Research 101 Parts I, II, and III" (http://www.informedesign.umn.edu) by Guerin and Dohr (2007).

We have also provided a brief overview of the programming process and have compared how the process for programming differs from the research process. Students who are interested in more detailed information on programming should consult, *Programming for Design* (1999) by Edith Cherry and *Architectural Programming* (1993) by Donna Duerk.

Table 2.1. Comparison of the Research Process and the Programming Process

Process	Research	Programming
Defining the Problem	The problem is clearly defined and is specific in nature.	The problems are broader in context but apply only to a specific client.
Literature Review or Existing State	The literature review essentially focuses on the variables of interest and rationalizes and justifies why the study is important to conduct.	The literature review is broader and covers all relevant background information for the project. It provides the conditions and constraints from which to design from.
Data Collection	Involves collecting data.	Involves collecting data. Data can be collected in a number of ways similar to what was discussed in the Research Process section.
Sampling	Sampling is an important part of research. The type of sampling technique used determines the external validity of the project.	Sampling has a different purpose. If we are completing a programming document for the Rainbow Riders Daycare Center in Blacksburg, VA, our sample might consist of a cross section of the staff who work in this facility. We would be interested in talking with a range of the staff including upper-level as well as lower-level positions to better understand the needs of this particular daycare center. We might also interview a cross section of parents and possibly observe the children who attend this facility. In this example, we would not be interested in probability sampling techniques.
Variables	We are interested in the variables. The research problem often defines the variables of interest, and the literature review is focused on what has been written about the variables of interest.	We are typically not concerned with variables.
Research Design	Research design involves which strategy the researcher will use prior to conducting the actual study. The strategy used typically depends on the definition of the problem. The type of research design is an important consideration during the research process, as some strategies will work better than others depending on the research problem.	Research design is not as important. Rather, we are interested in defining client needs, values, and problems. These are documented through various forms of data collection such as questionnaires and interviews. We usually do not conduct an actual research investigation because of time constraints in the profession. Instead, we would search for published research investigations to read as part of the background section or existing state.

BIBLIOGRAPHY

American Association of Retired Persons (AARP). (2000). *Fixing to stay: A national survey on housing and home modifications*. Washington, DC: AARP.

Brawley, E. C. (2006). *Design innovations for aging and Alzheimer's creating caring environments*. Hoboken, NJ: John Wiley & Sons.

Carpet Cushion Council. (1997). Carpet cushion your home [Brochure]. Riverside, CT: Author.

Connell, B. R., & Wolf, S. L. (1997). Environmental and behavioral circumstances associated with falls at home among healthy elderly individuals. *Archives of Physical Medicine Rehabilitation, 78*, 179–186.

Cooper Marcus, C. (1995). *House as a mirror of self: Exploring the deeper meanings of home*. Berkeley, CA: Conari Press.

Dickinson, J. I., Marsden, J. P., & Read, M. A. (2007). Empirical design research: Student definitions, perceptions, and values. *Journal of Interior Design, 32*(2), 1–12.

Dickinson, J. I., Shroyer, J. L., & Elias, J. W. (2000). The effect of residential carpeting on the gait of healthy, community-dwelling older adults. *Housing and Society, 27*(2), 1–18.

Dickson, A. W., & White, A. C. (1993). Are we speaking the same language? Practitioners' perceptions of research and the state of the profession. *Journal of Interior Design, 19*(1), 3–10.

Duerk, D. P. (1993). *Architectural programming information management for design*. New York: John Wiley & Sons.

Eckman, M., Clemons, S., & Oliver, B. (2001). An empirical analysis of the Journal of Interior Design. *Journal of Interior Design, 27*(2),1–13.

Eshelman, P. E., & Evans, G. W. (2002). Home again: Environmental predictors of place attachment and self-esteem for new retirement community residents. *Journal of Interior Design, 28*(1), 1–9.

Fisher, T. (2004, Fall). Architects behaving badly: Ignoring environmental behavior research. *Harvard Design Magazine*, 1–3.

Fraenkel, J. R., & Wallen, N. E. (1996). *How to design and evaluate research in education* (3rd ed.). New York: McGraw-Hill.

Fraenkel, J. R., & Wallen, N. E. (2006). *How to design and evaluate research in education* (6th ed.). New York: McGraw-Hill.

Gibson, L. (1998). How safe are your houses? *Professional Builder, 63*(3), 71–74.

Gray-Miceli, D. (1997). Falling among the aged. *Advance for Nurse Practitioners, 5*(7), 41–44.

Groat, L., & Wang, D. (2002). Architectural research methods. New York John Wiley & Sons.

Guerin, D. A., & Dohr, J. (2007). Research 101: Part 1 research-based practice. InformeDesign. Retrieved from http://www.informedesign.umn.edu

Guerin, D. A., & Thompson, J. A. (2004). Interior design education in the 21st century: An educational transformation. *Journal of Interior Design, 30*(1), 1–12.

Hamilton, D. K. (2004). Four levels of evidence-based practice. The American Institute of Architects. Retrieved from http://www.aia.org

Hasell, M. J., & Scott, S. C. (1996). Interior design visionaries' explorations of emerging trends. *Journal of Interior Design, 22*(2), 1–14.

Hausdorff, J. M., Edelberg, H. K., Mitchell, S. L., Goldberger, A. L., & Wei, J. Y. (1997). Increased gait unsteadiness in community-dwelling elderly fallers. *Archives of Physical Medicine and Rehabilitation, 78,* 278–283.

Howell, D. C. (1987). *Statistical methods for psychology* (2nd ed.). Boston: PWS-Kent Publishing Company.

Kaplan S., &Kaplan, R. (1989). The visual environment: Public participation in design and planning. *Journal of Social Issues, 45*(1), 59–86.

Kirk, R. E. (1995). Experimental design procedures for the behavioral sciences. Pacific Grove, CA: Brooks Cole Publishing Company.

Kuhn, D., Kasayka, R. E., & Lechner, C. (2002). Behavioral observations and quality of life among persons with dementia in 10 assisted living facilities. *American Journal of Alzheimer's Disease and Other Dementias, 17*(5), 291–298.

Lynch, K. (1960). *The image of the city.* Cambridge: MIT Press.

Maki, B. E. (1997). Gait changes in older adults: Predictors of falls or indicators of fear. *Journal of the American Geriatrics Society, 45,* 313–320.

Marsden, J. P. (2005). *Humanistic design of assisted living.* Baltimore: Johns Hopkins University Press.

National Center for Injury Prevention and Control (NCIPC). (2007). Falls among older adults: Figures and maps. Retrieved from http://www.cdc.gov

Pagano, R. R. (1994). *Understanding statistics in the behavioral sciences* (4th ed.). St. Paul, MN: West Publishing Company.

Pynoos, J., Rose, D., Rubenstein, L., Choi, I. H., & Sabata, D. (2006). Evidence-based interventions in fall-prevention. *Home and Health Care Services Quarterly, 25*(1/2), 55–73.

RBI International Carpet Consultants. (1997). Carpet styles and market areas. Dalton, GA: RBI.

Shin, J. H., Maxwell, L. E., & Eshelman, P. (2004). Hospital birthing room design: A study of mothers' perception of hominess. *Journal of Interior Design, 30*(2), 23–36.

Schoenfelder, D. P., & Why, K. V. (1997). A fall prevention educational program for community dwelling seniors. *Public Health Nursing, 14*(6), 383–396.

Shroyer, J. L., Elias, J. W., Hutton, J. T., & Curry, Z. (1997). *Preventing falls: A defensive approach.* Lubbock, TX: Neurology Research and Education Center.

Sommer, R., & Sommer, B. (2002). *A practical guide to behavioral research.* New York: Oxford University Press.

Stamps, A. (1990). Use of photographs to stimulate environments: A meta-analysis. *Perceptual and Motor Skills, 71,* 907–913.

Tinetti, M. E., & Williams, C. S. (1998). The effect of falls and fall injuries on functioning in community-dwelling older persons. *Journal of Gerontology: Medical Sciences, 53A,* M112–M119.

Touliatos, J., & Compton, N. H. (1988). *Research methods in human ecology/home economics.* Ames, Iowa: Iowa State University Press.

Tse, T. (2005). The environment and falls prevention: Do environmental modifications make a difference? *Australian Occupational Therapy Journal, 52,* 271–281.

Ulrich, R. (1984). View through a window may influence recovery from surgery. *Science, 224,* 420–421.

Ulrich, R., Quan, X., Zimring, C., Joseph, A., & Choudhary, R. (2004). The role of the physical environment in the hospital of the 21st century: A once-in-a-lifetime opportunity. Report for the Center of Health Design. Retrieved from http://www.healthdesign.org

Walliman, N. (2006). *Social research methods.* Thousand Oaks, CA: Sage Publications.

Wilson, E. B. (1998). Preventing patient falls. *American Association of Colleges of Nursing (AACN) Clinical Issues, 9*(1), 100–108.

Woolley, S. M., Czaja, S. J., & Drury, C. G. (1997). An assessment of falls in elderly men and women. *Journal of Gerontology: Medical Sciences, 52A,* M80–M87

Zeisel, J. (2006). *Inquiry by design.* New York: W. W. Norton & Company.

3 Sustainability and Information Gathering

Lisa Tucker

Abstract

C hapter 3 starts with an introduction to sustainability and provides background information on the importance of green design.
Next, terminology and relevant models and theories are discussed. In
the last section, both student and practitioner examples are provided
to illustrate informed design. For the first project, students relied on
published guidelines and product manufacturers' specifications to justify their decisions. They also read William McDonough and Michael
Braungart's book *Cradle to Cradle* (2002) and Daniel Quinn's *Ishmael*
(1995) to provide a theoretical underpinning to their design solutions.
Healthcare sustainable projects are discussed as well, and the students
relied on information obtained from the Center for Healthcare Design.
These projects tend to illustrate increased rigor in terms of information
gathering as the students read empirical research studies that guided
their work. The last example shows the connection between sustainability and historic preservation. This chapter illustrates different levels
of informed design as some projects rely more heavily on soft sources
of information, while others use hard sources (i.e., published investigations) to justify design decision making. In all of the project examples,
the students and practitioner are consumers of information gathering.

Introduction

During the past decade, sustainable design has become increasingly important to interior design, industrial design, and architecture as an awareness of the impact of design on the world's resources has come to the forefront. As early as the 1970s, Victor Papanek called for an end of wasteful design practices in the industrial design arena, claiming that design for obsolescence was unethical (Papanek, 1982). While his book was widely read, it had little overall impact on the processes of design or design education in the United States. For interior designers, it is critical that we ask ourselves "Why is sustainable design important?" To answer this question, we must first turn to the state of the world in which we are designing today.

In the twenty-first century, human beings live apart from the natural world. At some point during our evolution, we (in the West at least) chose to separate ourselves from the nature that surrounds us. We construct buildings in which we live and work that are totally insulated from the outside world. In our effort to expand our lifestyles, we have left a significant mark on the environment.

As humans, from our earliest history as a species, we have adapted to and shaped the world around us; we have gone from hunter-gatherer societies to agriculturally based ones. In the process we freed up an enormous amount of our time to think and create while also inventing culture. This ability to think and the time to do it has led to an amazing array of inventions and technological discoveries. In the mid- to late-nineteenth century, the Industrial Revolution radically changed the way we made virtually everything. Newly invented technology and machinery made it possible to create more items, gadgets, and machines for our human lives. We have focused on comfort and improving our lot in life for the most part since that time.

Living in the Built Environment

Several inventions have allowed us to progressively separate ourselves more each day from the world in which we live. Among these inventions are the automobile, the elevator, and air-conditioning. Our cities in the United States are designed around the use of the car. In choosing means of travel, we neglected to develop mass transit on a national scale in favor of the individualism made possible by the automobile. The advent of the elevator permitted us to build tall buildings high into the sky, leading to the skyscraper. Air-conditioning has led to thousands of buildings devoid of operable windows. The places where many of us work are controlled environments where the air temperature is between 65 and 75 degrees year round. During the winter, it is not uncommon to drive to work in the dark in our heated cars; stay in a heated room, perhaps without windows, all day; and then, at the end of the workday, drive home in our heated cars to our heated homes. Our only experience of nature is scenery along the way—assuming we look.

Our agricultural society has in fact been taken out of the hands of the local farmer for the most part. Food production is big business, handled by large conglomerates. When we go to buy our weekly groceries at the supermarket (a national chain), we can buy peppers from Guatemala, shrimp from Thailand, cheese from Wisconsin, milk from Indiana, corn from California, and wine from France. We can go literally weeks or months without eating a single item of food from within a 100-mile radius. Most of us are so far removed from the process of growing our own food, keeping our own livestock, or making our own cheese or butter that without the supermarket we would starve to death. So much of our food is prepackaged and overly processed that, in combination with our largely sedentary populations, we are forced to join a gym, buy a treadmill, or look for a miracle fat-burner on TV. Hospitals are being forced to install bariatric furniture because we are getting fatter and heavier and the chairs we designed in the last century cannot hold our twenty-first-century girth.

In our wake, we have left an indelible mark on the planet and have decimated many species. The World Watch Institute recently reported that species are going extinct at roughly 1,000 times the natural rate. Some 40 percent of the world's coral reefs are gone; the average atmospheric temperature increased .6 percent in the year between 2004 and 2005. In 2005, we experienced three of the ten worst hurricanes on record, and scientists attribute these severe hurricanes to global warming caused by emissions of carbon dioxide (Institute, 2006). Yet recently, National Public Radio reported that the average mileage of an automobile today is less than that of the original Model T (Kaufman, 2006)!

So why is sustainable design important? *Because our very survival as a species depends on it.* Designers have a tremendous role to play in the future of the planet. According to the Energy Information Administration, the United States consumed 99.89 quadrillion Btus of energy in 2005. This averaged out to 337 million Btus per person in the United States (EIA, Annual Review 2005, Table 1.5; DOE, 2005). According to the same report, the United States consumed 10,126,000 barrels of oil per day, resulting in a net dependence on import sources for 59.8 percent of this oil. In 2005, commercial buildings were responsible for the use of 5,820 trillion Btus of energy and residential buildings for 27.5 trillion Btus (DOE, 2005). As the population continues to explode around the world, and as other nations become more developed, the energy use in the world will be staggering.

As one of the primary users of energy, buildings must be designed to maximize efficiency, take advantage of natural light, embrace the prevailing climate, and reduce demand on power sources. Not only do the building systems need to reduce their fuel loads, but they must also be designed to incorporate materials that put less demand on manufacturing systems and energy use as well as be manufactured in a way that embraces environmental responsibility. Several programs are already in place to reduce fuel consumption including the ENERGY STAR program for houses and several initiatives through the Department of Energy. Little movement has taken place to completely redesign the way building materials are manufactured. Although several companies boast that their products are "green," there is no systematic way to make sure the processes used and resulting products are actually better for the environment. Notable exceptions to this include strides made within the textile industry, carpet manufacturing industry, and with some furniture manufacturers.

Definitions and Terminology

When we are gathering information on sustainability, it becomes apparent that there is not an agreed-upon definition. One of the most widely used definitions of sustainability was put forth by the Brundtland Commission in 1987. "Meeting the needs of the current generation without compromising the ability of future generations to meet their own needs" (Brundtland Report, 1987). Several experts in the area of sustainability find this definition lacking. The primary reason cited is that the definition is for sustainable development that implies a technologically based solution to the problems we face. An excellent article that describes several of the different theoretical frameworks for thinking about sustainability is "Reinterpreting Sustainable Architecture: The Place of Technology" by Simon Guy and Graham Farmer (2001). In the article, Guy and Farmer discuss six different frameworks or typologies they have identified on how people approach sustainable building design:

1. Eco-technic
2. Eco-centric
3. Eco-aesthetic
4. Eco-cultural
5. Eco-medical
6. Eco-social

Each type considers one area of emphasis to be of predominant concern. Integrated technology and a scientific approach to design and building characterize the *eco-technic* approach to sustainable design. An example of this type of approach would be the research being done across the United States for the Solar Decathlon competitions held by the Department of Energy. An *eco-centric* approach emphasizes harmony with nature and its systems such as is found in the work of Sym van der Ryn, an architect from California well known for his work in sustainable design. The *eco-aesthetic* paradigm calls for a new understanding of ecological knowledge and an expanded consciousness about nature. Vernacular local traditions highlight the *eco-cultural* method of design. The *eco-medical* typology stresses a nontoxic emphasis focused on health and well-being characteristic of much of the work being done with indoor air quality and low volatile organic compound (VOC) product development, while *eco-social* sustainability involves community participation to achieve an organic, decentralized, and democratic architecture.

Within the everyday world of design, the terminology vacillates between green design, sustainable design, eco-design, ecological design, environmental design, and some would even include universal design. *Cradle to cradle* has been singled out as a particular term for a subset of sustainable design concerns, as have biomimicry, biophilia, and permaculture. Some will differentiate sustainable design from green design through the claim that green design refers only to "green" materials and finishes, while sustainable design is broader in focus. Others, such as McDonough, identify shortcomings with the word "sustainable" because it implies the maintenance of a current state of being. Regardless of what one calls it or how one thinks about it, there is a clear call to the design professions to minimize the impact building design, construction, operations, and demolition have on the planet. What we call it is far less important than how we engage in change. For the purposes of this essay, I use the term sustainable design. By sustainable design, I mean design that works with the earth and natural systems and within which human beings adapt to their natural environments without forcefully adapting nature to mankind.

Theories

In this section, we consider three theoretical approaches to sustainability that provide a broad context within which design can occur: cradle to cradle, biomimicry, and biophilia.

Cradle to Cradle

Cradle to cradle, as presented and popularized by McDonough and Braungart (2002), describes a closed-loop system of production whereby biological nutrients (from nature) are separated from technical nutrients (man-made). By maintaining this separation, materials can be recycled infinitely into new products. McDonough has been instrumental in spreading the word about cradle to cradle and in working with client companies and manufacturers to create products that meet the stringent cradle-to-cradle protocol. In addition to his own architectural firm, McDonough created two spin-off companies—Green Blue and MBDC—to further the work outlined in *Cradle to Cradle*. McDonough and Braungart recognize that current manufacturing technologies and practices cannot produce cradle-to-cradle-compliant products, and it is therefore necessary to change the methods of entire industries. An excellent example of this change in industry practices is reflected by McDonough's work with DesignTex fabrics. According to McDonough, "waste = food." The goal is to eliminate all waste and to make everything usable. Infinite recycling eliminates this concept of waste.

Biomimicry

Janine Benyus used the term *biomimicry* for the title of her revolutionary book. Biomimicry regards nature as a model for design. Nature's systems and methods provide information for our species and how we can adapt to our surroundings without damaging the environment (Benyus, 1997).

Biophilia

The Biophilia Hypothesis is the title of a book of commentaries on the writings of E. O. Wilson. This collection, coedited by Stephen R. Kellert and Wilson, assembles articles that both promote and argue against the hypothesis. *Biophilia* describes the human need to associate with other life forms. Research reflecting support of this hypothesis demonstrates the therapeutic benefits of nature on the human condition (Frumkin, 2001). As humans, we are drawn to nature and benefit from our association with it.

Models

The following models of sustainable design differ from the preceding theories in that they provide a more concrete set of actions one can take to meet a more sustainable way of life. Included in the discussion are permaculture, ecological footprint, factor 4/factor 10, and ecological design.

Permaculture

Bill Mollison originally published a book about permaculture in Australia in 1978. The concept of *permaculture* calls for a completely integrated agricultural system in which local plants are used to create a self-contained ecological system that produces food and sustains itself over time (Mollison, 1978). Through the use of natural systems, the permaculture environment is able to feed itself and subsist without the addition of artificial intervention.

Ecological Footprint

One's *ecological footprint* refers to the impact one person has on the world. Various Web sites allow people to enter basic information about their personal consumption patterns. The results show how many planet Earths it would take if everyone on the planet maintained the same usage patterns. One site created by the Earthday network can be found at the following link: http://www.myfootprint.org/.

Factor 4 / Factor 10

Originally conceived as factor 4 and now expanded to a factor of 10, the concept behind this movement is to maintain the same standard of living as today, making the resources we use ten times more productive. Like McDonough and Braungart's cradle-to-cradle proposal, Factor 10 seeks to eliminate waste of resources. According to the *Factor 10 Manifesto,* "Violent and life-threatening reactions to the ecosphere to the stresses imposed by human activities are still growing in all parts of the world. Humanity continues to live in an increasingly dangerous and unsustainable environment. Essential environmental services are declining at an alarming pace" (Schmidt-Bleek, 2000, p. 1). The *Manifesto* goes on to say that "based on observations, the worldwide consumption of natural resources has to be lowered by at least one half on the average before a state of balanced co-evolution between the human economy and the ecosphere can be expected" (Schmidt-Bleek, 2000, p. 1). Factor 10 dictates that the 20 percent of the population that uses the 80 percent of resources (as we do in the United States) must increase resource productivity by at least a factor of 10.

Ecological Design

The title of a book by Sym Van der Ryn, *Ecological Design,* provides a framework for ecologically sound building design. The five principles of *ecological design* are as follows:

1. Solutions grow from place.
2. Make nature visible.
3. Design with nature.
4. Ecological accounting informs design.
5. Everyone is a designer (Van der Ryn, 1996).

Models for Implementation

Models for implementation provide guidelines or checklists for achieving specific sustainable design measures and can be measured quantifiably.

BEES

Building for Environmental and Economic Sustainability (BEES) is a software package that allows building designers to select economically viable and environmentally preferable materials while working on a project. For more specific information, see http://www.bfrl.nist.gov/ oae/software/bees.html.

LEED

Leadership in Environmental and Energy Design (LEED) consists of several building rating systems developed with and administered by the United States Green Building Council. Within the LEED system, buildings receive points for various categories when in compliance with the standard. If a building obtains enough points, it can become LEED Certified. The professional consultants trained to facilitate this process are LEED Accredited Professionals.

The Hannover Principles

Written by William McDonough for the 2000 EXPO world's fair in Germany, the *Hannover Principles* provide a series of broad theoretical sustainable design guidelines for participants in the fair to use when designing their own pavilions for the EXPO (McDonough, 1992).

The Natural Step

Established in 1988, the Natural Step seeks to provide business and industry with guidelines for a sustainable economic future. According to the Natural Step/U.S. Web site, the goal of the organization is "to accelerate global sustainability by guiding companies, communities and governments onto an ecologically, socially and economically sustainable path" (Gateway to the Natural Step, 2007).

The State of Minnesota Sustainable Design Guidelines

The University of Minnesota wrote and published the *Minnesota Sustainable Design Guidelines*. Currently in Version 2.0, the online guidelines contain a guidelines section, a worksheet to use, and appendices with more specific information (Minnesota Sustainable Guidelines, 2006).

Informed Design Examples

In 2005, the Interior Design Educator's Council created a resolution that stated, "Be it resolved that IDEC supports the concept of socially responsible design including the *Cradle to Cradle Paradigm* as an integral part of interior design education" (IDEC meeting, March 2005). In the same year, the Council for Interior Design Accreditation released revised standards with many new indicators about including sustainable design into an interior design education. As a result, much work has been done across the country to begin to incorporate sustainable design issues into the classroom or coursework as well to apply principles of sustainability to interior design projects. Following are several examples of student projects and a professional project for which information gathering about sustainability had an impact on design decisions.

Cradle-to-Cradle House Design Competition

For this project, students were challenged to design a single-family residence that would meet cradle-to-cradle protocol. The students each first selected one of four sites in Roanoke, Virginia. Having selected a building site, each student then undertook an extensive information gathering process to determine (1) what cradle-to-cradle design entailed and (2) how his or her specific design might meet this challenge. The project

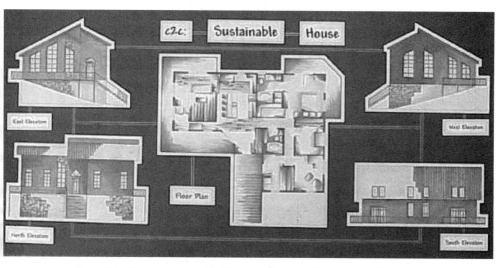

Figure 3.1. Student project: Cradle-to-cradle house design (Carly Olmstead).

description was part of an international design competition sponsored by cradle-to-cradle homes and based on the book by McDonough and Braungart. At the time of the competition, fewer than ten products actually met Cradle-to-Cradle protocol; thus, the project required significant innovation on the part of the students as to how to interpret cradle to cradle using existing materials combined with new processes.

Figure 3.1 shows one of the competition entries completed by a third-year student in a residential design studio. As mentioned, the students had to go through a rigorous information-gathering process prior to making any selections or completing any design work. This process involved using resources that were available at the time, including books, sustainable design guidelines, and online resources. The books were used primarily to provide an introduction to the issues facing the planet, of which many of the students were unaware. First, the students read *Cradle to Cradle*. They were also encouraged to read *Ishmael* by Daniel Quinn as a way of shifting their thinking about mankind's relationship with the natural world. Class discussion followed the readings. The second phase of the information gathering was to find out about the proposed locations for the houses they would be designing. During the semester, all students visited the building sites located in Roanoke, Virginia, to understand how each felt and how each one was oriented, and to get a sense of the neighborhood within which the house would be built. The final phase of information gathering before the students started to design involved an extensive search for existing guidelines on sustainable house design and sustainable materials. The students used several resources available to them including *New Home Construction Green Building Guidelines* produced by Alameda County Waste Management Authority and Recycling Board and available on the Internet.

As the student designs were developed, the students had to determine, based on a list of questions, whether "green" materials actually met the cradle-to-cradle requirements. In most cases, they did not. In fact, at the time of the project, there were approximately five cradle-to-cradle-compliant products. One of these products was a wool baby blanket.

The students implemented several strategies for sustainable house design that they had discovered during the information-gathering process. Some of the decisions that the students made based on their findings about how to make a property sustainable and have it respond to a specific site and location included: integration of rainwater catchment systems, orientation to maximize natural light and prevailing breezes, and use of energy-efficient heating systems and windows, sustainable materials and finishes, and locally available products.

During the materials and finishes phase of the projects, students had to be able to make informed decisions about the products they selected. Most of the product choices for interior finishes met sustainability criteria but were not produced in a cradle-to-cradle-compliant manner. For example, students used Richlite recycled paper countertop materials, low-VOC paints and adhesives, bamboo and cork flooring, DesignTex fabrics, and recycled glass tiles. Low-flow toilets were specified, as were faucets with automatic sensors. Students chose low-water-use showerheads as well to further reduce water us-

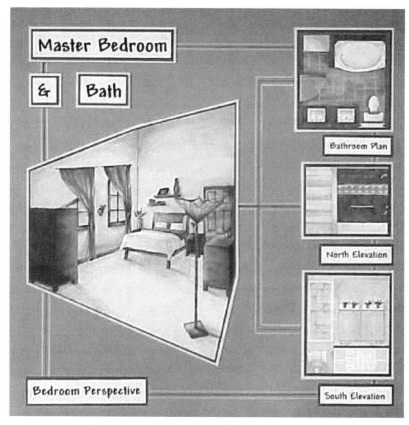

Figure 3.2. Student project: Cradle-to-cradle house design (Carly Olmstead).

age. Much of the information gathering conducted by the students involved the use of online sources and green product guides provided by the cradle-to-cradle home competition providers and the United States Green Building Council. Links to online resources for sustainable design materials can be located on several Web sites including those of the American Society of Interior Designers (ASID), International Interior Design Association (IIDA), and the American Institute of Architects (AIA).

The design shown in Figures 3.1 and 3.2 demonstrates how one student integrated her information gathering. The main façade faces south and has an overhang to shield the interiors from direct sunlight in the summer months. The exterior of the house uses Forest Stewardship Council (FSC) certified wood siding and a locally harvested stone for the foundation. The windows are energy-efficient. All interior lighting is fluorescent, and the fixtures are ENERGY STAR rated, as are all appliances included in the design. The wall and ceiling paints are low VOC. The flooring throughout is bamboo, which was found to be a rapidly renewable resource.

Healthcare and Sustainability Projects

Students in the healthcare studio followed a similar information-gathering methodology as the cradle-to-cradle house design participants (see Figures 3.3 through 3.6). Added to the required reading was the Center for Healthcare Design's Sustainable Design guidelines, which are closely aligned with the LEED Rating System. The majority of the information gathering completed for this project focused on finding viable sustainable substitutes for healthcare mainstays such as vinyl flooring. The information-gathering phase included site visits to local hospital facilities so that students could see the impact of heavy wear on building materials. Research studies completed through the center for Healthcare Design were used by the students during the design process. These included some empirical research studies about specific healthcare issues. For example, students referred to studies on privacy and how this influenced health and well-being. Specific case studies available through the Web site and through the hard copy *Healthcare Design* magazine provided students with multiple examples of projects using emerging sustainable technologies. Some of the articles used by the students included Adams and Courage (1998), Carrol (2004), and Critchfield (2005). Also viewed were several projects from the *Healthcare Design* Architectural Showcase issues 2004, 2005, and 2006. Student research articles ranged from

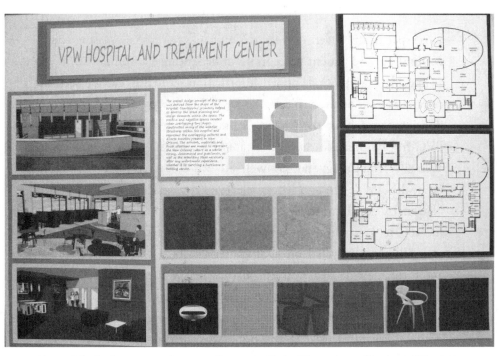

Figure 3.3. Student project: Senior studio sustainable healthcare design (Stephanie Westrick).

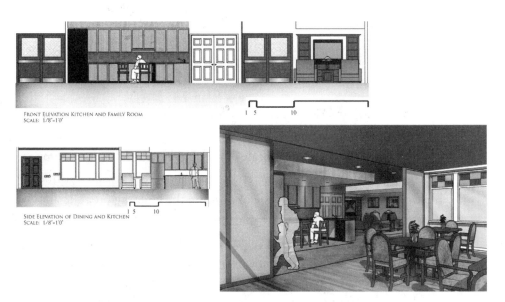

FRONT ELEVATION KITCHEN AND FAMILY ROOM
SCALE: 1/8"=1'0"

SIDE ELEVATION OF DINING AND KITCHEN
SCALE: 1/8"=1'0"

Figure 3.4. Student project: senior studio sustainable healthcare design (Olivia Ackerman).

those specifically covering green design issues to those discussing color, wayfinding, and patient perceptions of healthcare environments.

Specific examples of applied information gathering can be seen in certain aspects of the projects shown in Figures 3.3 through 3.6. The flooring throughout the project is linoleum, as shown in Figure 3.3. PVC-free synthetic leather was located through the ATex Technologies Web site. The EnergyStar.gov Web site was consulted for information on healthcare design and led to selections for lighting and lamps. The National Geographic Green Guide listed the criteria it used to select the top 10 green hospitals. These criteria included low-VOC paints and adhesives, recycled building materials, local and certified wood, and formaldehyde-free products, all of which were implemented in the schemes shown in Figures 3.3 and 3.4. LEED-certified projects served as case study models for how to approach the interior design. Actual product selections used in the projects shown include Sherwin-Williams low-VOC paint, Benjamin Moore Eco Spec products, Maharam and Design Tex textiles, natural beech furniture made from FSC wood, and 100 percent recycled polypropylene chairs.

IDEC Student Competition

The 2006–2007 Interior Design Educator's Council International Student Design Competition was for the design of a sustainable women's shelter to be located within a locale of the student team's choice. Teams were composed of two or three students who were given an existing building shell. The students were to position the building on a site and provide all interior design for the facility.

This women's shelter project (Figures 3.7, 3.8., and 3.9) occurred during the same semester as the previously mentioned healthcare project. As a result, much of the information gathered for the 13-week-long project was applicable to the 2-week competition project. Students also

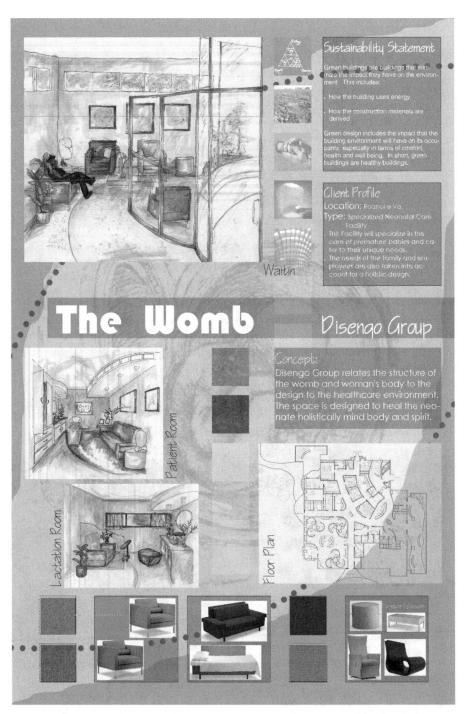

Figure 3.5. Student projects: Sustainable healthcare design (April Compton and Heather Bryan).

Figure 3.6. Student projects: Sustainable healthcare design (April Compton and Heather Bryan).

Figure 3.7. IDEC Student design competition project panels: Sustainable women's shelter (Heather Bryan and April Compton).

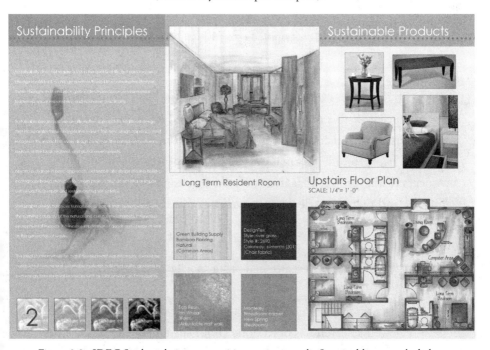

Figure 3.8. IDEC Student design competition project panels: Sustainable women's shelter.

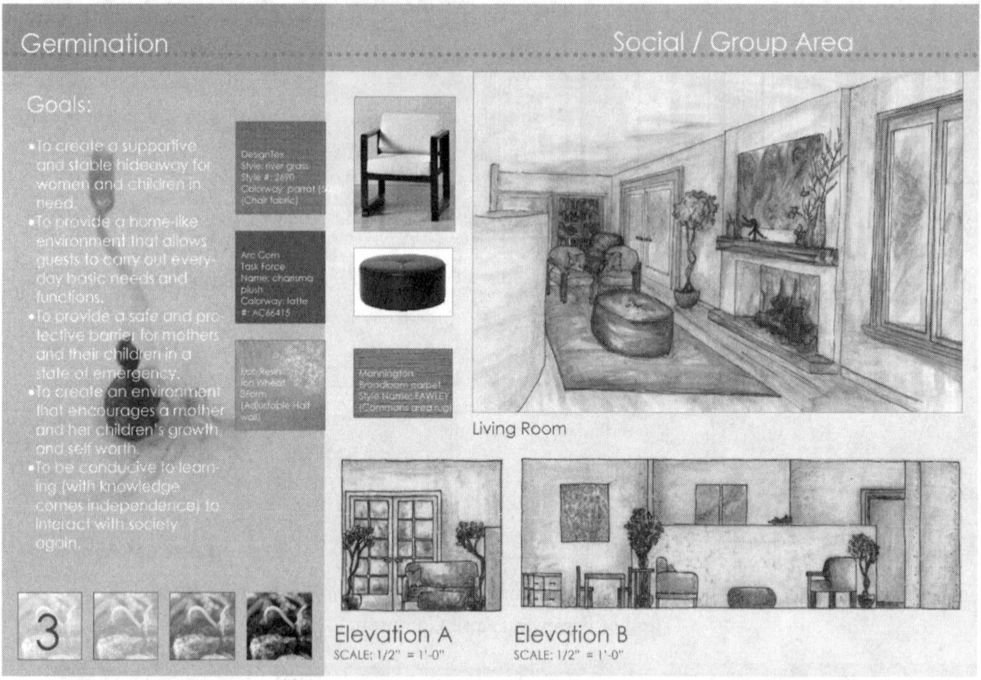

Figure 3.9. IDEC student design competition project panels: Sustainable women's shelter.

met with the director of a local women's shelter to learn more about the specific needs of this user group. This combined with previous materials information and additional guidelines on women's shelters rounded out the background information used to complete the final project. Aspects of the project that incorporated sustainable design include all finishes and materials selections as well as fixtures and furnishings.

Research and Sustainability

While many disciplines have completed research on sustainability, little peer-reviewed research has been done about sustainable design as a holistic approach to building design. The existing articles focus on sus-

tainable urban development and universal design, with the majority focusing on indoor air quality (Bentivegna, Curwell, Deakin, Lombardi,
Mitchell, & Nijkamp, 2002; Bontje, 2004; Hanna, 2005; Philip, Berke,
& Conroy, 2000; Price, Zavotka, & Teaford, 2004). Unfortunately, the
information was not found to be directly applicable to student design
work.

Many of the journal articles for the architecture discipline highlight the
eco-technic approach to architectural design. Technology provides the vehicle to solve our environmental problems. One such example is an article
in the *Journal of Architectural Education* by Dunay, Wheeler and Schubert
where they present a case for increased energy efficiency (2006).

Sustainability and Historic Preservation

The connection between historic preservation and sustainability is one
area that has received a great deal of attention in recent years (Hyllegard, Ogle, Dunbar, 2003; Tucker, 2002). As a result, the Association
for Preservation Technology created a task force to look at Sustainable
Preservation in 2002. Since this time, papers about sustainability and
historic preservation have been presented at each annual international
conference.

One example from my own work of a project bridging sustainable
design and historic preservation is a circa-1830s farmhouse that was re-
habilitated in 2005 into a bed and breakfast to serve hikers along the
Appalachian Trail (Figures 3.10, 3.11, and 3.12). Originally constructed
in 1830, the Huffman House was added to circa 1920 and again in the
1960s. The 2005 work included the following: National Register nomination, tax credit forms, and design work. The first step was to write a
National Register Nomination form, which resulted in listings on both
the National and Virginia Landmarks Registers. Second, part one of
the historic tax credit forms for both state and federal tax credits were

Figure 3.10. Restored parlor ca. 1830.

submitted for review. While under review, the design for the addition of a new master bedroom suite and a gourmet kitchen began. Once part one was approved, the Department of Historic Resources in Virginia was contacted to ensure that all design work was consistent with the Secretary of the Interior's Standards for Rehabilitation. Finally, the plans and specifications as well as "before" photographs and a description of the proposed work were submitted as part two of the tax credit application.

The approach to this project was sustainable. Most importantly, an existing building was used for a new and compatible purpose, thus reducing material use. The existing house was restored to its original condition circa 1920. All historic fabric was retained, and a 1960s-era bathroom was removed from the main parlor. The existing windows were rebuilt in compliance with the Secretary of the Interior's Standards and were made energy-efficient through the addition of interior, removable storm windows. They were also repaired so that they are operable. The floors were sealed with wax instead of polyurethane. Low-VOC paint

Figure 3.12.
Master bedroom showing
reclaimed lumber as
flooring and structure.

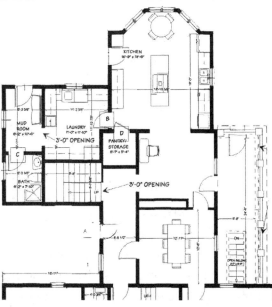

Figure 3.11.
First-floor plan showing
existing dining room
(1830) and new
addition to rear.

FIRST FLOOR

was used to reduce toxins in the interior environment. Product information gathering was completed using independent research test data that informed the decision-making process. For example, many new green product certifications exist. These are sometimes first-party certifications/labels, sometimes second party, and sometimes third party. With first-party labels, the manufacturers have tested the product and labeled it "green" themselves. Third -party labels are tested by an independent agency outside the industry and are considered more reliable. Second-party labels are based on consensus standards within an industry. Knowing which type of testing and labeling has been used helps a designer make an informed decision. Manufacturer data was also consulted.

The new addition used reclaimed lumber for exposed framing on the second floor and as flooring. Low-VOC paint was used throughout. Some of the kitchen cabinets were fabricated on-site using salvaged wood. The cast-iron kitchen sink was also salvaged. Though reclaimed materials were used in the new addition, it was clear what was original versus what was new, in compliance with the Secretary of the Interior's Standards.

In addition to the above-mentioned sustainable design initiatives, the entire house is heated by a wood pellet stove located in the adjacent garage building. Energy-efficient windows were used throughout the addition. The porch located on the west side of the house was reopened and restored to its historic appearance, allowing natural breezes into the dining room and kitchen areas.

Summary

Ideally, all design decisions would be based on peer-reviewed articles from respected journals. While some examples are available (as mentioned above), much of this work is yet to be completed. Most of the projects in this chapter illustrate that designing sustainable interiors at this point in time is dependent on manufacturer data, books, and guidelines. GreenBuild is conducting product testing for cradle-to-cradle compliance as an independent agency. There are also several manufacturer-led product certification and endorsement programs; however, there is little consensus on what these programs mean and how products actually compare. Some of the more holistic issues related to sustainable design—such as the need for a team approach and a new way of thinking about design—have been addressed.

BIBLIOGRAPHY

Adams, J., & Courage, M. (1998). *Human newborn color vision: Measurement with chromatic stimuli excitation purity.* Retrieved from InformeDesign http://www.informedesign.umn.edu/.

Bentivenga, V., Curwell, S., Deakin, M., Lombardi, P., & Nijkamp, P. (2002). A vision and methodology for integrated sustainable urban development. *Building Research & Information, 30*(2), 83–94.

Benyus, J. (1997). *Biomimicry: Innovation inspired by nature.* New York: William Morrow and Company.

Berke, P. (2000). Are we planning for sustainable development? *Journal of the American Planning Association, 66*(1), 21–33.

Bontje, M. (2004). From suburbia to post-suburbia in the Netherlands: Potentials and threats for sustainable regional development. *Journal of Housing and the Built Environment, 19*(1), 25–47.

Carrol, R. (2004). Applying design and color to healing. *Healthcare Design, 4* (3), 29–31.

Critchfield, S. (2005). Pragmatic strategies for green design in healthcare. *Healthcare Design, 5*(2), 16–19.

DOE. (2005). *Annual review.* Retrieved from http://www.eia.doe.gov/basics/energybasics101.html

Duany, R., Wheeler, J., & Schubert, R. (2006). No compromise: The integration of technology and aesthetics. *Journal of Architectural Education, 60*(2), 8–17.

Edwards, A. (2005). *The sustainability revolution.* Gabriola Island, BC: New Society Publishers.

Gateway, T. N. S. (2007, January). *The natural step/U.S.* Retrieved from http://www.naturalstep.org/com/nyStart/

Guy, S., & Farmer, G. (2001). Reinterpreting sustainable architecture: The place of technology. *Journal of Architectural Education, 54*(3), 140–148.

Hanna, K. (2005). Planning for sustainability: Experiences in two contrasting communities. *Journal of the American Planning Association, 71*(1), 27–40.

Hyllegard, K., Ogle, J., & Dunbar, D. (2003). Sustainability and historic preservation in retail design: Integrating design into a model of the REI Denver decision-making process. *Journal of Interior Design, 29*(1, 2), 32–49.

Institute, W. W. (2006). *State of the world 2005.* Retrieved from http://www .worldwatch.org/node/3942

Kaufman, W. (2006). Mileage ratings drop as EPA changes car tests.[Radio broadcast]. Morning Edition. National Public Radio. Retrieved from http:// www.npr.org/templates/story/story.php?storyId=6612913

McDonough, W. (1992). *The Hannover principles: Design for sustainability.* Retrieved March 26, 2007, from http://www.mcdonough.com/principles.pdf

McDonough, W., & Braungart, M. (2002). *Cradle to cradle: Remaking the way we make things.* New York: North Point Press.

McLennan, J. (2004). *The philosophy of sustainable design.* Kansas City, MO: Ecotone Publishing.

Papanek, V. (1982). *Design for the real world: Human ecology and social change* (2nd ed.). Chicago: Academy Chicago Publishers.

Price, C., Zavotka, S., & Teaford, M. (2004). Implementing a university-community-retail partnership model to facilitate community education on universal design. *The Gerontologist, 44*(5), 697–702.

Research, C. F. S. D. (2006). *The state of Minnesota sustainable design guidelines (MSBG).* Retrieved March 26, 2007, from http://www.msbg.umn.edu/ downloads_v2_0/guidelines.pdf

Schmidt-Bleek, F. B. (2000). *Factor 10 manifesto.* Retrieved March 26, 2007, from http://www.factor10-institute.org/pdf/F10Manif.pdf

Tucker, L. M. (2002). *The void between sustainability and historic preservation.* Paper presented at the Interior Design Educators International Conference, Sante Fe, NM.

Van der Ryn, S. (1996). *Ecological design.* Washington, DC: Island Press.

4   Design of the Workplace: Programming

Elizabeth Riordan, Heather Modzelewski,
and Erik Lucken

Abstract

In this chapter, design decisions are informed by collecting data through interior design programming. The first part of the chapter provides an introduction to workplace design and gives a thorough description of various data collection methods a designer might use during the programming process to better understand client needs, values, and goals. These data collection methods illustrate the variety of ways that designers can gain knowledge about a project and also show that information can be obtained through qualitative or quantitative methods. In the last part of the chapter, informed design examples are given to demonstrate how the programming process was used to verify and solidify design decision making.

Introduction

Today, we are witnessing the birth of a new age in business. A thriving knowledge and services sector is now at the heart of the economy, with strong demand for smart, skilled, and creative professionals. Globalization is connecting nations, companies, and people and creating new market opportunities. Technology has empowered work to happen everywhere, and employees are working remotely—from different cities, from airports and hotels, and from client sites. To adapt to the new demands and realities of global business, companies must develop strategies to maximize culture, collaboration, and workflow.

The forces creating new markets have also brought into daily contact a workforce of unprecedented diversity. People from different cultures, countries, races, and religions are working together. Adding to the mix is the fact that the workplace now hosts four generations of people. Organizations must offer a range of workplace options to meet the needs of different groups of workers.

We are also seeing the advent of increased social consciousness in the business world. This consciousness is acutely focused on sustainability and extends to our collective use of the Earth's resources. Sustainable environments are no longer an option, but a mandate, both to realize energy savings and to provide a healthy workplace and a healthy planet. Recognizing this context of new markets, new workforce, and new responsibility, the workplace designer must ask: What is the new definition of success for business, and how does the office environment play a role?

The design of the workplace has always paralleled what is happening in business. When we look at past changes in the workplace, we look at what has changed about work itself. In the 1980s, the workplace was seen as a tool to support company process. Process flow and efficiency metrics were introduced as workplace success measures. Spaces were formal in their arrangement and feel. In the 1990s, increased emphasis was placed on technology, with workplace environments moving beyond process and actually enhancing the ways work was conducted. Spaces were casual and less refined.

Today, process and technology have leveled the field of business. People alone create the strategic competitive advantage. By fully supporting them, design has the potential to enable organizations to leverage their human capital more effectively. Maximizing human potential requires a deep understanding of the role of workplace environments in competitive companies. With careful study and analysis of the various work models utilized—by individual, by team, and by company—an office can be more than just an overhead expense; it can be a dynamic workplace environment with the power to enhance a company's business goals. Information gathering can help align the design of workplaces with business strategy, allowing designers to create office environments that sustain, retain, and engage collaborative and productive employees.

Information Gathering Methodology

Information gathering addresses both qualitative and quantitative aspects of workplace strategy, such as culture, values, communication, space requirements, adjacencies, and the ultimate impact these requirements have on programming and design strategies. These two kinds of analysis—qualitative and quantitative—occur as a fluid series of interactive work sessions and studies that inform one another. Using data collection efforts such as questionnaires and focus group sessions as well as ethnographic methods such as conducting field observations of users in their "natural habitat," designers can gain insight into how people use their environment.

The findings enable the design of integrated workplace strategies that work at individual, departmental, and company-wide levels. In addition, the information gathering process fosters company-wide communication between groups, leveraging amenities, promoting operational efficiencies, and facilitating expansion, contraction, and even exit strategies for the future.

Employing an inclusive information gathering process ensures optimal understanding of an organization and its cultural practices. Allowing everyone—from entry-level staff to senior-level managers—to have a voice in the design of a new facility promotes a sense of ownership and strong acceptance of the resulting solution. "Engaging participant involvement in the change process is critical to any project's success," according to

Strombom and Kifer (2002). "Engagement is about inspiration . . . exploring the possibility among those who will benefit most from the results."

There are several steps in a successful assessment process:

1. Understanding client goals
2. Collecting data
3. Documenting existing conditions
4. Documenting design changes based on study input

1. Understanding Client Goals

What is the client's vision not only for the space but also for its enterprise? How can design support the client in achieving this vision?

Projects are most successful when expectations are clear to all team members. Visioning sessions bring the project team together with the client to mobilize and start the project on the best foot. These initial work sessions ensure that everyone has a clear understanding of the project objectives and the information and background materials needed to begin the project. Topics include determining the level of staff participation in the design process, assigning team roles and responsibilities, scheduling key work sessions and milestones, reviewing data collection tools and methodologies, and establishing project protocols and desired communication methods (Figure 4.1).

Visioning sessions are most valuable when participants include all those with a vested interest in the finished design. Specific issues or topics may benefit from a similar session with select participants—for example, a visioning session where a client's executive team defines the company's vision, culture, and ways of working and discusses how the business might change in the future.

It is critical to clearly articulate the vision for a design project (Figure 4.2). How does it enable the client's business to be more responsive?

Figure 4.1. Example of a visioning session.

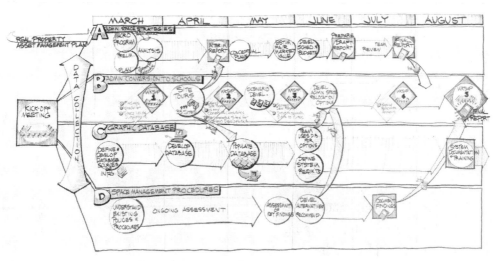

Figure 4.2. Outcome from visioning session.

How does it encourage employees to be more innovative, to think differently, and to behave differently? "The primary purpose, beyond securing early engagement and building consensus, is to discover breakthrough opportunities—those areas where (design) can really make a difference," write Strombom and Kifer (2002).

2. Data Collection

What kinds of data are needed to attain the desired outcome? How do the end users feel about their current space? What resources and practices need to remain? What changes can or should be made?

To explore important qualitative aspects of work (i.e., collaboration and teaming, access to information, task flow, and creative workplace strategies), the design team needs to get to know the client leadership as well as the people who will inhabit the newly designed workspaces on a daily basis. What are their daily habits and work processes? In addition to qualitative data, it is also important to have hard, quantitative facts on hand when making planning and programming decisions in order to give a clear picture of the existing conditions. Data collection activities may include the following:

- Interviews
- Focus groups
- Surveys
- Pre- and post-occupancy assessment
- Camera journaling
- User segmentation
- Relationship mapping
- Workplace audits
- Facility planning
- Computer-aided facilities management-based documentation tools

Focus Group Analysis

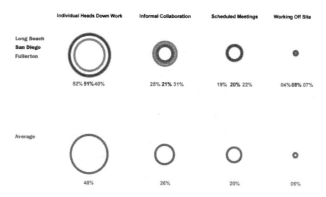

Figure 4.3. Graphic representation of focus group analysis.

Interviews

Speaking directly to the people who work within a client organization, both management and staff, is critical to developing an appropriate and effective needs assessment. *Interviews* focus on understanding strategic initiatives, organizational culture, workplace objectives, and deficiencies in the current facility, as well as exploring opportunities and determining criteria for the ideal environment and spatial configuration. Several interviews may be performed with the same groups of people over the course of the data collection process in order to clarify survey responses, explore alignment with the executive leadership team's vision, and to challenge how employee groups may work differently in the future. These interviews provide opportunities for the design team to hear the issues personalized.

Focus Groups

Focus groups are an excellent means for surfacing, concerns, and identifying opportunities by bringing a cross section of staff together around issues such as amenities or collaboration. Gaining consensus on a direction and communicating ideas back to the rest of the client organization builds collective support and excitement about upcoming change (Figure 4.3). A number of focus groups are typically conducted, with the goal of a diverse constituency base being heard.

"It's important to ask about the 'givens' in focus group sessions—those items considered sacred cows, like 'all managers will have corner offices,'" according to Strombom and Kifer (2002). Some organizational or cultural reasoning will make sense to all involved, while other issues or decisions may cause concern or disagreement. "By flushing out these issues of disconnect in the discovery phase of the project, the designer can offer tremendous value by resolving the conflict," writes Strombom and Kifer (2002).

Surveys

Surveys are a valuable tool for assessing needs and levels of satisfaction with current conditions, as well as soliciting ideas and opinions about potential future directions. Designers meet with the client team members to determine to whom the survey is sent, and to discuss the specific content of the questions. Surveys may be paper-based or electronic. Employees who feel they had a voice in the design of their new space are far more satisfied with their new work environment than employees who do not (Figure 4.4).

Pre- and Post-Occupancy Assessment

This survey-based tool is used to understand the gaps in the performance of the existing workplace at the outset of a project and to measure the impact of the design intervention after a project is completed. (Figure 4.5). The resultant data is used to understand the relative qualities of the work environment. The workplace can then be evaluated by job type, space type, or activity type. This information can be compared to the findings from the other data collection methods to help establish benchmarks against which future solutions may be measured. After a project is complete, the same questions are issued again to understand how effectively the design solution solved for the identified issues.

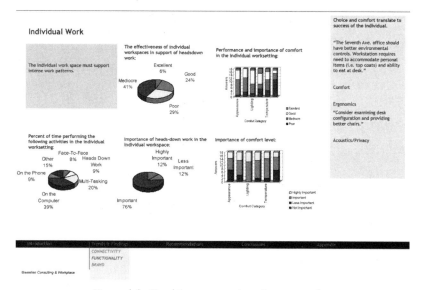

Figure 4.4. Graphic representation of survey results.

Camera Journaling

Camera journaling allows the designer to see the environment through the eyes of the users. Participants are provided a digital camera and journal instructions and asked to document specific aspects of their work environment (e.g., "Take a picture of where you are most productive"; "Take a picture of the something that hinders communication with your colleagues"). In addition, employees may be asked to comment on how well the work environments support their activities. This self-directed technique is useful for prompting users of the space to reveal points of view and patterns of behavior not otherwise identified through traditional data collection methods. It also provides a visual record of perspectives, activities, and issues that might otherwise be missed.

User Segmentation

User segmentation studies are a means of discovering the kinds of experiences that a building or workplace might offer. By combining interviews with other company information, designers can create composite

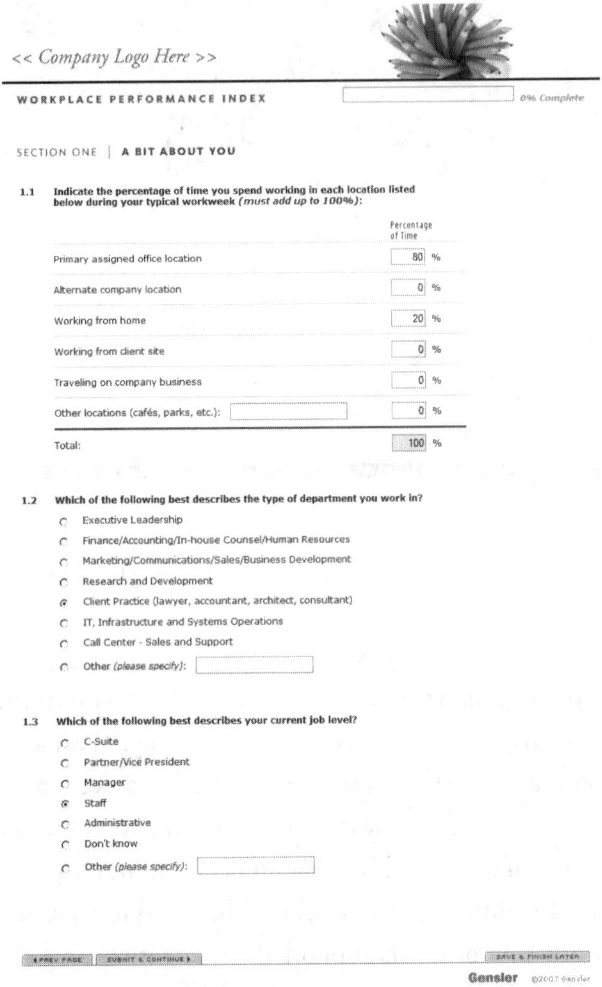

Figure 4.5. Screen shot from pre- and post-occupancy assessment.

identities for various hypothetical users of an office building or work-place environment, complete with life stories. A story is then developed about the kinds of unique experiences these people might have in the building. This storytelling approach often leads to revelations about the design that could not be arrived at through a traditional programming interview. The stories also provide a way to help end users envision an interaction with the space outside of their own personal experience.

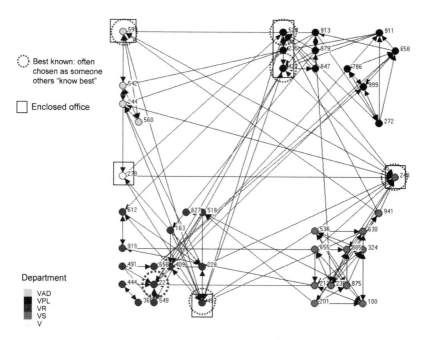

Figure 4.6. Example of relationship mapping.

Relationship Mapping

Relationship mapping is a tool that determines the need for adjacencies within an organization by analyzing certain key factors. The analysis results in "mapping" a plan for the optimum location for each employee based on his or her weighted relationship values with all other staff members (Figure 4.6). "[Relationship maps depict a] firm's invisible inner mechanisms, the relationships and networks and patterns of trust that arise as people work together over time, and that are hidden beneath the organization chart," according to Gladwell (2000). Collocating staff members who interact infrequently can promote impromptu meetings and conversations, increasing the potential for collaboration between work groups.

Workplace Audits

Workplace audits, often referred to as programming, are used to determine what?, how big?, and how many? people and/or things are required in a given facility. An audit usually has three components:

1. *Headcount.* Determining the projected quantities of people who will be using the space
2. *Storage audit.* Identifying the types of storage to be found within a facility (such as files, supplies, high-density storage, libraries, dead files, etc.)
3. *Equipment audit.* Identifying types, quantities, and sizes of equipment required within a facility

Facility Planning

Space requirements for amenities such as food services and wellness centers, and support facilities such as learning/training spaces, mail, reprographics, information technology, and so on, are typically based on meetings with the client's facilities group and are informed by benchmarking information gathered from similar, competitive facilities. To determine issues of sharing, utilization of space, and alternative work scenarios, the data gathered in a workplace audit is integrated with data gathered via some of the other methods described in this chapter to determine the most effective location of required items within the facility (Figure 4.7).

Computer-Aided Facilities Management (CAFM)–Based Documentation Tools

In order to adequately track headcounts and user needs, *CAFM-based documentation tools* are employed to confirm move requirements. These tools are used to coordinate move-related planning activities with the client and space management, design and construction, and technology. Related survey documentation drawings are formatted to convey occupancy by line of business and department, highlighting vacant space for deployment by space management.

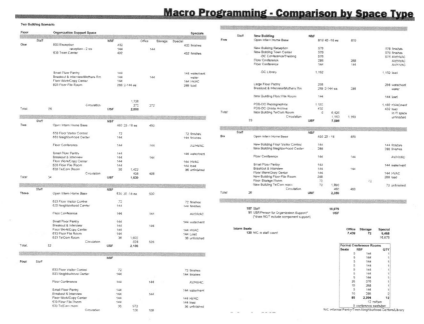

Figure 4.7. Example of facility planning.

3. Documenting Existing Conditions

What resources currently exist? How is the current space allocated? Beyond simple walk-throughs by the design team, the following methodologies are employed to uncover work patterns, social networks, desired/undesired behaviors, and possibilities for the ways that a new work environment can help reach business goals:

- Field surveying
- Time utilization analysis
- Work process mapping

Site Observations: Walk-Throughs

As part of the information gathering process, the project team walks through the existing space and observes how the space is actually being

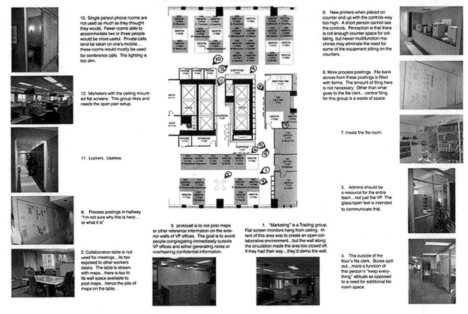

Figure 4.8. Graphic representation of site observation analysis.

used, which can sometimes differ from how employees report they use it. The observer notes space usage, where/how work is occurring, space inefficiencies, redundant activities, and informal communication patterns. The goal is to identify potential opportunities for alternative work environments that could accommodate more efficient work patterns or make better use of space (Figure 4.8).

Field Surveying

Field surveys are conducted to identify the location of departments and teams, and occupied and vacant seats, and to establish a reliable set of departmental boundaries. The process typically involves designers routinely walking through areas to document current occupancies and organizational groups.

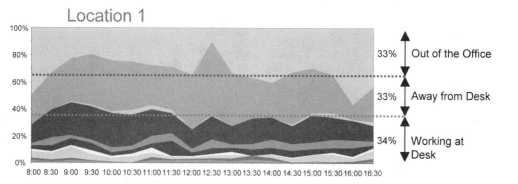

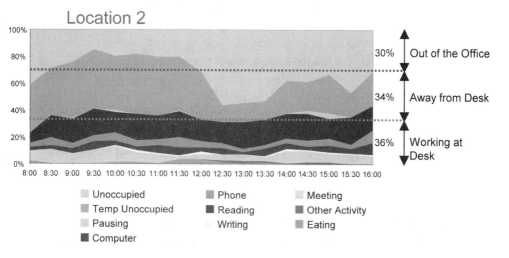

Figure 4.9. Graphic representation of time utilization analysis.

Time Utilization Analysis

Time utilization analysis is used to observe the pattern of use of the office environments over a period of time. Time spent in and out of the office by job type, workspace type, or by activity type over the period of a typical day is documented (Figure 4.9). This information can then be used to more effectively distribute workspace on the basis of the work being done and can be used to verify the other survey methods discussed.

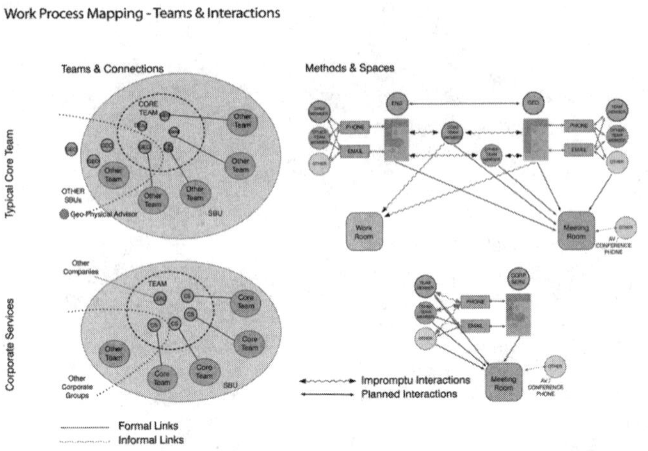

Work Process Mapping - Teams & Interactions

Figure 4.10. Example of work process mapping.

Work Process Mapping

Work process mapping looks at the ways work is conducted by analyzing team makeup and interactions and the space in which these take place. The mapping process seeks to understand how the work is achieved, above and beyond the formal definition of a particular business unit, monitoring work styles, meeting arrangements, and other aspects of the work process (Figure 4.10).

Designers may ask participants to show and describe their flow of work (What work is being done? What is the typical process for completing that work? How much work is there? What is the typical timetable for completing the work?) and walk them through where it takes them both within their own workspace and in the office as a whole, paying particular attention to how embedded this practice is in the work culture as well as how the process is supported in terms of architecture, interior design, technology applications, and furniture selection. Detailed examination of existing individual and group workspaces can yield essential information about how work is changing over time and how roles shift and can even provide insight into social networks, essential input into adjacency planning.

4. Document Design Changes, Based on Study Input

What does the gathered information show? How can the results be applied to the design?

Once the space projections are finalized, recommendations and planning strategies are presented to the client. The project team presents workplace strategies that will affect the design process, including the final space projections (this may be a square footage range to provide the client maximum flexibility), adjacencies, and workflow between groups or functional areas. Planning strategies to support corporate culture, multiple/single building strategies, expansion/contraction strategies, shared functions, and amenities are analyzed for their potential to foster communication between groups and to enhance a company's image. In addition, designers share any relevant planning trends, change management programs, and/or case studies for comparison.

Informed Design Examples

In this section, we look at three examples of office design projects to see how information gathering and research informed the design decisions.

Leading High-Tech Firm: Supporting Globalization

Faced with a corporate real estate portfolio approaching millions of square feet in more than 100 countries, a leading high-tech firm realized it needed to develop a new, comprehensive workplace strategy to align its work environments with contemporary work styles, sustainable practices, and its brand's core values. The firm retained Gensler to initiate a program that would ultimately consolidate owned and leased office locations around the world into core sites.

In creating work environments that promote collaboration by making use of current technology, the design became less about the physical space and more about the connection of the people that use that space. The firm's intranet became the "place," while the office building was designed to provide a series of flexible office spaces that accommodated the constantly changing project teams.

The goals for the project were to establish a leadership position regarding how work environments can create synergies between user experience, brand awareness, a mobile workforce, and sustainability. Moreover, these synergies needed to be achieved with neutral or even lower costs than with a traditional facilities approach.

The project began with a workshop-style visioning session. The goals were aggressive: aligning how the firm's principles translate into a common global vision for its work environments. Participants tackled the challenges of diversity of materiality, density, worker type, and context on a global scale. Every statement, recommendation, or standard discussed had to pass the global translation test. Would the same planning approach apply as effectively in the Americas as in Thailand?

The visioning session identified that the firm's projects often have very short life cycles, requiring a flexible workspace that can adapt to the frequent team changes and the need to connect teams whose members reside in different locations. The global lens challenged the design team to explore how different work modes can relate to the firm's values, policy, economics, and employee experience.

The design team surveyed and interviewed firm leaders and staff to better understand how and where their time is spent over an average workday, what tasks they perform, and how the global nature of the firm affects their ability to communicate and collaborate with each other.

Using time utilization studies, the design team examined the work patterns in various offices and was able to demonstrate to the firm's leadership that its staff was often in the office less than half of the time. This aligned with a global trend that mobility is a dominant characteristic of modern work, fast becoming the rule rather than the exception.

The studies found that many of the firm's employees spend a large percentage of their time at client sites or find that they are more productive doing heads-down work at home or away from ringing phones and constant distraction. Taking a cue from surveys, interviews, and time utilization studies, the design team incorporated flexible workstations in the design, accommodating "hoteling," whereby employees reserve a workstation on the days they need to be in the office to meet with co-workers and clients or to participate in interactive activities, and spend the rest of the time working remotely from client sites or their homes.

These touchdown spaces can be reserved on the intranet or booked on the spot. The flexible workstations are identically equipped and arranged around shared facilities, such as conference rooms, copy centers, and cafes and dining facilities, providing a wide range of services within easy reach.

By locating office buildings in areas centrally located to offer easy public transportation and traffic access, employees are able to work efficiently without a permanently assigned desk. This design approach allows the company to support more employees with less space, saving the company money while providing the necessary infrastructure and services for successful business.

Conference rooms are equipped with videoconferencing features, allowing employees to connect with each other and their clients for virtual meetings from locations around the globe. The ability to interact at the touch of a button helps achieve a sense of community among team members and a feeling of accessibility between the company and its clients. These features were directly in line with the company's goals of a common global vision as informed by the visioning session.

By harnessing the available technology and implementing new strategies, the firm achieved improved productivity, employee satisfaction, and reduced energy costs by decreasing the number of unused workstations. The collaborative methodology and approach allowed the design team to explore the complexity of the global workplace culture from many angles, gathering valuable information to bring to the design process.

Leading Media and Communications Company: Supporting Diversity

A media and communication giant's headquarters building conveys a very un-corporate feel, appropriate for a company whose success is built on defying corporate cultural norms. The company makes a business of being open and creative, breaking down hierarchies and embracing the newness of ideas, growing from one small cable channel to a global entertainment leader. The design of its work environment needed to be as unconventional.

In order to translate the company's culture and vision into the design of its workspace, the design team employed a series of focus groups to capture and discuss ideas and employee observations. The focus group sessions facilitated a dialogue between company leaders and employees, conversations about work modes and workspace design that took place across the spectrum of skills and experience levels. The concerns and impressions of leaders and employees alike were heard and recorded.

With a staff nearing 2,000 people, one significant challenge was how to maintain the entrepreneurial spirit and small company feel at the heart of the operation. Using feedback from the focus group sessions, the design team organized the new office environment into a series of neighborhoods, with multipurpose community centers at their hub, to foster a sense of belonging. The focus groups relayed employees' and management's dislike of cube workstations and their interest in increased spontaneous collaboration. This was reflected in the open workstation plan.

The design team also employed camera journaling, to capture and record employee impressions of an average workday, showcasing what types of space were most effective from an end-user perspective. These journals documented both pros and cons of the existing workspaces and became important foundations for the new design, supporting the shift to a more open, collaborative environment and generating a very positive response from the company community because of the inclusiveness of the process.

In addition, to supplement the two previous data collection techniques, the design team selected a series of people throughout the company to participate in a show-and-tell exercise, asking them to lead the project team through various interactions with their workspace, exploring working relationships between employees and between departments, as well as opportunities for collaboration and unplanned interaction.

The information gathered in these sessions, combined with the design team's field survey work, which documented existing office space conditions, provided descriptive insider data on the working relationships and needs of the company.

The resulting design features a flexible and contemporary-style furniture system, selected to address the client's "anti-cube" mentality, while making use of the building's large floor plates and high ceilings. In addition, the primarily open workspace is complemented by "phone booths," or small meeting rooms that provide private space for one or several employees to collaborate and escape the confines of their desks.

Modular offices away from the window wall offer enough privacy for managers' needs while encouraging them to get out among their groups to collaborate. Video walls and graphic elements reinforce identities for the company's many divisions, promoting the company's brand as well as pride and awareness of the exciting multimedia projects underway throughout the office.

Leading Financial Services Firm: Acting Responsibly

A leading financial services firm was faced with the challenge of recruiting and retaining the talent necessary to meet strong projected growth over the next decade. Understanding that large cities provide an unmatched pool of creative and diverse people, management decided to develop a high-rise office tower in a dense urban setting. They felt the high cost of prime real estate and new construction would be offset by the level of talent they could attract and support with a best-in-class facility that takes a proactive approach to environmental sustainability.

The design team approached the data collection process from several angles. Employees were asked to participate in a workplace occupancy assessment. An electronic questionnaire was distributed to gauge employee impressions of their current workspaces. The data collected identified key issues to consider during the design process, such as employees' desire to control personal work environments—temperature, lighting, and other personal preferences, and an overall demand for clean, healthy air quality. In addition to engaging workers directly, the design team performed a workplaces audit, surveying the existing office to better understand current workspace environmental conditions and overall facility needs.

Once the initial data collection was complete, focus groups were held with firm leadership, individual business units, and cross-pollinated groups that were structured to represent the firm as a whole to explore some of the issues that came to light during the initial studies. In addition, the focus group sessions explored the state of environmental awareness among company employees and tested reactions to trends in sustainable office design.

The resultant design was influenced by the study findings and conversations with end users. The new design included commercial underfloor air systems, which require significantly less energy while providing even temperature and allowing employees to control the environment individually to suit their personal preferences. Using advance filtrations systems and carbon dioxide monitors, the air system provides not only more comfort but also cleaner, healthier air, a direct response to employee input expressed in the focus group sessions.

Sustainable building materials were used as extensively as possible, including recycled metal in the ceiling grid and tiles; recycled steel studs; and formaldehyde-free paints, coating, and adhesives. All wood used was FSC-certified. All interior furnishings were sourced from green manufacturers, and all designed for long life. Fabric panels were made of 100 percent recycled polyester, a direct response to the perceived interest in sustainable office design and environmental awareness expressed during the focus group sessions.

Maximum daylight and views were incorporated into the design through high ceilings and insulated windows. Glass front offices, low-height workstation partitions, reflective ceiling tiles, and light reflective wall paint and interior surfaces all encourage the flow of natural daylight throughout the interior. For artificial lighting, modular lighting positions, occupancy sensors, energy-efficient fixtures, and indirect lighting strategies increase efficiency and productivity while providing sufficient light levels and access to daylight, issues that registered as important to employees during the initial workplace occupancy assessment.

The firm's overarching aim was to be not just a business, but a true community of people. The resulting workplace is the physical representation of the firm's commitment to excellence and will have a huge impact on the way clients and employees live and experience the firm's brand on a daily basis, reinforcing its values and mission. The new facility will be the physical embodiment of the commitment to excellence to both customers and employees. By developing a design that celebrates core values and reflects the firm's brand and by demonstrating environmental commitment, the design creates an innovative workplace environment with state-of-the-art technology and establishes a strong urban presence.

BIBLIOGRAPHY

Becker, F., & Steele, F. (1995). *Workplace by design: Mapping the high-performance workscape* (The Jossey-Bass Management Series). New York: John Wiley & Sons.

Beckmann, W. (2000, January). Bigger than the boomer cohort: A new and different office worker generation. Herman Miller Research Report.

Brown, J. S., & Duguid, P. (1998). Organizing knowledge. *California Management Review,* 40(3), 90–111.

Buckingham, M., & Coffman, C. (1999). *First, break all the rules: What the world's greatest managers do differently.* New York: Simon & Schuster.

Chermayeff, S., & Alexander, C. (1963). *Community and privacy: Toward a new architecture of humanism.* New York: Doubleday.

Donnellon. A. (1996) *Team talk: The power of language in team dynamics.* Cambridge: Harvard Business School Press.

DYG, Inc. (n.d.) The second bottom line: Competing for talent using innovative workplace design: Results of qualitative research among high tech workers. Knoll, Inc. Retrieved from http://www.knoll.com/research/docs/Second_Bottom_Line.pdf

Franklin, B., & Steele, F. (1995). *Workplace by design: Mapping the high-performance workscape.* NY: John Wiley & Sons.

Gladwell, M. (2000, December). Designs for working. *New Yorker,* 60–70.

Henderson, J. (1998). *Workplaces and workspaces: Office designs that work.* Gloucester, MA: Rockport Publishers.

Horgen, T., Schon, D., Porter, W., & Joroff, M. (1998). *Excellence by design: Transforming workplace and work practice.* New York: John Wiley & Sons.

Kirkpatrick, K. (2002). A roadmap for the integrated work environment, Gensler white paper.

Leiserowitz, N. R. (2001). Future imperfect: the world of work in 2010. Prepared for the American Society of Interior Designers' FutureWork 2020, Phase Two: Presenting the Future of the Workplace. White paper.

McIntosh-Fletcher, D. (1995). *Teaming by design: Real teams for real people.* New York: McGraw-Hill Professional Publishing.

Pfeffer, J. (1998). *The human equation: Building profits by putting people first.* Cambridge: Harvard Business School Press.

Robinson, A., & Stern, S. (1998). *Corporate creativity: How innovation and improvement actually happen.* San Francisco: Berrett-Koehler Publishing.

Schrage, M. (1995). *No more teams! Mastering the dynamics of creative collaboration.* New York: Bantam Doubleday.

Schrage, M., and Peters, T. (1999). *Serious play: How the world's best companies simulate to innovate.* Cambridge: Harvard Business School Press.

Smith, P. and Kearny, L. (Contributor). (1994). *Creating workplaces where people can think* (The Jossey-Bass Management Series). New York: John Wiley & Sons.

Stone, P. J., & Luchetti, R. (1985, March–April). Your office is where you are. *Harvard Business Review.*

Strombom, D., & Kifer, C. (2002). Fanatical design/smart business, Gensler presentation at Neocon.

Zelinsky, M. (1998). *New workplaces for new workstyles.* New York: McGraw-Hill Professional Publishing.

Zucker, D. (2002). The next big thing: design to enhance creativity and innovation, Gensler white paper.

5 Supermarket Retail: Programming

Stephanie Heher and John P. Marsden

Abstract

This chapter is dedicated solely to the exploration of supermarket retailing. General background information is provided about non-traditional and traditional grocery retailers, the needs of customers, and theories related to consumer behavior. In addition, information gathered through focus groups with customers of two different supermarket chains is used to inform the design of the supermarkets. Just as in programming, the market research in both examples is project specific and is not intended for dissemination to advance the field.

Introduction

The use of empirical research to inform design is most often used by professionals responsible for creating educational, healthcare, workplace, and senior living environments. Recognizing the relationship between scientific breakthroughs or advances can improve the quality of life and safety for individual users. Yet, in other areas of practice, design decisions based on research may not be so apparent, nor do the outcomes always have such widespread results or humanitarian intent.

In retailing, design typically has a more deliberate purpose: to create an environment that provides an enjoyable experience causing consumers to make purchases, thereby enhancing the bottom line for a retailer. Baker, Levy, and Grewal (1992) found that "retailers do not generally engage in systematic research that enables them to examine the environmental factors that may influence the patronage decision" (p. 446). Architects and designers working in the retail industry, more often than not, rely on market research provided by retailers gathered from customer surveys, focus groups, demographic data, sales figures, and so forth. The retail design practice remains a bit reluctant to share this market research, perhaps to avoid scrutiny due to the ever-changing retail landscape or the fear of disclosing advantages to the competition (Hamilton, 2004).

Other sources of information that can inform retail design exist. An abundance of scholarly research related to the psychological, sociological, and economical drivers of consumer behavior in retail settings has been conducted by behavioral scientists. In addition, because the retail business changes dramatically over very short periods of time, architects and designers are exposed to a substantial amount of information sourced by the retail industry itself in the form of trade journals, books, studies, papers, and project evaluations, along with a significant amount of facts and figures as reported in newspapers and periodicals.

Conventional supermarket design has changed dramatically over the past decade as competition intensified because of the growth of club shopping, the entrance of national discounters into the market, the expansion of specialty stores, and the changing demands for services and products by consumers (Lindeman, 2006). Progressive grocery retailers are spending considerable amounts of money in pursuit of the design solutions that create the atmosphere and provide the shopping experience required to retain their customers (Kaltcheva & Weitz, 2006; Lindeman, 2006). In this chapter, general background information will be provided about nontraditional and traditional grocery retailers, the needs of customers, and theories related to consumer behavior. In addition, information gathered through focus groups with customers of two different supermarket chains is used to inform the design of the supermarkets. The two examples involve programming for a specific project and demonstrate the architectural features and design elements currently utilized by retailers to achieve the store format and environment that successfully entice and draw customers to the destination.

Traditional and Nontraditional Grocery Retailers

Traditional grocery retailers not only compete with each other but also with the nontraditional grocery retailers who have successfully incorporated groceries into super/power shopping centers and warehouse/discount shopping centers (Arnold & Reynolds, 2003). These discount retailers along with countless other retailers are selling grocery items or offering meal solutions in specialty food stores, convenience stores, drugstores, and even in dollar stores, and those factors have affected the supermarket trade dramatically (Hibbard, 2006; Purcell, 2006; Reda, 2005).

Discount Retailers

Discount retailers or box retailers are successful for a number of reasons. Their commanding distribution networks and impressive buying power provide their customers with vast supplies of products at extremely low prices. The box retailer's ability to cater to the lifestyles of consumers, including the need for one-stop shopping, is yet another element of success. As determined by Leszcyzc, Sinha, and Sahgal (2004) in referring to an increase in one-stop shopping, "One reason for this change in consumer grocery shopping behavior is the increased need for shoppers to optimize their time spent shopping, since demands of everyday professional and

personal life have increased for most shoppers" (p. 85). With stores ranging in size from just under 100,000 square feet to nearly 260,000 square
feet, box retailers easily satisfy consumer demands for products and services housed under one roof (Wal-Mart, 2007).

In 1988, Wal-Mart introduced its Supercenter store concept, which
included a full line of grocery products (Wal-Mart, 2007). Within the
first decade of the Supercenter's existence, Wal-Mart found itself quickly climbing to the top position in grocery sales in America and holds
the number one ranking at the time of this writing (Progressive Grocer,
2006; Supermarket News, 2008). With nearly 2,200 Supercenters in
operation and the addition of the neighborhood market concept in
1998 (which currently includes over 100 stores), Wal-Mart has grown
its market share to nearly 20 percent in a relatively short period of time
(Reda, 2005, Wal-Mart, 2007).

Specialty Food Retailers

The entrance and growth of specialty stores in the marketplace has also influenced the supermarket business. Retailers like Whole Foods Markets
have been enormously successful with niche market concepts. Whole
Foods distinguishes its place in the industry by catering to consumer demands for a variety of organic and natural product choices with an emphasis on quality and excellence in its source selection (Hibbard, 2006; Purcell, 2006). Additionally, in fulfilling consumer's ethical beliefs by setting
high standards for environmental stewardship and by acknowledging the
social issues surrounding food production, Whole Foods' approach has
been extremely lucrative (Whole Foods, 2007). At the time of this writing, Whole Foods is the fastest-growing supermarket chain in America
and holds the 13th position in grocery sales; all of this accomplished with
just over 180 store locations ranging in size from 18,000 to 80,000 square
feet (Progressive Grocer, 2006; Purcell, 2006; Whole Foods, 2007).

Other Food Retailers

By expanding food and grocery selections in store locations, convenience store, drugstore, and dollar-store chains have played a major role in challenging the revenues and profits of traditional grocery retailers. Beyond the typical offerings of gasoline, cigarettes, milk, and bread, convenience stores provide today's consumer with an assortment of prepared meal options as well as an ever-expanding variety of fresh foods and staple grocery items (Caffarini & Cavanaugh, 2006; Convenience Store News, 2007).

Because of the sheer number of store locations, estimated to be at least 19,000 for each format, coupled with strong distribution channels that keep products flowing and prices low, drug and dollar stores also provide a convenient and satisfying option to busy consumers (Howell, 2002; Caffarini & Cavanaugh, 2006). Convenience, drug, and dollar stores are using food as a key strategy to boost sales, and with continued growth projected for these store formats, the resulting competition can only have a negative effect on the revenues of traditional grocers (Howell, 2002; Caffarini & Cavanaugh, 2006).

Needs of Customers

Grocery shopping has moved beyond the mere acquisition of perishables and dry goods and, for many consumers, has become more about convenience and services offered by the retailers. As Reda (2005) points out, supermarket retailers need to employ a "customer-centric strategy" in response to the demands of the modern consumer. Otherwise, today's grocery shopper will go elsewhere (Litwak, 2006). With competition intense and profit margins slim, it is essential for supermarket retailers to join forces with members of the design community to create the store environments that prevent this from happening.

Store image, the shopping experience, and changing demands due to consumer lifestyles and food interests are factors that supermarket retailers should take into account when they focus their effort on improving customer satisfaction.

Store Image

Baker, Levy, and Grewal (1992) stated in their study, "In a time when retailers are finding it increasingly difficult to create a differential advantage on the basis of merchandise, price, promotion, and location, the store itself becomes a fertile opportunity for market differentiation" (p. 446). Supermarket retailers are making large investments to improve and create an image that distinguishes their stores from other grocery retailers and certainly from nontraditional grocery retailers. In fact, one major supermarket retailer reported a budget of $1.6 billion to be spent in 2006 alone on new construction and store renovations, to create that distinguished or differentiating store environment (Progressive Grocer, 2006). New construction, along with perpetual renovations and expansions to existing stores, has proven to be successful in retaining customers and increasing sales (Hibbard, 2006; Progressive Grocer, 2006).

Shopping Experience

Store image is paramount, but grocers must go further to "identify their market niche in order to transform the shopping experience in their realm into something extraordinary" (Ibrahim & Wee, 2002, p. 240). According to Arnold and Reynolds (2003), the entertainment factor is an important and key tool recognized by progressive retailers determined to remain competitive, and the term *entertailing* has been coined to describe the entertainment aspect demanded in current retailing. With strength of sales as the central factor, Kim (2001) found that retailers are defining a new business category composed of a crossover between hospitality management and retail merchandising, which he refers to as "experiential retailing." Riewoldt (2005) surmises that retail should be staged in order to be an exciting experience, saying, "with the same care and professionalism as the theatre, the sequence of events must be worked out in detail . . . in order to transform the sale of merchandise" into what he describes as an "experience-intensive act" (p. 9).

Studies show that if all things are equal as far as selection, price, and customer service, an entertaining store atmosphere will cause consumers to travel, even considerable distances, to shop (Ibrahim & Wee, 2002; Tauber, 1972). For some consumers, the grocery shopping experience has evolved into a form of entertainment, with the stores themselves becoming a destination point.

Lifestyles

The demands of hectic lifestyles filled with activities and events have produced distinctive needs for grocery shoppers. Busy consumers tend not to rely on the weekly grocery run to satisfy all food and meal demands and are willing to make frequent midweek stops for fresh ingredients or for ready-to-cook and ready-to-eat meal options. Convenience and choice of solutions are major considerations in determining where to grocery shop during midweek excursions. And the lion's share of supermarket retailers are catering to the demands of busy lifestyles by including fresh and prepared foods in a myriad of formats, to be consumed either in the store or at home (Din, 2000).

Interest in Food

Some shoppers focus attention on certain types of food or express awareness of food issues that surpass the concerns of price or convenience. Savvy shoppers call for an increased assortment of ethnic, organic, natural, and health food options. As a result, features like kosher delis, sushi bars, charcuteries, and wellness or lifestyle centers are now included in some store designs (Purcell, 2006).

In addition, food ethics has surfaced as a reason for store selection with consumers conscientious of quality and safety issues relating to the origin and production of food. Supermarket retailers are factoring in these interests by providing a wide array of choices, together with the critical facts concerning food selection and delivery methods.

With the increase of exposure to various culinary options, scores of shoppers express more than a casual interest in food, and the industry refers to them as foodies. As Hanson (2006) indicates, "Foodies are passionate about food and flavors and are constantly exploring and seeking eclectic tastes" (p. 40). Retailers are especially interested in foodies because, in their quest for gourmet options, these shoppers are eager to learn about products, strive to discover new ones, repeatedly experiment with uncommon ingredients, and, in the process, buy more merchandise (Schooley, 2005). Most supermarket retailers are paying particular heed to the requests of foodies by providing an assortment of products. Some go even further and supply consumers with demonstration areas and professional chefs to showcase and instruct on the use of uncommon products.

Psychological Models or Theories of Consumer Behavior

A significant amount of scientific research with reference to consumer behavior is most often found in peer-reviewed retail and marketing journals where social scientists expound upon the motivational, emotional, and environmental dimensions of shopping. Several of the prominent models and theories focused specifically on consumer behavior are discussed below. Almost all of this research is associated with retail shopping in general, but much of it can be applied by retailers and designers to grocery shopping as well.

Motivational Dimensions

Most behavioral studies conclude that shoppers can be categorized into two basic and distinct groups centered on motive or reason for shopping. The two primary types of shoppers are referenced in various ways; however, the research predominantly describes them as shoppers who consider shopping a chore or task and those who view shopping as a form of entertainment or recreation (Bellenger & Korgaonkar, 1980; Tauber, 1972). For ease of discussion in this chapter, the terms task-oriented shopper and recreational shopper will describe the two categories of shoppers.

The body of research consistently states that the task-oriented shopper follows specific shopping patterns, strives to minimize the amount of time spent shopping, frequents stores in close proximity to home or work, spends as little time in the store as possible, and focuses on the acquisition of the product (Bellenger & Korgaonkar, 1980). On the other hand, the recreational shopper enjoys shopping, views it as a leisure-time activity, seeks more information with regard to products, keeps current with trends, and spends longer amounts of time in the store (Bellenger & Korgaonkar, 1980; Ibrahim & Wee, 2002; Tauber, 1972).

As a result of diverse shopping motives, store environment affects task-oriented and recreational shoppers in different ways (Bellenger & Korgaonkar, 1980). Task-oriented shoppers identify with and are loyal customers of stores who provide uncomplicated atmospheres and convenient locations. Bellenger and Korgaonkar (1980) found that task-oriented shoppers "dislike shopping or are neutral toward it, and thus approach retail store selection from a time- or money-saving point of view" (p. 78). Recreational shoppers, on the other hand, require more from retailers. "To attract the latter group the retailer must offer an attractive décor and an exciting shopping experience" and create a "recreational experience for shoppers that goes beyond the purchase of goods" (Bellenger & Korgaonkar, 1980, p. 92).

Early research recognized shopper motivation as an important consideration for retailers. Tauber (1972) determined that motivation could affect market differentiation, stating that "in the future, the ability to gain a distinct differential advantage may depend on catering to shopping motives that are not product related" (p. 49). And more recent research concludes that shopper motivation should be considered in the overall shopping experience (Ibrahim & Wee, 2002).

Emotional Dimensions

Beyond shopper type, the existing research presents further information on consumer behavior concerned with the emotions of shoppers. Three often-studied emotional dimensions, described by Donovan and Rossiter (1982) as the Mehrabian-Russell environmental psychology model, are pleasure, arousal, and dominance, and these dimensions influence attitude and affect behavior as to approach or avoidance of an environment. Studies show that emotional dimensions affect purchasing behavior and influence shoppers in the following ways: attitude toward and enjoyment of the store, time spent browsing, willingness to talk to salespeople, tendency to spend more money than intended, and probability to return to the store (Donovan & Rossiter, 1982; Lam, 2001).

Pleasure and Arousal

Going further, the store environment affects the emotional dimensions of pleasure and arousal of consumers distinctively. For this reason, the research suggests that to increase pleasure, retailers "create a high-arousal environment for recreational customers and low-arousal environment for task-oriented consumers" (Kaltcheva & Weitz, 2006, p. 115). Further, in comparing the two shopper types, this team of researchers found that recreational shoppers "desire rich experiences from shopping and therefore would find high energy demands in high-arousal environments to be pleasant; conversely, they would view environments that call for less energy mobilization as unpleasant" (Kaltcheva & Weitz, 2006, pp. 109–110). In contrast, the task-oriented shopper "would find that the high energy demands in high-arousal environments require more effort to complete the shopping activity and therefore would find such environments to be unpleasant" (Kaltcheva & Weitz, 2006, p. 109).

In addition, with regard to the emotional dimensions of pleasure and arousal, "shoppers experiencing relatively high pleasure and arousal generally spend more time in a store and are more willing to make a purchase than are their displeased or unaroused counterparts" (Babin & Darden, 1995, p. 49). Other research concludes that increased arousal and pleasure equates to more time spent in the store, and the inclination to visit the store more often, thereby leading to improved sales (Donovan, Rossiter & Marcoolyn, 1994; Lam, 2001).

Dominance

Dominance can be described as the sense of control or the perception of command experienced by a person in a particular environment (Donovan & Rossiter, 1982). Many of the studies conclude that pleasure and arousal are the primary dimensions affecting behavior, with dominance being rendered "ineffective" (Babin & Darden, 1995). However, despite these findings, dominance is "of key interest to retailer practitioners because of the close link between store layout and control of shopper movement through a store" (Babin & Darden, 1995, p. 49). This dimension can be a critical factor in the behavior of the task-oriented shopper because "designs encouraging shoppers to spend more time and money in a store may be harmful in building customer loyalty" (Babin & Darden, 1995, p. 61).

Catering to the Emotional Dimensions

Comprehension of the effects of these *emotional dimensions* presents retailers with the clues and evidence to determine what factors relating to the retail environmental could be controlled in order to foster the shopping experience for consumers (Jones, 1999). By manipulating the store environment and creating the required levels of emotion to suit shoppers, retailers are capable of promoting customer satisfaction. At the same time, a direct correlation will result between an increase in customer satisfaction and an increase in sales due to customer approach and store loyalty (Ang, Leong & Lim, 1996).

Environmental Dimensions

Further research focused on an additional conceptual framework known as *servicescape* is concerned with consumer behavior resulting from the physical environment. Bitner (1992) enumerates "three composite dimensions" most relevant in constituting servicescape: ambient conditions; spatial layout and functionality; and signs, symbols, and artifacts and states further that these dimensions, like emotional dimensions discussed above, contribute to approach and avoidance behavior.

Broken down in more detail, ambient conditions are those factors that affect any of the five senses such as temperature, lighting, air quality, noise, music, odor, and so forth (Bitner, 1992). The dimension of spatial layout and functionality incorporates the physical layout of machinery, equipment, and furnishings, taking into consideration their shape, size, and the effect their spatial relationship to each other has on performance (Bitner, 1992). The image communicated by means of the aesthetic quality of materials used in decor, along with signs, symbols, and any artwork or artifacts placed in an environment, constitute the last physical dimension of servicescape (Bitner, 1992).

The framework of servicescape has numerous implications that can be applied to retail environments. In general, Bitner (1992) tells us that in order "to secure strategy advantages from the servicescape, the needs of ultimate users and the requirements of various functional units must be incorporated into environmental design decisions" (p. 67). Other researchers regard the importance of servicescape and agree that environmental dimensions influence consumer behavior, enhance emotional dimensions, and thereby improve attitude and approach toward a retail location (Ang, Leong & Lim, 1997).

Informed Design Examples

It appears to be a straightforward formula: address the needs of the targeted customer, create a store format that is both convenient and functional, produce a means of differentiation through store image, and roll it all into an exciting, entertaining, and distinguished design that encourages a positive shopping experience. The end result: an environment that attracts and satisfies the desired customer, encourages that customer to shop and return, and increases revenues for the supermarket retailer. Yet supermarket store design is tremendously complex. In order to avoid costly design mistakes, supermarket retailers and design professionals focused on successful store design collect market data from their customers for specific projects to inform design solutions. This section examines two supermarket chains and the processes they followed.

Chain A

Even prior to drawing up plans for a new retail location or a store re-model, the management of Chain A surveys its own customers to determine the features to be incorporated into store design. With the help of outside consultants to organize, proctor, and compile the data, Chain A's management, along with internal operational, merchandising, marketing, and design professionals, work together as a team and analyze the results of the information garnered from customer focus groups. Chain A's customers contribute valid and meaningful insight into what design elements are essential to develop a shopping environment that attracts them to the retailer. The time and effort taken by the management of Chain A to uncover and examine this information has a distinct effect on store design and the ultimate success of a retail location.

The focus groups not only provide Chain A's management with innovative ideas but do, on occasion, substantiate that long-established design approaches remain valid. For example, Chain A's management recognizes that store layout plays a significant role in customer satisfaction. Certain departments like produce and floral have historically been positioned near the front of the store, where high-impulse items are displayed and merchandised early in the shopping trip, when consumers are most likely in the mood to make purchases. Customer feedback not only confirms preference for this layout, but sales data support the success of this configuration.

Additionally, Chain A's management understands the importance of situating the produce and floral departments in this locale because it provides the retailer with the opportunity to generate an ideal first impression with its customers. Well-stocked and well-lit produce and floral departments filled with fragrant, colorful, and quality merchandise also set the tone for a meaningful and memorable shopping experience. The management of Chain A counts on customers to remember that first image of quality and to envision the positive experience encoun-

Figure 5.1. High-impulse items, like those in the floral department, are displayed and merchandised near the front of the store when consumers are most likely in the mood to make purchases.

tered while shopping at its store locations. This successful store image presents Chain A with the means to gain a competitive advantage by differentiating its stores from those of other retailers and in promoting customer loyalty (Figures 5.1, 5.2, and 5.3).

In supporting the demanding and active lifestyles of its customers, the management of Chain A also utilizes store layout to cater to convenience. Overall store layout must incorporate easy access to a wide array of perishable products and ready-to-cook or ready-to-eat meal solutions. Chain A is leaning toward the "power alley" concept, whereby perishables and home meal replacements are logically merchandised in close proximity near the front of the store. Coordinating the adjacency of these departments enhances the lifestyles of consumers by providing convenient, quick, and effortless access to products while simultaneously eliminating the need to shop the entire store. This emphasis on perishable products

Figure 5.2. Produce departments, filled with fragrant, colorful, and quality merchandise located near the front of the store, set the tone for a memorable shopping experience.

Figure 5.3. Focus groups confirm that the location of a well-stocked and well-lit produce department near the front of the store is preferred by customers.

and meal solutions offers yet another vehicle for Chain A to differentiate its locations from those of the competition (Figures 5.4 and 5.5).

The opinions solicited from focus groups also verify that the gourmet tastes and heightened food interests of consumers have a tremendous influence on the grocery retail environment. Chain A's management is long aware that the products and choices offered and sold in stores even as recently as ten years ago no longer sustain the worldly and epicurean appetites of today's shopper. Flexibility in layouts and merchandising for the ever-evolving selection of products to be sold is an ongoing space-planning issue that affects current and future store design (Figure 5.6).

Focus group feedback also reveals that consumers would prefer that essential products be conveniently located near the front of the store. Yet certain preferences produce spatial layout and functionality challenges for the management of Chain A. For example, locating products like dairy near the front of the store creates unnecessary construction expenditures

Figure 5.4. The emphasis on perishable products, like cheese, provides a retailer with the means to differentiate its stores from the competition.

Figure 5.5. Overall store layout must incorporate a wide array of perishable products including ready-to-cook and ready-to-eat meal solutions.

Figure 5.6. The ever-evolving selection of products offered is an ongoing space-planning issue that affects current and future store design.

for the retailer because of the duplication of refrigeration and mechanical systems. Production inconveniences, due to the distance between the location of product delivery and/or storage and the product merchandising area, require employees to transport perishable products through often-congested store aisles. Store layouts that promote production and operational efficiencies encourage employee satisfaction and keep labor costs down; conversely, poor layouts with the resulting inefficiencies negatively affect store employees and often produce unwanted turnover. Chain A recognizes that staff retention is paramount to maintain quality customer service. Therefore, a delicate balance must exist between satisfying the preferences of customers and supporting efficient operational issues. Now more than ever, store design influences labor relations; with profit margins slim and competition intense, the significance of these labor issues obviously must be a consideration in store design (Figure 5.7).

Figure 5.7. Customers prefer that essential dairy products be located near the front of the store; however, some retailers, in order to support production and operational efficiencies, locate the dairy section near the rear of the store.

Figure 5.8. Features like demonstration kitchens incorporated into store
design serve as another channel to differentiate retail locations.

Customer feedback also offers clues into the significance of fostering a
meaningful connection between the retailer and the consumer. Chain A's
management comprehends that this connection can be enhanced through
elements of design. An in-store feature like a demonstration kitchen, for example, provides Chain A with an avenue to educate its customers on food
products and preparation techniques. Consumers enjoy these educational
experiences because they generate that sought-after meaningful connection that enhances the overall shopping experience. Incorporating features
like demonstration kitchens into store design serves as yet another channel
to successfully differentiate Chain A from its competition (Figure 5.8).

Figure 5.9. Skylights provide natural light while reducing or eliminating the use of overhead lighting during daylight hours, thereby reducing energy consumption and operational costs.

The management of Chain A has also learned from its customers that environmental stewardship, sustainability, and green design are noteworthy issues. Not only do Chain A's customers expect environmental responsibility, they expect Chain A to communicate its stewardship efforts, articulate their effect, and convey how they, the customers, can support Chain A's sustainability activities. In response, more current store designs include skylights that provide natural lighting into the retail space, thereby allowing Chain A to save on energy costs by reducing or eliminating the use of overhead lighting during the day (Figure 5.9).

As illustrated in this example, Chain A's management bases numerous design decisions on the data collected from consumer focus groups, and as a result, Chain A continues to be competitive in the supermarket industry. The data reveal that informed design decisions can differentiate store locations, enrich the meaningful connection made with its customers, and provide measurable benefit when enhancing the overall shopping experience.

Chain B

The approach used in this example is slightly different from that of the previous example, as Chain B, a large retailer with at least five formats in its cadre of stores, looks to outside professionals for design solutions. In this instance, Chain B commissions a professional design firm to create a successful store prototype for a newly acquired chain of stores.

Members of the firm will first absorb and catalog all marketing and demographic information provided by the management of Chain B. Once complete, they will establish a team, composed of individuals with varied retail expertise, to carry out an objective evaluation. This team will literally become immersed in the areas where Chain B's newest stores are located in an effort to assess the stores, observe regional shopping habits, and interview consumers. This method of investigation is programming for a specific project and enables the firm to capture the essence of the targeted customers.

As learned from past practice, producing a visual report reflecting the lifestyles, habits, expectations, and desires of targeted customers enables these design consultants to convey a powerful, comprehensible, and memorable image to the client. Visual reports, coupled with statistical and demographic information as to the buying habits, income levels, and cultural differences, become valuable devices that enhance and drive store designs. This imagery lends itself to objective decision making, keeping the client focused on the targeted customer, and creates the checks and balances required to eliminate subjective design decisions.

The professional team will then embark on creating the schematic designs and internally choose the best to present to its client. Once the store prototype is determined, these consultants remain engaged through the entire process from the construction and fabrication documentation phase, to the construction and fabrication administration, through post-construction evaluation. Any adaptations or changes made during this process will be incorporated into the next rollout of the format. Along the way, consumer testing will continue to be employed, with store concepts, store layouts, and 3-D models being evaluated by focus groups prior to construction and additional consumer feedback generated from surveys and interviews post-construction.

The strategy of Chain B's management to hire experienced professionals to create store prototypes assures the retailer that the needs and desires of its customers will be addressed in design. Professional design firms that utilize the best available information enable retailers like Chain B to remain competitive in the supermarket industry.

Summary

Supermarket retailers rely on design professionals to create store environments that provide the atmospheres to support their business goals. In taking the time to examine data and information derived from several approaches, design professionals have an opportunity to be successful in creating destinations where consumers browse, shop, and spend money. Store design that is cognizant of the desires of today's consumer; supports their fast-paced and urbane lifestyles; differentiates a retail grocer from others through store image; and provides an entertaining, exciting, and educational shopping experience will appeal to shoppers and foster satisfaction. Ultimately, by increasing customer satisfaction, architects and designers will enhance customer loyalty and improve sales, thereby fulfilling the objectives of the supermarket retailer.

BIBLIOGRAPHY

Ang, S. H., Leong, S. M., & Lim, J. (1996). The mediating influence of pleasure and arousal on layout and signage. *Journal of Retailing and Consumer Services, 4*(1), pp. 13–24.

Arnold, M. J., & Reynolds, K. E. (2003, February). Hedonic shopping motivations. *Journal of Retailing, 79,* pp. 77–95.

Babin, B. J., & Darden, W. R. (1995). Consumer self-regulation in a retail environment. *Journal of Retailing, 71*(1), pp. 47–70.

Baker, J., Levy, M., & Grewal, D. (1992, Winter). An experimental approach to making retail store environmental decision. *Journal of Retailing, 68*(4), pp. 445–459.

Bellenger, D.N., & Korgaonkar, P.K. (1980, Fall). Profiling the recreational shopper. *Journal of Retailing, 56*(3), pp. 77–93.

Bitner, M.J. (1992, April). Servicescapes: The impact of physical surroundings on customers and employees. *Journal of Marketing, 56,* pp. 57–71.

Caffarini, A. J., & Cavanaugh, K. (2006, July). The future of food retailing. Willard Bishop. Retrieved from http://www.willardbishop.com/filebin/200607FFR.pdf

Convenience Store News. (2007). 7-Eleven becomes a foodie. Convenience Store News. Retrieved from http://www.csnnews.com/csm/news/article_display.jsp?vnu_content_id=1003546547

Din, R. (2000). *New retail.* London: Conran Octopus Limited.

Donovan, R. J., & Rossiter, J. R. (1982, Spring). Store atmosphere: An environmental psychology approach. *Journal of Retailing, 58*(1), pp. 34–59.

Donovan, R. J., Rossiter, J. R., & Marcoolyn, G. (1994). Store atmosphere and purchasing behavior. *Journal of Retailing, 70*(3), pp. 283–294.

Hanson, A. (2006, May). Food savvy. *VM + SD, 137*(5), pp. 38–42.

Hamilton, D. (2004). Four levels of evidence-based practice. *AIA Journal of Architecture.* Retrieved from http://www.aia.org/nwsltr_aiaj.cfm?pagename=aiaj_a_20041201 fourlevels

Howell, D. (2002, July, 29). Dollar stores cash in on food offerings; Success seen on dry goods, perishables. *DSN Retailing Today.* Retrieved from http://www.findarticles.com/p/articles/mi_m0FNP/is_14_4l/ai_90189108l/print

Hibbard, J. (2006, September 18). Put your money where your mouth is. *Business Week, 4001,* pp. 61–63.

Ibrahim, M. F., & Wee, N. C. (2002). The importance of entertainment in shopping center experience: Evidence from Singapore. *Journal of Real Estate Portfolio Management, 8*(3), pp. 239–254.

Jones, M. A. (1999). Entertaining shopping experiences: An exploratory investigation. *Journal of Retailing and Consumer Services, 6,* pp. 129–139.

Kaltcheva, V. D., & Weitz, B. A. (2006, January). When should a retailer create an exciting environment? *Journal of Marketing, 70*(1), pp. 107–118.

Kim, Y. K. (2001). Experiential retailing: An interdisciplinary approach to success in domestic and international retailing. *Journal of Retailing and Consumer Services, 8,* pp. 287–289.

Lam, S. Y. (2001). The effects of store environment on shopping behaviors: A critical review. *Advances in Consumer Research, 28*(1), pp. 190–195.

Leszczyc, P. T., Sinha, A., & Sahgal, A. (2004). The effect of multi-purpose shopping on pricing and location strategy for grocery stores. *Journal of Retailing, 80,* pp. 85–99.

Lindeman, T. F. (2006, June 27). Giant Eagle woos foodies with "Market District." *Pittsburgh Post-Gazette.* Retrieved from www.post-gazette.com/pg/pp/06178/701433.stm

Litwak, D. (2006). Keeping customers in mind. *Grocery Heaquarters.* Retrieved from http://www.groceryheadquarters.com/?pg=contents&spg=edo&spg_num=1&print=true

Progressive Grocer. (2006). Super 50. *Progressive Grocer.* Retrieved from http://www.progressivegrocer.com/progressivegrocer/images/pdf/Super_50_PG_2006.pdf

Purcell, D. (2006, May 2). Supermarkets go specialty. *Specialty Food Magazine.* Retrieved from http://www.specialtyfood.com/do/news/ViewNewsArticle?id=2365

Reda, S. (2005, February). Marsh Supermarkets takes on the Bentonville champ. *Stores, 87*(2), pp. 30–36.

Riewoldt, O. (2000). *Retail Design.* New York: Neues Publishing.

Schooley, T. (2005). Giant Eagle creates own upscale brand. *Pittsburgh Business Times.* Retrieved from http://www.bizjournals.com/pittsburgh/stories/2005/11/28/story7.html?t=printable

Supermarket News. (2008). SN's Top 75 Retailers for 2008. Retrieved from http://www.supermarketnews.com/profiles/2008-top-75/

Tauber, E.M. (1972, October). Why do people shop? *Journal of Marketing*, 36, pp. 46–59.

Wal-Mart (2007). Retrieved from http://www.walmartfacts.com/FactSheets/

Whole Foods Market (2007). Retrieved from http://www.wholefoodsmarket.com/investor/index.html

6 The Design of Neonatal Intensive Care Units: Information Gathering and Practioners as Consumers of Research

Anna Marshall-Baker

Abstract

This chapter begins with a description of the development of neonatal intensive care and illustrates the importance of informed decisions in both medicine and design. Critical to the treatment of infants requiring intensive care was the incubator, an invaluable medical marvel whose design evolved with advances in science and medicine. Yet despite an increasing body of knowledge fueled ultimately by empirical research, the design of the infant incubator and of neonatal intensive care units (NICUs) exposed vulnerable infants to detrimental effects of their immediate environments. An awareness of the critical relationship between infants and their social, medical, and physical environments fostered changes in the care and treatment of preterm infants that required complementary changes in the design of NICUs, including integration of natural objects and conditions. The work of two healthcare designers, Kristi Ennis and Lynne Wilson-Ore, illustrates the intersection between the NICU environment and green design principles. In the first project, design decision making is influenced by empirical research, and in the second, design decisions are informed by detailed information gathering related to product manufacturer specifications. The chapter concludes with a description of the author's own empirical work regarding the air quality in infant incubators.

Introduction

The evolution of neonatal intensive care has been characterized at times by either a lack or a profusion of research that has proved problematic in both instances. Scientific inquiry was limited during the early years of neonatal care, and later development of NICUs reflected trends in design and medicine that were so heavily influenced by the technological advances of an Industrial Age that the relationship between human beings and their physical, social, and natural environments often was neglected, ignored, or disparaged. One particular technological advance, the infant incubator, came to prescribe rather than support the care and treatment of newborn infants requiring intensive care. In its more recent history, investigators involved in neonatal intensive care have focused their efforts on the vital relationships between infants and their environments, which depend on the integration of biological systems with environmental stimulation. The purpose of this chapter is to provide an overview of the design and development of NICUs and to emphasize the critical role that informed design plays in the process of designing interiors to enhance the care and treatment of critically ill infants.

Development of Neonatal Intensive Care

Contemporary NICUs belie their initial celebrity as curiosities in amusement pavilions of world's fairs and expositions during the late nineteenth and early twentieth centuries (e.g., Gustaitis & Young, 1986; Silverman, 1979). Physicians, particularly Martin Couney, arranged exhibitions of premature infants in Europe and the United States, and argued that their display reflected significant advances in medicine that warranted inclusion in science and technology pavilions (Silverman, 1979). Yet promoters viewed the tiny infants as entertain-

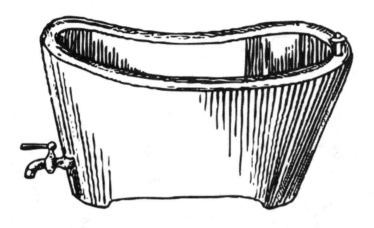

Figure 6.1. Double-walled metal incubator typical for the care
of preterm infants in the early nineteenth century.

ment and often positioned the exhibits on the Midway among bearded
women, dog-faced boys, and fan dancers or in the Agricultural Hall
with exotic animals and dirt tracks for bicycle racing. At other shows,
such as the Victorian Era Exhibition at Earl's Court in 1897, the infants
were exhibited in a specially designed building with spaces for nurses
and wet nurses, a nursery where infants were fed and bathed, and a
central viewing room for the public. This precursor of a specialized care
nursery included, as did all the exhibits, "hot air chambers," or infant
incubators.

The original, fundamental medical concern for premature infants was
temperature regulation, and this became the primary function of the
earliest incubators. One of the first known incubators was developed in
1835 in St. Petersburg, Russia, and resembled a small tub with doubled
iron walls that held heated water (Cone, 1980). See Figure 6.1.

The first enclosed incubator was developed in 1880 at the request of
E. S. Tarnier, an obstetrician, after he observed the incubation of chick-
ens at the Paris Zoo (Hess, 1922; Hess & Lundeen, 1941). The Tarnier

Figure 6.2. Iron-framed glass wall incubators vented to indoor air
during a World's Fair in the early twentieth century.

incubator held several infants in a double-walled wooden box that measured about 2 feet by 3 feet by 3 feet (Budin, 1900/1907; Hess, 1922).
A metal reservoir beneath the infant chamber held approximately 18
gallons of heated water. Sawdust insulated the space between the walls
and the top was a glass pane that allowed the infant to be viewed from
above. A later modification of this incubator replaced the wooden walls
with thick panes of glass fixed in an iron frame that enabled observation
of the infant from any area of a room (Figure 6.2). Successive modifications to incubator design considered not only the source of heat (e.g.,
hot water or warmed air) but also the source of air (Hess, 1922). Some
models vented into the ward with a "chimney" attached to the side of
the incubator. Other models required a stack through the building that

Figure 6.3.
During the mid-twentieth century, incubators became more tightly fitted to facilitate new treatments such as oxygen therapy. These more tightly controlled environments also affected access to the infant occupants.

connected to a supply of fresh air and used an electric fan to control the air currents and direction of the airflow.

As the growth and development of the premature infant became better understood, issues other than temperature regulation such as gestational age at birth, feeding, weight gain, prenatal health, deformities, and infectious disease had to be addressed (Hess, 1922). Oxygen therapy was introduced in an effort to support the development of the infants' immature lungs, and incubators were fitted with oxygen tanks. Increased awareness of the need to control the incubator environment, in the case of oxygen therapy, for example, resulted in infant incubators that were more tightly fitted. In the Chapple incubator (Figure 6.3), portholes fitted with fabric sleeves provided access to the infant without compromising the controlled environment (Robertson, 2003). Air pressure in the infant chamber was greater than that in the nursery and prevented any airborne infection in the nursery from entering the incubator. More tightly fitted incubators that had portholes and sleeves to access the infant enabled sustained environments that controlled temperature, humidity, and oxygen levels.

The Chapple incubator of 1938 was the predecessor of the Isolette that was manufactured by Air Shields following World War II. These two incubators mark a critical point in incubator design and care procedures for preterm infants. They provided the industry with a design that has remained relatively unchanged for more than 60 years: infant chamber over mechanical system over storage cabinet. By the very nature of their design, the Chapple incubator and the Isolette determined how infant care would be provided: with hands through portholes that flip, turn, and manipulate infants—types of touch that contrast to the cradling support more typical of care of healthy newborns. Further, these incubators with their ability to provide each infant an individualized, controlled environment fostered a "hands-off" caretaking practice. As a result, contact unrelated to medical care was discouraged and challenges to this passive approach of care and treatment were believed to be unwarranted and, thus, unwelcome (Silverman, 1989).

The hands-off, passive approach to care assumed that the NICU and the incubator, specifically, provided favorable conditions for the growth and development of preterm infants. Infants needed controlled environments with constant temperature, levels of humidity and oxygen, and medical care—all of which were provided by or within the incubator environment. The negative consequence of this approach was care and treatment of the preterm infant that emerged as a consequence of technology: nurses interacted with the infants as the incubator allowed. Instead, the appropriate types of care necessary for the growth and development of preterm infants should direct technological advances. The danger of this hands-off approach became obvious in the 1950s with the discovery that the routine use of high levels of oxygen, believed to be a "favorable condition" for the infants' respiratory systems, created devastating eye damage to over 10,000 children across a 12-year period (Day, 1980; Silverman, 1989). Although oxygen levels seemed to be related to blindness, the medical establishment offered all kinds of alternative hypotheses to explain away the devastating outcomes of such a "long-trusted therapeutic agent" (Silverman, 1989, p. 164). Silverman (1989) notes that it became "painfully clear that none of the time-honored routines to provide 'favorable conditions for survival' had ever been rigorously tested" (p. 164).

With the collapse of the hands-off, passive approach to care came an exponential increase in research and study of all aspects of preterm infant behavior and development, accompanied by a plethora of new drugs and other physical agents (Day, 1980; Silverman, 1989). A more aggressive outlook toward care and treatment of preterm infants developed, one that seemed boundless and bountiful. This new approach fueled the widespread growth of neonatology as a medical specialty in the 1960s and 1970s (Gustaitis & Young, 1986), and the result was an NICU that was alive with medical staff, activity, and technology. These new NICUs were bright, boisterous, and nonsocial environments filled with physicians, nurses, specialists, technicians, and state-of-the-art equipment (Figure 6.4).

Soon these NICUs once heralded for the intensity of investigation and technology, came to be recognized as environments that were "overstimulating" (Cornell & Gottfried, 1976)—characterized by elevated levels of handling (Korones, 1976), noise (Linn, Horowitz, Buddin, Leake, & Fox, 1985), light (Glass et al., 1985), and activity (Gottfried et al., 1981). The opportunity for infants to experience the typically occurring progression of sensory system development was not only disrupted but further compromised by sensory experiences that were dissynchronous. Voices or sounds that the infant may hear were not connected to a particular source, and a stomach filling with food (from a tube) was not associated with sucking. The intensity of the NICU environment and the various types of care

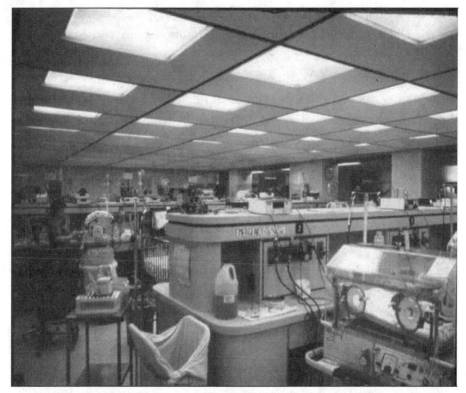

Figure 6.4. An overstimulating environment typical of NICUs in the 1970s.

and treatment of preterm infants ushered in an array of harmful environmental effects resulting in conditions such as disorganized behavioral states of sleeping and waking, hearing disorders, and chronic respiratory disease caused by prolonged mechanical ventilation.

As we reflect on the development of the modern newborn intensive care unit, we see a fundamental piece of medical equipment, the infant incubator, dominating the care and treatment of the preterm infant. And as it evolved, reports of infant successes did appear. The 66 percent mortality rate in 1879, for example, fell to 38 percent in 1882 as a consequence of Tarnier's incubator (Cone, 1980). Reports such as these inspired successive modifications to the infant incubator, but these reports were reactive, documenting quantitative outcomes such as mortality or survival rates. In addition, these reports, which qualified the success of medical equipment and caretaking practices, also fueled the passive, favorable conditions or "hands-off" method of care. Perhaps inadvertently but none the less devastating, this approach disparaged the role of the mother in her infant's life (Baker, 1996). Even Couney in the early part of the twentieth century noted the effects of mother/infant separation when he despaired that parents visited their infants (in the exhibitions) infrequently and that he had difficulty persuading them to take their infants when it was time to send them home (Silverman, 1989).

This brief history of the development of the NICU demonstrates not only the danger of technology as the driving force of medical care, but also the critical need for systematic development and testing of hypotheses with a careful interpretation of results that contribute to a growing body of knowledge. The wide array of investigations that occurred following the collapse of the passive approach to care offered significant insight into the care and treatment of preterm infants, but unintentionally hosted a plethora of harmful environmental effects (Cone; 1983; Day, 1980; Gustaitis & Young, 1986; Silverman, 1989) and conditions such as learning and attention deficit disorders (Harrison, n.d.), sensory impairments (e.g., D'Agostino & Clifford, 1998), and language comprehension difficulties (Luoma, Herrgard, Martikainen, & Ahonen, 1998). At the same time, the parental role was degraded to the point that parents sometimes were not allowed to visit their infants (e.g., Cone, 2007). The outcome was a gradual awareness that infants' relationships with their environments are critical.

Developmental Care

Documentation of harmful environmental conditions in NICUs in the United States during the 1970s and 1980s focused the attention of investigators on the seemingly complex relationship between hospitalized infants and their environments. Investigations such as those by Hofer (1981), Thoman (1986), Als and colleagues (1982), and Garbanati and Parmelee (1987) revealed that infant development resulted from the organization of component behaviors into hierarchically more complex behavioral systems, a process that involves integration of the infant's biological systems with environmental stimuli. Yet sensory integration is difficult for infants whose systems are fragile, and behavioral organization is further compromised by environmental stimulation in the NICU that is particularly intense and untimely. Infants trying to sleep, for example, were bombarded constantly with high levels of light. Thus, a new approach to care was required, one that recognized infants' individual abilities and the important role that the environment played in their development. This approach is known as "developmental care."

At the core of developmental care is the understanding that the environment of the NICU affects infants and their families. In developmental care, the term environment is used in the broadest sense and represents aspects of the

- Physical environment such as levels of light and noise
- Medical environment, which includes interventions and procedures
- Social environment provided by the parents of the infant

The purpose of developmental care is to individualize and modify the infant's environments to promote the integration of stimuli with the infant's biological systems (Als, Lester, Tronick, & Brazelton, 1982; Thoman, 1986) in nonstressful ways that preserve the infant's energy, promote growth, enhance recovery, and enable self-induced soothing and organizing behaviors (Royal Women's Hospital, 2006). This approach to neonatal care represents a significant shift in care practices.

The traditional clinical delivery of care was procedure-based and directed by the caregiver, typically a nurse. In this model, nurses' schedules determined when babies were fed, changed, and examined and when procedures occurred. In contrast, developmental care is a relationship-based model guided by the infant patient (Ballweg, 2004; Pressler, Turnage-Carrier, & Kenner, 2004). With developmental care, babies are fed, changed, and examined when they are ready for interaction. For example, an infant who is calmly awake may be held, engaged in social interaction with a parent, and then fed. A baby in a sound sleep is not awakened for a diaper change or to replace an IV line. Developmental care, then, requires that caregivers be educated and trained to recognize infants' behavioral and developmental status and cues. Caregivers also have to be flexible to provide appropriate types of care at the moment that the infant is best organized to receive the care (Als & Lawhon, 2004).

Physical Environment

As a model of caregiving in the NICU, developmental care provides a framework for the array of investigations related to the care, treatment, and development of the preterm infant. For example, studies that investigate the effects of light on preterm infants enable informed decisions regarding the design of a supportive physical environment. We know, for example, that infants in cycled light have lower heart rates, quieter activity levels, and more hours of sleep than infants exposed to constant levels of light (Grauer, 1989; Miller, White, Whitman, O'Callaghan, & Maxwell, 1995; Holditch-Davis, Blackburn, & Vandenberg, 2003). Cycled light also fosters development of a circadian rhythm, which becomes evident in infant activity levels that correspond to day and night (see Rivkees, 2004), and this knowledge coupled with that regarding benefits of natural light has resulted in NICUs designed to take advantage of daylighting conditions. Thus, within our model of developmental care, designing the NICU to accommodate daylighting and cycled light conditions reduced infants' stress, helped them conserve energy, fostered their self-regulatory capabilities, and promoted growth (Figure 6.5).

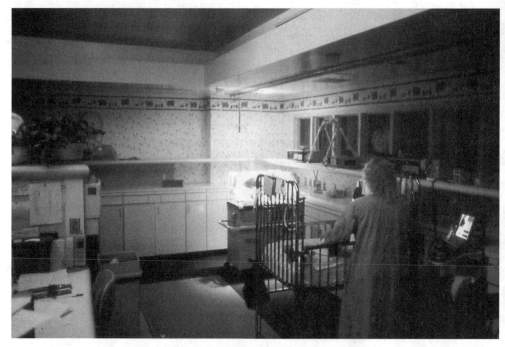

Figure 6.5. Cycling light in the NICU is representative of developmental care practices, in this instance adjusting light levels to support infants' sleeping and waking states as well as the development of their circadian rhythms, which are entrained to a 24-hour cycle of daylight and darkness.

Medical Environment

In terms of the medical environment, awareness of infants' responses to interventions has altered the traditional delivery of care to be sensitive to the infant's ability to receive and recover from a particular procedure. The intent of "clustered care," for example, is to protect infants from interruptions and stressful conditions across the course of the day by combining like procedures and to provide infants an opportunity to rest between events. Clustering events or procedures, whether routine, such as changing a diaper and replacing the infant's blankets, or painful, such as suctioning the baby's lungs and collecting a blood sample, when the infant is aware and organized causes less stress than unexpected, isolated events (Turnage-Carrier, 2004). During the procedures, caregivers recognize when an infant has had enough treatment and needs a rest or whether the infant can tolerate a longer episode of procedures. Slevin and colleagues (1999) found that nesting, a form of swaddling, helped preterm infants tolerate a visual screening for eye disease and recover from the procedure more quickly. A contained baby is an organized baby who is conserving energy and facilitating development of self-regulatory systems (Browne, 2004).

Social Environment

Developmental care emphasizes, particularly, the infant's social environment, which involves patients, families, and professional caregivers. An approach to care that recognizes family members as vital participants in decisions regarding their infants is known as "family-centered" (Institute for Family Centered Care, n.d.).

The intent of family-centered care is to acknowledge parents' perceptions and reactions to their infants and to the NICU experience, and to promote their participation in decision making involving individualized and comprehensive care of their babies (Harrison, Lotas, & Jorgensen, 2004). Family-centered care is based on open, honest, and inclusive communication between family members and medical professionals and is characterized by these four components:

- *Dignity and respect.* Healthcare practitioners listen to and honor patient and family needs, perspectives, and choices.
- *Information sharing.* Healthcare practitioners communicate and share complete and unbiased information with patients and families in ways that are affirming and useful.
- *Participation.* Patients and families are encouraged and supported for participating to the degree they feel comfortable in care and decision making.

- *Collaboration.* Healthcare leaders collaborate with patients and families in policy and program development, implementation, and evaluation; in healthcare facility design; and in professional education, as well as in the delivery of care (adapted from Institute for Family-Centered Care).

For family-centered care to occur, parents need to "know" their baby. When they do, they are prepared to engage in conversations regarding care and treatment of their infant family member. But knowing their baby results from spending time with the baby, and this means that the family needs space at the baby's bedside for privacy and intimacy. These needs have fueled a recent trend in NICU design for individual neonatal care rooms (e,g., Shepley, Harris, & White, 2008).

Single-family rooms (SFRs) enable parents to nurture their infants away from staff and other families (see Chapter 10 for further discussion of single-family rooms). In addition, SFRs ensure that conversations between parents and medical professionals are private (Harris, Shepley, White, Kolberg, & Harrell, 2006). SFRs also empower families to control temperature, lighting, and noise, and enable them to shield themselves from traffic and other distractions in the NICU by closing the doors to their rooms or securing visual barriers such as blinds, curtains, or panels. But perhaps most importantly, SFRs afford parents an opportunity to stay overnight with their infants, to live with their babies, despite the continued need for neonatal intensive care (Figure 6.6). Because of overnight stays, SFRs provide more amenities for parents such as desks and full-size beds, kitchens, bathrooms with showers, laundry facilities, and family lounges that encourage interaction with other parents. Various studies have revealed that infants in SFRs spend fewer days in the hospital and are readmitted less often than infants in open-bed wards, and parents have lower levels of anxiety and are more confident in their ability to care for their infants (e.g., Kolberg, n.d.).

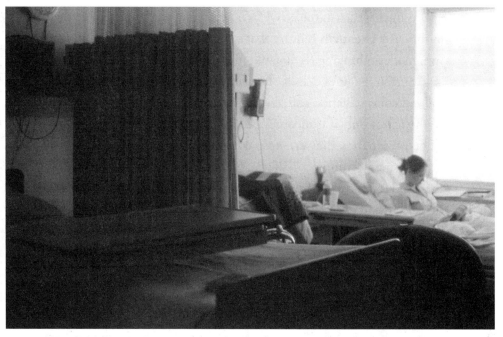

Figure 6.6. This mother stays in a single-family room with her infant, who still requires intensive care. She is enjoying a quiet moment to read by a window while her infant sleeps in an incubator, covered by a quilt that lowers the light level.

In summary, developmental care acknowledges the confluence of physical, medical, and social conditions that affect infant behavior and development. Developmental care provides a framework for the study of appropriate care and treatment of preterm infants that crosses various disciplines such as social science, medicine, and design. Importantly, attention has focused recently on conditions important to human well-being that still are not typical of hospital environments—conditions of nature.

Green Healthcare

As we have seen, care of the preterm infant evolved as a consequence of advances in medical technology. The evolution of high-tech medical environments such as the NICU was accompanied by a design aesthetic in the early twentieth century that was intended to symbolize progressive, modern thinking (Kellman, 1995). This aesthetic was characterized by clean, sterile lines; a lack of ornamentation; geometric shapes; neutralized color schemes; and abstracted images. Kellman notes that this aesthetic not only was incorporated into hospital design but also came to be accepted as the way hospitals should be designed. Thus, both modern architecture and design and modern medical advances reflected the trend to turn away from nature and toward technology and science (for discussion of the influence of the medical model and medicine on the design of nursing homes, see Chapter 8). William McDonough and Michael Braungart (2002) describe this period as a time when nature was viewed for its potential to provide tools and materials—in other words, "resources"—to human beings who could capitalize and improve upon nature's efforts, thereby producing goods and services of the Industrial Age. Yet people began to realize the unintended and often negative consequences of the detachment of human beings from nature. In healthcare, people began to be dissatisfied with the aesthetic, realizing that beyond actual procedures, the healthcare environment was not meeting other needs such as emotional well-being.

In a pioneering study by Roger Ulrich (1984), patients with a view of nature were found to have fewer post-surgical complications, require less pain medication, and spend fewer days in the hospital than patients with a view of a brick wall. Ulrich's work fueled significant advances in the field of environmental health during the last 20 years, work that often is grounded in the theory of biophilia (Wilson, 1984; for additional discussion of biophilia, see Chapter 3). Proposed by biologist E. O. Wilson, biophilia describes an innate affiliation of human beings toward other living organisms. This theory has been extended to include inanimate natural objects or conditions such as waterfalls, landscapes, and wind. To illustrate, consider healing environments such as therapeutic gardens that promote physical, physiological, and emotional well-being (Smith, Roehll, & Bonnell, 2007). A number of studies indicate that people feel calmer and more relaxed around plants (Butterfield & Relf, 1992) and prefer windows that face landscaped views (Browne, 1992). Even inanimate illustrations of natural scenes that include plants and streams or pools of water have a positive effect on patients. Ulrich (1993) reported that patients recovering from heart surgery experienced less post-operative anxiety when they looked at pictures of nature. Others experienced better pain control when they listened to natural sounds and viewed natural images on cubicle curtains (Lechtzin, Withers, Devrotes, & Diette, 2001). Clearly a positive relationship exists between human beings and natural objects and conditions, yet for decades this affiliation was ignored in the design of healthcare facilities.

Informed Design Examples

Boulder Community Foothills Hospital

Kristi Ennis is a senior associate and the sustainable design director for Boulder Associates in Colorado. Ms. Ennis also is a LEED-accredited professional who played a significant role in the design and development of Boulder Community Foothills Hospital (BCFH), the first healthcare facility ever to be LEED certified, earning a Silver designation in 2003 (see First-LEED, 2004).

Boulder Community Hospital (BCH) began its environmental stewardship decades ago with an award-winning recycling program. Since then, BCH has secured alternative forms of energy, provided bus passes to its 3,000 employees, and recommitted itself to environmental principles intended to "protect and preserve the environment" (Ruzzin, 2004). After a site was selected for the new women's and children's hospital, for example, the BCH Board was confronted immediately with

Figure 6.7. A resident of Boulder, Colorado.

a question regarding protection of the environment. The site of the proposed BCFH would have an impact on a wetland and displace a colony of prairie dogs. The designers responded with a plan to construct another wetland on the hospital site that was six times the size of the original and to relocate the prairie dogs, which are not only important to the diversity of the regional ecosystem but also provide delightful entertainment (Figure 6.7).

Use of native plants, locally manufactured face brick, and locally harvested sandstone further assured a fit of the facility with the environment (see McDonough & Braungart, 2002). Bike racks and shower facilities encouraged employees to ride bicycles to work, and the transportation authority agreed to develop a new bus stop at the hospital. These strategies reduced the overall number of cars and enabled a smaller amount of paved surface for parking.

Figure 6.8. Daylighting of the two-story atrium in Boulder Community Foothills Hospital.

As with preterm infants, lighting conditions that fluctuate and cycle during the course of the day also are important to the well-being of adult patients, staff, and visitors. A two-story atrium in BCFH positioned at the entrance where the hospital intersects with the medical office building not only fills the space with natural light but also serves as a wayfinding device (Figure 6.8). A short circulation spine that wraps three sides of the building admits daylighting, facilitates wayfinding, and provides continuous views of the nearby foothills and of frolicking prairie dogs. Mansard overhangs were used to fully shade windows on the south and west sides to prevent solar gain, though daylight still enters the space. Overhangs were not included on the east and north sides of the building, where solar gain is not a problem. These types of design decisions not only enable *daylighting* and *wayfinding* but also acknowledge the work of scholars like E. O. Wilson and Roger Ulrich, who document the positive effects of nature on health and wellness.

Further informed from the literature of the benefits of single-family rooms (e.g., Harris, Shepley, White, Kohlberg, & Harrel, 2006, and Kohlberg, n.d.), the design of Boulder Community Foothills Hospital includes six individual rooms for infants and their families. Each single-family room has a door that opens into the hospital corridor and a second door that opens into an individual infant room. The infant's room also has a second door that opens into the corridor. This arrangement not only enables access into either the parents' or infant's rooms but also allows parents to move privately between their and their baby's rooms (Figure 6.9). Importantly, fresh air enters the single-family rooms through operable windows fitted with contacts that monitor when windows are open or closed. Opened windows send a signal that dials back the variable air otherwise controlled by the energy system. Should the window in the parents' room be open when the door to the infant's room also is open, preterm infants who still require intensive care may breathe fresh air.

To further address indoor air quality, a two-week building flush with 100 percent outside air preceded occupancy. This was important despite Ms. Ennis' careful specification of environmentally responsible substances and materials that included low-VOC paints, adhesives, sealants, insulation, and carpet and formaldehyde-free composite wood products. Specifying "green" materials is not easy, and Ms. Ennis laments that there is not a coordinated, organized resource that serves as a type of clearinghouse for information. She notes that many designers continue to choose materials based on a single issue such as durability or cost, and most designers continue to "juggle individual information" that they have gathered through their own search process. Yet the issue of specifying materials that are not harmful to human or environmental health is pervasive, particularly in healthcare design.

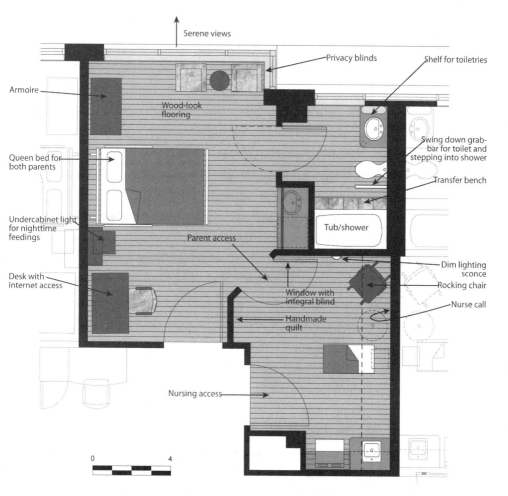

Serene views

Privacy blinds

Shelf for toiletries

Armoire

Wood-look flooring

Swing down grab-bar for toilet and stepping into shower

Queen bed for both parents

Transfer bench

Undercabinet light for nighttime feedings

Parent access

Tub/shower

Desk with internet access

Dim lighting sconce

Rocking chair

Window with integral blind

Nurse call

Handmade quilt

Nursing access

0   4

Figure 6.9. This floor plan of a single-family room at Boulder Community Foothills Hospital shows accommodations and privacy afforded infants and their families.

Sunnybrook Health Sciences Center

Lynne Wilson-Orr is an interior designer, architect, and principal at Parkin Architects in Toronto, Ontario. While developing the design for the new NICU at Sunnybrook Health Sciences Center in Toronto, Ms. Wilson-Orr and the design team of interior designers, architects, and nurses realized that many of the standard or typical materials and substances installed in healthcare settings were harmful to human and environmental health. Launching its own educational journey, the group searched and found an overwhelming amount of information from various sources such as government agencies, individual manufacturers, sales reps, and private institutions. This sea of resources was very different from Ms. Wilson-Orr's first search for information in 2001 when she recalls searching for two days to finally locate a single source. She credits two factors for the vast array of resources now available. First, success stories from healthcare institutions report that economic barriers such as up-front and operational costs are coming down as green healthcare becomes more cost-effective, particularly in terms of energy use. This stimulates a rapidly emerging interest in sustainable healthcare design, which includes specifying materials that do not negatively impact human and environmental health. The second factor that has fueled the wealth of information now available to interior designers and architects is an ethical concern felt by medical staff who were unaware that standardized practices and typical materials and products were actually hazardous or toxic to the preterm infants the staff was working so hard to support (e.g., Marshall-Baker, 2006).

At a recent presentation, Ms. Wilson-Orr and colleagues (2007) illustrated a typical space in a healthcare setting and annotated the usual placement and installation of hazardous substances and materials such as polyvinyl chloride (PVC; Why Health Care, 2006; see Figure 6.10). Informed by sources such as manufacturer's product information and best practices, the design team of the Sunnybrook project looked for alternative products that were natural, such as linoleum and rubber flooring, and specified adhesives that did not degrade indoor air quality (Figure 6.11). They also did not specify any material such as floor or wall covering that was made with PVC. They found pressed-wood products that were formaldehyde free and used solid polymer countertops. They identified polyester fabrics that were inherently stain-resistant, and they avoided or reduced the use of upholstery foam. They also searched for

Hiding places of PBTs / VOCs

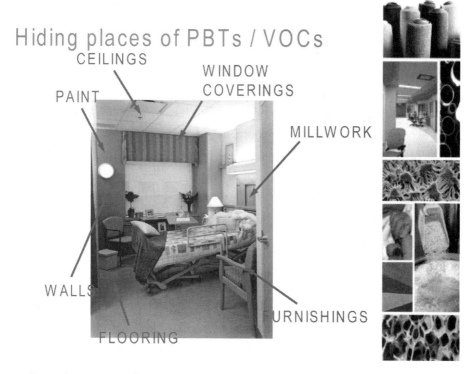

Figure 6.10. Annotated image indicating common placement of materials that typically contain persistent bioaccumulative toxins (PBTs) or volatile organic compounds (VOCs) such as polyvinyl chloride (PVC).

alternatives for PVC piping that included cast iron and polyethylene.

Yet despite the number of resources available, the learning curve regarding substances and materials remains steep, even for those seasoned to the search. Part of the challenge is collecting data from manufacturers who may not know what substances are in their products or, if they do, may consider that information proprietary. Other manufacturers that are aware of the substances in their products may "greenwash" or "spin" the healthful qualities of their products while omitting information regarding the harmful substances. Ms. Wilson-Orr notes that additional concerns facing the use of new materials involve the "newness" of the products—whether they will meet infection control, maintenance, and durability standards, for example. There also is the challenge of facing people's expectations. Floors in hospitals are expected to be shiny, but rubber flooring, for example, is not. To complicate the materials issue further, cleaning staff who may have always stripped, waxed, and polished floors may easily ruin a different type of floor because they were not aware of the required maintenance procedure. Collectively, these current concerns regarding the development of healthful NICUs are reminiscent of periods early in the development of medical equipment and special-care nurseries when staff and parents struggled to provide environments that take into account all aspects of infants' health and well-being.

We have observed in the evolution of neonatal intensive care the dangers of proceeding with practice that has not been "rigorously tested" (Silverman, 1989). Designers who are aware of the importance of research and understand research methods are positioned to make informed design decisions whether they are determining lighting conditions for a particular space or selecting materials that are not harmful to human or environmental health. To extend a step further, designers who are informed about research will be able to conduct their own investigations. Regardless of the challenges associated with either sustainable or green design, designers have little choice but to be well-informed regarding the complexities associated with the spaces they design. This is particularly important in healthcare settings, where patients come seeking wellness. And for preterm infants, the concern for environmental quality begins not with a building or room but with their nearest environment, the incubator.

Full Circle: Infant Incubators

My own work brings this chapter full circle with a return to infant incubators. Just as substances typical of healthcare environments actually may be harmful to human and environmental health, so may be the materials and equipment used in the care and treatment of the preterm infant. To determine whether that was true, we borrowed an incubator from a nearby NICU (Marshall-Baker, 2007). The incubator was still in use by the hospital when we placed it in a testing chamber, turned it on, and took samples of air during a 24-hour period. The results revealed 20 individual chemicals emitting into the air within and around the incubator. The chemicals ranged from fragrance in a cleaning solution that dissipated rapidly to substances with a constant presence and to others with a presence that increased across the 24-hour period. Although the effects of some substances are unknown, others are suspected developmental or neurotoxicants, and others, such as formaldehyde and acetaldehyde, are known human carcinogens and strong upper respiratory and mucosal irritants. These two substances were present at levels twice those recommended by the state of California for indoor environment exposure, and this incubator was eight years old.

This study serves as a seed project for future investigations to further examine the presence and effect of substances and materials common in the incubator environment. Because this was a test of a single incubator, one selected for convenience and availability, we do not know whether these substances appear in all incubators. We also do not know, for example, how these emissions affect air quality over time or whether these substances affect the immature systems of preterm infants. Nor do we know if certain amounts or periods of exposure to the substances are detrimental to infant health. This study also provides support for development of new nontoxic materials and substances that may be used in healthcare environments. In contrast to the early, limited study of infant incubators and their effects on preterm infants, this seed project reflects an approach to the care and treatment of preterm infants that is framed by the integration of biological systems with environments that are physical, medical, social, and natural.

Summary

In this chapter, we have seen the costly effects of practices that initially seemed benign and indeed favorable, and later we realized that rigorous investigation of factors affecting all aspects of the health and wellness of preterm infants is imperative. Developmental care, which emphasizes the role of the infant patient, provides a framework for investigation of physical, medical, and social environments and their effects on infant development. Research in these areas also has revealed the critical relationship between human beings and nature. Neglected in a rush to use nature and trust technology, we thankfully have regained awareness that a connection with nature improves our quality of life and, in fact, is *critical* to our quality of life. Kristi Ennis with Boulder Associates acknowledges that most clients still need to be convinced that sustainable design in healthcare is a good fit with their project, but she believes that we are on a cusp of acceptance of green healthcare design because of the strength of the relationship between health, sustainability, and the building.

Awareness of the importance and complexity of relationships between individuals and their environments transcended neonatal intensive care in the later part of the twentieth century. Developmental and family-centered care, which focus on the integration of infants' biological systems with physical, medical, and social environments, emerged to complement advances in design, medicine, and technology. The resulting body of knowledge, fed by various fields, enables interior designers and architects to make informed decisions regarding the design and development of neonatal intensive care units.

This project was partially supported by a Special Projects Grant from the Interior Design Educators Council (IDEC) in 2005.

BIBLIOGRAPHY

Als, H., & Lawhon, G. (2004) Theoretic perspective for developmentally supportive care. In C. Kenner & J. M. McGrath (Eds.). *Developmental care of newborns and infants: A guide for health professionals* (pp. 47–63). St. Louis, MO: Mosby.

Als, H., Lester, B. M., Tronick, E. Z., & Brazelton, T. B. (1982). Toward a research instrument for the assessment of preterm infants' behavior (APIB). In H. E. Fitzgerald, B. M. Lester, & W. Michael (Eds.), *Theory and research in behavioral pediatrics* (pp. 35–63). New York: Plenum Press.

Baker, J. P. (1996). *The machine in the nursery: Incubator technology and the origins of neonatal intensive care.* Baltimore: Johns Hopkins University Press.

Ballweg, D. D. (2004). Individualized care: Actions for the individualized staff member. In C. Kenner & J. M. McGrath (Eds.), *Developmental care of newborns & infants: A guide for health professionals* (pp. 35–45). St. Louis, MO: Mosby.

Browne, A. (1992). The role of nature for the promotion of well-being in the elderly. In D. Relf (Ed.), *The role of horticulture in human well-being and social development: A national symposium* (pp. 75–79). Portland, OR: Timber Press.

Browne, J. V. (2004). Early relationship environments: Physiology of skin-to-skin contact for parents and their preterm infants. In R. D. White (Vol. ed.), Clinics in Perinatology: Vol. 31(2). *The sensory environment of the NICU: Scientific and design-related aspects* (pp. 287–298). Philadelphia: Saunders.

Budin, P. (1907). *The nursling: The feeding and hygiene of premature and full-term infants* (W. J. Maloney & A. R. Simpson, Trans). London: The Caxton Publishing Company. (Original work published 1900).

Butterfield, B., & Relf, D. (1992). National survey of attitudes toward plants and gardening. In D. Relf (Ed.), *The role of horticulture in human well-being and social development: A national symposium* (pp. 211–212). Portland, OR: Timber Press.

Cone, S. (2007). The impact of communication and the neonatal intensive care unit environment of parent involvement. *Newborn & Infant Nursing, 7*(1), 33–38.

Cone, T. E., Jr. (pub. 1980). Perspectives in neonatology. In G. F. Smith & D. Vidyasagar (Eds.), *Historical review and recent advances in neonatal and perinatal medicine: Vol. 1. Neonatal Medicine* (pp. 9–33). Evansville, IN: Mead Johnson Nutritional Division.

Cornell, E. H., & Gottfried, A. W. (1976). *Intervention with preterm infants. Child Development, 47,* 32–39.

D'Agostino, J. A., & Clifford, P. (1998). Neurodevelopmental consequences associated with the premature neonate. *American Association of Critical Care Nurses (ACCN) clinical issues: Advanced practice in acute and critical care, 9*(1). Retrieved from http://www.aacn.org/AACN/jrnlci.nsf/GetArticle/ArticleTwo91?OpenDocument

Day, R. L. (pub. 1980). Retrolental fibroplasia: A medical and legal tragedy. In F. Smith & D. Vidyasagar (Eds.) *Historical review and recent advances in neonatal and perinatal medicine: Vol. 2. Perinatal Medicine* (pp. 39–43). Evansville, IN: Mead Johnson Nutritional Division.

First LEED-certified healthcare facility (2004). Retrieved from http://www.buildinggreen.com/auth/article.cfm?fileName=130104d.xml

Garbanati, J. A., & Parmelee, A. (1987). State organization in preterm infants: Microanalysis of 24-hour polygraphic recordings. In N. Gunzenhauser (Ed.), *Infant stimulation: For whom, what kind, when, and how much?* (pp. 51–64). Skillman, NJ: Johnson & Johnson.

Glass, P., Avery, G. B., Subramanian, K. N. S., Keys, M. P., Sostek, A. M., & Friendly, D. S. (1985). Effect of bright light in the hospital nursery on the incidence of retinopathy of prematurity. *The New England Journal of Medicine, 313*, 401–404.

Gottfried, A. W., Wallace-Lande, P., Sherman-Brown, S., King, J., Coen, C., & Hodgman, J. F. (1981). Physical and social environment of newborn infants in special care units. *Science, 214*, 673–675.

Grauer, T. T. (1989). Environmental lighting, behavioral state, and hormonal response with the newborn. *Scholarly Inquiry for Nursing Practice: An International Journal, 3*, 53–69.

Gustaitis, R., & Young, E. W. D. (1986). *A time to be born, a time to die: Conflicts and ethics in an intensive care nursery.* Reading, MA: Addison-Wesley.

Harris, D. D., Shepley, M. M., White, R. D., Kolberg, K. J. S., & Harrell, J. W. (2006). *Journal of Perinatology, 26*(Suppl. 3), 38–48.

Harrison, H. (n.d.). ADHD in children born premature. Retrieved June 19, 2007, from http://www.prematurity.org/research/helen-adhd.html

Harrison, L. L., Lotas, M. J., & Jorgensen, K. M. (2004). Environmental issues. In C. Kenner & J. M. McGrath (Eds.), *Developmental care of newborns and infants: A guide for health professionals* (pp. 229–269). St. Louis, MO: Mosby.

Health Care Without Harm (2006). *Why health care is moving away from the hazardous plastic polyvinyl chloride (PVC).* Retrieved April 15, 2007, from http://www.noharm.org/details.cfm?ID=1277&type=document

Hess, J. H. (1922). *Premature and congenitally diseased infants.* Philadelphia: Lea & Febiger.

Hess, J. H., & Lundeen, E. C. (1941). *The premature infant: Its medical and nursing care.* Philadelphia: J.B. Lippincott Company.

Hofer, M. A. (1981). *The roots of human behavior: An introduction to the psychobiology of early development.* San Francisco: W. H. Freeman.

Holditch-Davis, D., Blackburn, S.T., & VandenBerg, K. (2003). Newborn and infant neurobehavioral development. In C. Kenner & J. W. Lott (Eds.), *Comprehensive neonatal nursing: A physiologic perspective* (3rd ed., pp. 236–284). St. Louis, MO: W. B. Saunders.

Institute for Family-Centered Care. (n.d.). *Newborn intensive care bibliography.* Retrieved from http://www.familycenteredcare.org/advance/nicu_bib.pdf

Kellman, N. (1995). History of healthcare environments. In S. O. Marberry (Ed.), *Innovations in healthcare design* (pp. 38–48). New York: Van Nostrand Reinhold.

Kolberg, K. J. S. (n.d.). *Family-centered care: Rooming in.* Retrieved from http://www.pediatrix.com/documents/famsupp_roomingin.pdf

Korones, S. B. (1976). Disturbance and infants' rest. In T. D. Moore (Ed.), *69th Ross conference on pediatric research: Iatrogenic problems in neonatal intensive care* (pp. 94–96). Columbus, OH: Ross Laboratories.

Lechtzin, N., Withers, T., Devrotes, A., & Diette, G. (2001, May). Distraction using nature sights and sounds reduces pain during flexible bronchoscopy. Abstract retrieved November 22, 2006, from American Thoracic Society Access at http://www.abstracts2view.com/atsall/view.php?nu=ATS1P1_433

Linn, P. L., Horowitz, F. D., Buddin, B. J., Leake, J. C., & Fox, H. A. (1985). An ecological description of a neonatal intensive care unit. In A. W. Gottfried & J. L. Gaiter (Eds.), *Infant stress under intensive care: Environmental neonatology* (pp. 83–112). Baltimore: University Park Press.

Luoma, L., Herrgard, E., Martikainen, A., & Ahonen T. (1998). Speech and language development of children born at < or = 32 weeks' gestation: A 5-year prospective follow-up study. *Developmental Medicine & Child Neurology, 40*(6), 380-387.

Marshall-Baker, A. (2006). Healthy buildings/sustainable design: Cradle to cradle healthcare. Invited as a member of the Conference Faculty at the 19th Annual Conference on the Physical and Developmental Environment of the High-Risk Infant: Human Factors and Research in the NICU. Orlando, FL.

Marshall-Baker, A. (2007). Assessing indoor air quality in infant incubators. Syllabus of the 20th Annual Gravens Conference on the Physical and Developmental Environment of the High-Risk Infant: Communication: Defining, designing and delivering effective human interaction in the NICU.Clearwater Beach Florida.

McDonough, W., & Braungart, M. (2002). *Cradle to cradle: Remaking the way we make things.* New York: North Point Press.

Miller, C. L., White, R., Whitman, T. L., O'Callaghan, M. F., & Maxwell, S. E. (1995). The effects of cycled versus noncycled lighting on growth and development in preterm infants. *Infant Behavior and Development, 18,* 87–95.

Pressler, J. L., Turnage-Carrier, C. S., & Kenner, C. (2004). Developmental care: An overview. In C. Kenner & J. M. McGrath (Eds.), *Developmental care of newborns and infants: A guide for health professionals* (pp. 1–34). St. Louis, MO: Mosby.

Rivkees, S. A. (2004). Emergence and influences of circadian rhythmicity in infants. In R. D. White (Vol. ed.), *Clinics in Perinatology:* Vol. *31*(2). The sensory environment of the NICU: Scientific and design-related aspects (pp. 217–228). Philadelphia: Saunders.

Robertson, A. F. (2003). Reflections on errors in neonatology: I. The "hands-off" years, 1920–1950. *Journal of Perinatology, 23,* 48–55.

Ruzzin, M. (2004, September–October). An industry first: Boulder foothills community hospital sets an example for the health care industry, *Eco-Structure,* 14–22. Retrieved from http://www.eco-structure.com/docs/archives%20 2004/eco_oct04%20for%20web/eco_ oct%20feature.pdf

Shepley, M. M., Fournier, M.-A., & McDougal, K.W. (1998). *Healthcare environments for children and their families.* Dubuque, IO: Kendall/Hunt Publishing Company.

Shepley, M. M., Harris, D., & White, R. (2008). Open-bay and single-family room neonatal intensive care units: Caregiver satisfaction and stress. *Environment and Behavior, 40*(2), 249–268.

Silverman, W. A. (1979). Incubator-baby side shows. *Pediatrics, 64*(2), 127–141.

Silverman, W. A. (1989). Neonatal pediatrics at the century mark. *Perspectives in biology and medicine, 32*(2), 159–170.

Slevin, M., Murphy, J. F. A., Daly, L. (1999). Retinopathy of prematurity screening, stress related responses, the role of nesting. *British Journal of Ophthalmology, 81,* 762–764.

Smith, J., Roehll, G., & Bonnell, L. M. (2007, February). *Design with nature. Healthcare Design, 7*(1), 36–38, 40–41.

The Royal Women's Hospital (2006). Developmental care. Retrieved from http://www.rwh.org.au/nets/handbook

Thoman, E. (1986). The time domain in individual subject research. In J. Valsiner (Ed.), *The individual subject in scientific psychology* (pp. 181–200). New York: Plenum Press.

Turnage-Carrier, C. S. (2004). Caregiving and the environment. In C. Kenner & J. M. McGrath (Eds.), *Developmental care of newborns & infants: A guide for health professionals* (pp. 271–297). St. Louis, MO: Mosby.

Ulrich, R. S. (1984). View through a window may influence recovery from surgery. *Science, 224,* 420–421.

Ulrich, R., & Lundén, O. (1993). Effects of nature and abstract pictures on patients recovering from heart surgery. First International Congress on Behavioral Medicine, Sweden, 27–30.

Wilson, E. O. (1984). *Biophilia: The human bond with other species.* Cambridge: Harvard University Press.

Wilson-Orr, L., Archer, J., MacMillan-York, E., Macisaac, E., & Reid, A. (2007). Greening of a nursery. Syllabus of the 20th Annual Gravens Conference on the Physical and Developmental Environment of the High-Risk Infant: Communication: Defining, designing and delivering effective human interaction in the NICU. Clearwater Beach, Florida.

7   Child Development Centers:
Students as Consumers of Research

Marilyn Read

> From childhood I remember a geode my brother had that
> fascinated me. I would constantly borrow it and he would take
> it back—this geode would travel back and forth between my
> desk and his. He still has it.　(Lin, p. 2:07)

> My grandmother used to get a sack of wood cuttings from the
> wood store. Every once in a while she would open the sack of
> wood cuttings and throw them out on the floor and we would start
> building things.　(Frank Gehry, *Sketches of Frank Gehry*)

Abstract

This chapter begins with background information related to the importance of child care in the United States. A description of the educational approaches found in child care centers is provided along with an explanation of how the physical environment is influenced by the educational model selected by the facility. Next, research in the area of design for child care centers is summarized. In the last section, design projects are shown that illustrate how students can utilize findings from research investigations to justify design decision making for preschool environments. This chapter provides an example of students as consumers of research.

Introduction

Childhood memories remain with us for a lifetime. Maya Lin and Frank Gehry recall specific items from their past that inspired their future design endeavors. The geode from Lin's childhood was the inspiration for the Vietnam Veteran's Memorial (Lin, 2000). The wood chips Gehry played with when he was a young boy were fundamental to his understanding of form and space, laying the foundation for his future architectural creations (Guilfoyle & Pollack, 2006). Gehry's quotation also brings to mind Frank Lloyd Wright's recollections of the Froebel blocks his mother gave him to play with as a young child. He reminisced of how he still felt those maple blocks in his fingers at 88 years of age. The influences that childhood experiences with the environment have on adult cognition, emotion, and behavior are profound, steadfast, and enduring. Cooper Marcus (1988) interviewed adults about their feelings, emotions, and attitudes toward their home environments. A consistent theme that emerged from the interviews was the detailed descriptions people gave of the memorable places of childhood including childhood experiences of notable hiding places and child-created dwellings. Undoubtedly, children's experiences with the environment play a significant role in their development.

The places of early childhood experiences typically include the home, child development and care environments, and outdoor settings. Child development environments are settings that support the education and care of young children. The focus of this chapter is on the impact the environmental design of child development centers has on children's behavior. From six weeks of age on, young children are spending increasing numbers of hours in noncustodial care, meaning they are being cared for by care providers other than parents or guardians. In 1999, 9.8 million children in the United States were spending 40 or more hours each week in child care (Committee on Family and Work Policies, 2003). According to the U.S. Department of Education (2006), 57 percent of children aged three to five years were enrolled in center-based early childhood care and education programs. As more young children enter center-based programs each year, from 53 percent in 1991 to 57 percent in 2005, there is clearly a need to create well-designed, functional, and engaging child development centers.

There are many different types of child development centers, including for profit, nonprofit, public, private, and church-sponsored programs and family child care. This chapter focuses on a general type of center and does not include family child care providers who care for children in the provider's own home. The number of children enrolled at a child development center is determined by state licensing regulations. The children's age range at a center is often from six weeks old through five years of age. Classrooms tend to be divided by broad age groups. For example, one classroom may be for infants six weeks to eighteen months; another classroom may include children from eighteen months to three years; another room may be for children from three years through five years. Some centers separate the age groups, while some organize the children in mixed-age groupings. The educational curriculum the center uses determines the method by which the children are grouped by age.

Other program considerations include the

- Child-to-caregiver ratio
- Program length: Half-day or full-day programs
- Weekly length: Part-time (three days each week) or full-time (five days each week)

Definition of Quality Childhood Education

In order to understand the complexity of child development center programs, the following sections define and describe quality childhood education. The physical design of a child development center is determined by multiple factors including the program's objectives and curricular approach, the site characteristic requirements, and the center's structural and process quality characteristics. *Process quality* consists of those experiential aspects of a setting, such as teacher-child and child-child interactions. Other process quality characteristics include the types of spaces, activities, and materials available to children; and how everyday personal care routines, such as meals, toileting, and rest, are handled. *Structural quality* consists of the factors that influence the processes children actually experience. Examples of structural quality characteristics include measures of group size, adult-child ratios, and education and experience of the staff members (Cryer, 2003). Taken together, process quality characteristics and structural quality characteristics help define the quality characteristics of a multitude of types of child care centers.

The professional definition of quality early childhood education and care that is widely held in the United States includes the following core elements (Cryer, 2003):

- *Safe care*, with sufficient, diligent adult supervision that is appropriate for children's ages and abilities and safe toys, equipment, and furnishings.
- *Healthful care*, in a clean environment where sanitary measures to prevent the spread of illness are taken and where children have opportunities for activity, rest, developing self-help skills in cleanliness, and having their nutritional needs met.

- *Developmentally appropriate stimulation* where children have wide choices of opportunities for learning through play in a variety of areas such as language; creativity through art, music, and dramatic play; fine and gross motor skills; numeracy; and nature/science.
- *Positive interactions with adults* where children can trust, learn from, and enjoy the adults who care for and educate them.
- *Encouragement of individual emotional growth,* allowing children to operate independently, cooperatively, securely, and competently.
- *Promotion of positive relationships with other children,* allowing children to interact with their peers with the environmental supports and adult guidance required to help interactions go smoothly (Cryer, 1999, p. 42).

Center Assessment

Child development centers must be licensed through the state in which they are located. Additional accreditation may be sought through the National Association for the Education of Young Children (NAEYC), which is the accrediting body for early childhood education programs. If a center is NAEYC- accredited, it is determined to be a high-quality child development center. Standard 9 is the NAEYC accreditation standard for the physical environment. "The program has a safe and healthful environment that provides appropriate and well-maintained indoor and outdoor physical environments. The environment includes facilities, equipment, and materials to facilitate child and staff learning and development" (NAEYC, 2007). The NAEYC describes appropriate features for indoor and outdoor spaces in the center.

Assessments that focus specifically on the physical environment of child development centers include the following:

- The Early Childhood Environment Rating Scale, Revised Edition, often shortened to the ECERS-R (Harms, Clifford, & Cryer, 1998). This assessment is the most comprehensive assessment scale in terms of reliability and validity; however, only eight items measure the physical environment of the space. In the ECERS-R scale, items are rated from 1 to 7 and are described as inadequate, minimal, good, and excellent. The physical environment section focuses on indoor space; furniture for routine care, play, and learning; furnishings for relaxation and comfort; room arrangement for play; space for privacy; child-related display; space for gross motor play; and gross motor equipment.
- The Early Childhood Physical Environment Rating Scale (Sugiyama & Moore, 2005) is a 142-item scale; it measures the quality of the physical environment of early childhood centers. This scale is in the development phase. Item 2.3 under the Image and Scale Subscale is: "The interior finishes appear welcoming and natural (e.g., use of carpets, warm colors, soft lighting, curtains, etc)." Raters use a five-point Likert-type scale from not met (0) to fully met (4).
- Maxwell (2007) has developed a rating scale that focuses on the physical environment of the preschool classroom and children's competency. This scale is designed similarly to the ECERS-R scale. Each item is rated excellent (0), adequate (1), or inadequate (2). Items on the scale include social spaces, boundaries, privacy, personalization, complexity, and scale.
- Sanoff (1995) proposed a rating scale for specific learning centers that identifies factors of the learning or activity area that are evident in the space. Items are divided by learning areas or centers and rated on three points minimal, fair, and good. For example, the art area has low tables accommodating three to five children, secluded from circulation paths (M for minimal), plus individual easels and low tables, for solitary and group work, storage for art materials accessible to children; drying and dis-

play area; floor easily cleanable (F for fair), plus individual and group work surfaces visible, impervious and washable; natural lighting; materials and drying and display area accessible to children; sink present (G for good).

Decisions about the interior and architectural design of the space should be made collaboratively among the center director, staff, parents, architect, and interior designer. Including children in the decision-making process would be an additional benefit for the design development phase because their perspectives are valuable for creating an environment that reflects their own experience (Day, 1998; Dudek, 2000; Rivlin & Wolfe, 1985). The environment communicates many messages to young children, and they clearly are influenced by those messages over the course of the day. A clear interpretation and understanding of these messages is one of the tasks of the designer of the center.

The goal of the designer of a child development center is to fuse the knowledge from research in the various disciplines with the design recommendations specific to the educational approach of the center. There are as many different "designs" for the preschool classroom environment as there are preschool teachers and children in the classrooms. After the professional designers have completed their work, teachers and children personalize the spaces and adapt the environments, depending on the curriculum. The interior designer or architect must therefore provide teachers and children with a setting that can be designed with flexibility and functionality as core objectives of the program.

Educational Approaches

An overall framework for categorizing early childhood education approaches is outlined by Wolfgang and Wolfgang (1999). This framework has been adapted for this discussion to include the most widely

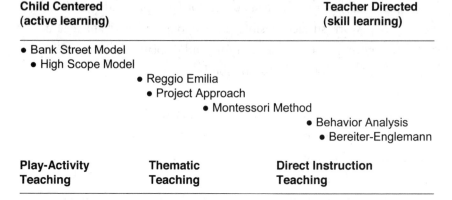

Figure 7.1. Early Childhood models or approaches continuum.

adopted early childhood education models or approaches across the United States (Figure 7.1). The continuum ranges from child-centered learning or play-activity teaching on one end to teacher-directed learning or direct instruction learning at the other end. In the middle of the model is thematic teaching, which uses a project approach to children's learning. Teachers set up projects and plan the curriculum in concert with children's input. The following section describes each curriculum approach or model.

The Constructivist Approach

Constructivist models are based on the learning theories of John Dewey, Jean Piaget, and Lev Vygotsky. Examples of constructivist programs include the Bank Street Model and the Cognitively Oriented Curriculum or High/Scope Model. While the goals of all constructivist programs are not the same, they are all concerned with the expansion of children's reasoning capabilities and their abilities to represent experiences in meaningful ways. Each program depends on children's dynamic involvement

Figure 7.2. A classroom designed for a constructivist curriculum.

with materials and teacher's guidance in helping children reflect on their experiences. The development of physical, social, emotional, and intellectual competence is the program's focus. The curriculum is integrated; therefore, the content is not arranged by subject matter areas. Figure 7.2 illustrates an example of a constructivist model program. Content areas in the learning centers are integrated across the curriculum.

The Developmental-Interaction Approach
at Bank Street College of Education

In the model favored by Bank Street College of Education, children are the initiators and teachers take their cues from the child's activities. Learning results from the children's active participation with their social and physical world. Learning is experience-based, interdisciplinary, and collaborative. The teacher's role is to provide an enriched, safe, and stimulating environment in which children are free to play, select activities and materials, and determine their own goals. The classroom is an inspiring learning environment that contains a wide variety of materials. Activity materials are organized around learning or interest centers to facilitate children's interactions with them (Cuffaro, Nager, & Shapiro, 2005).

The Cognitively Oriented Curriculum Model (High/Scope)

The Cognitively Oriented Curriculum Model or High/Scope approach has its foundation in the work of Jean Piaget and strongly emphasizes cognitive development. Piaget (1954) believed that children learn best when they are actually doing the work themselves, creating and constructing their own understanding of the world. Children make sense of the objects in their world by engaging in symbolic play, for example, using a blanket and a box to make a house. This program emphasizes careful and systematic observations of the child and organizes the curriculum around key experiences that are identified in the categories of social and emotional development, movement and physical development, and cognitive development. Children have a great deal of freedom to plan and carry out their objectives while providing teachers with a basis for planning the curriculum so that activities are not random. The physical arrangement consists of a large, open area for group activities and games in addition to centers or work areas for specific activities such as sand and water play, art, music, movement, and blocks (Weikart & Schweinhart, 2005).

The Reggio Emilia Approach

The Reggio Emilia approach to early childhood education fully integrates the physical environment as "the third teacher." The teacher is a researcher who documents children's learning experiences (Thornton & Brunton, 2005). Many of Reggio Emilia's principles about how children learn are embedded in Vygotsky's theoretical construct of the zone of proximal development. The child is able to develop a skill at a higher level of development with the assistance of a peer, older child, or adult. This is termed *scaffolding* in child development. If a child is on the verge of learning a new concept, an adult or classmate can assist him or her with advancing to the next level to complete the task.

Reggio Emilia schools in Italy are characterized by environmental features purposefully designed to create a school culture that reflects and promotes the values of the community (Fleet & Robertson, 1998). In the facility, the piazza is a large central space where children, parents, and teachers meet. The atelier, a place of experimentation, is located off the piazza. The classrooms are located off the piazza with direct access to outdoors. Classrooms are divided into spaces for group gatherings, dramatic play, and large and small construction activities. An internal courtyard is typically located off the piazza. The dining room is a separate space. Design features include the following:

- Use of light sources. Natural and artificial windows are large and placed to offer children a variety of views. Reflective surfaces are seen throughout the center, with mirrors on walls and at right angles to each other.
- Visibility and interconnectedness as concepts that underpin the internal designs.
- Subtle finish colors with vibrant colors used for large structural pieces of equipment.
- Materials and finishes selected for their aesthetic, sensorial, and functional qualities (Thornton & Brunton, 2005).

The Project Approach

Main features of project work that distinguish it from the traditional didactic way of introducing children to new knowledge are as follows:

- The direct involvement of the children in identifying the topic to be studied
- The children's role in formulating the questions to be answered by their investigation
- Openness to possible shifts in the direction of the inquiry as it proceeds
- The children's acceptance of responsibility for the work accomplished and for the kinds of representations of findings that are prepared and reported (Katz & Chard, 2005, p. 297).

The project method was inspired by the ideas of John Dewey. The four types of learning goals in the project approach are knowledge, skills, dispositions, and feelings. Learning in all four goal categories is facilitated in different ways. Children work on projects in a variety of group sizes. Project development requires children to apply many intellectual dispositions along with academic and social skills. Project work may involve a variety of tasks including gathering and recording data, sketching, painting, and dramatic play. The space in the classroom is arranged by providing areas for various kinds of work. The furniture layout should be flexible for individual and group work. Walls should be designed to accommodate display of children's work products, objects of interest, instructions, work in progress, and lists. Children assist with managing the space, work areas, and resources.

The Montessori Model

Maria Montessori developed an activity-based, sensory education model involving didactic materials, emphasizing the importance of children's learning through hands-on activity. A basic premise of the

Montessori philosophy is that the child copies reality rather than constructs it. Key elements of the Montessori philosophy include the ideas of the prepared environment, sensitive periods, the absorbent mind, and the principle of freedom for each child (Montessori, 1976). The children organize their world and their own thinking from watching and then doing activities. The Montessori didactic materials are a variety of materials that children learn to use from a teacher's demonstration. Examples of the materials are a set of cylinders decreasing in diameter only, a set of cylinders decreasing in height only, a set of cylinders decreasing in height and diameter, and a set of cylinders decreasing in diameter and increasing in height (Montessori, 1965). Montessori curriculum presents the materials in a sequence, from simplest to most difficult, so that the child learns concepts logically. Most of the learning tasks have a series of steps and must be learned in a prescribed order.

Six essential components of the Montessori learning environment are freedom, structure and order, reality and nature, beauty and an atmosphere that encourages a positive and spontaneous response to life, Montessori learning materials, and the development of community life (Montessori, 1965). The Montessori approach calls for low, open shelves to be accessible, holding many carefully arranged materials from which the children can choose to play. Extensive shelving is needed to hold the required Montessori materials, with all walls of the classroom typically containing some shelving. Tables and desks are grouped to facilitate individual or small-group work. Open floor space allows for work on the floor. Plants, animals, and small gardens cared for by the children are standard in the Montessori setting. Figures 7.3 and 7.4 depict Montessori classrooms, with extensive shelving and well-organized materials. The walls are devoid of display projects, thereby helping children to focus on the learning materials. Wood is used throughout the centers in the furnishings and manipulatives.

Figure 7.3. A Montessori classroom.

Figure 7.4. A Montessori classroom showing extensive shelving and windows for natural light.

Behavior Analysis Model

The theories of Skinner (Neisworth & Buggey, 2005) and Bandura are the foundation of the Behavior Analysis Model. The child is considered to be a "blank slate" to be written on by the teaching environment. Behavioral changes occur as a result of reinforcing events. There are two fundamental principles of behavior. First, behavior is controlled by its consequences, meaning that when a behavior is positively reinforced, it becomes stronger. Second, circumstances that exist when a behavior is reinforced become cures, or signals, for the behavior. This principle is also known as *stimulus control*. Behavioral changes and individual differences are explained in terms of learning, not development. This idea is quite different from the less-structured models previously discussed. In the classroom, children are seated before the teacher in a structured manner. The teacher uses scripted lessons, which are organized with the intent to teach children language skills, math concepts, and prereading and reading skills. Blocks of time are short, with a fast-paced program dictated by the clock.

The environment should be physically responsive, meaning that it is a setting that provides instant and steady feedback, thereby permitting children to have a sense of control over the space (Neisworth & Buggey, 2005). The setting should also include areas for quiet, individual time. The classroom in the structured model is not a roomy, open space. It is designed to focus the children's attention on the teacher by reducing peripheral distractions. High dividers are used in the space to define areas.

Bereiter-Englemann (DISTAR) Model

The Bereiter-Englemann Model was developed in the 1960s for teaching disadvantaged children language and verbal reasoning skills. Presently, the Direct Instructional System for Teaching and Remediation

(DISTAR) curriculum is designed for children in kindergarten through third grade; however, some preschools use the DISTAR materials with younger children. The main goal of direct instruction is to increase academic achievement through focused instruction (Neisworth & Buggey, 2005). Instruction is task-oriented, and children respond to teacher prompts in a rapid, repetitive manner. Direct instruction also covers science, social science, cultural literacy, and handwriting. The curriculum is carefully planned and scripted. Teachers ask hundreds of questions of the children each day. Children have heavy work demands, which are rewarded if they work hard and pay attention to the teacher and task at hand. Children meet with teachers in small groups and focus on individual or choral responses to the teacher's questions.

Influence of the Curriculum Model on the Design of the Facility

The variety of early childhood education curriculum models is diverse and complex. The range of types of programs from a child-centered approach to a teacher-directed approach prescribes many different physical design elements in the setting. Clearly the design of the classroom environment will be dictated by the curriculum model used by the center. It is important to note that seldom does one find a "pure" example of a curriculum model reflected in the physical environment. Typically, center staff members adapt a model to suit the specific needs of the staff, children, parents, and community at large (Table 7.1).

Research

The design of early childhood environments has been broadly investigated by, among others, researchers in child development and education (Kritchevsky, Prescott, & Walling, 1969; Olds, 2001; Weinstein,

Table 7.1. Characteristics of Environments Supporting Various Curricula

Curriculum Type	Characteristics of the Physical Environment
The Constructivist Approach	• Activity areas are learning centers • Centers offer a wide variety of materials
Bank Street College of Education	• Centers are defined reading, science, art, etc. • Display area
The Cognitively Oriented Curriculum Model (High/Scope)	• Centers offer defined play opportunities, e.g., sand and water, art, music, movement, blocks, reading • Display area
The Reggio Emilia Approach	• Facility has central open area for engagement opportunities; a large area for experimentation positioned next to the central open area • Internal courtyard; multiple light sources, including natural light • Classrooms have direct access to outdoors • Divisions in classrooms include group, dramatic play, and large/small construction activity areas; smaller art areas located off the main classrooms • Display area
The Project Approach	• Spaces are provided for a variety of large-scale and small-scale projects • Spaces must accommodate long-term project work • Child-scaled storage for materials • Display area
The Montessori Model	• Accessible, low, open shelves • Grouped tables and chairs • Open floor space • Display area • Garden
Behavior Analysis Model Bereiter-Englemann (DISTAR) Model	• Closed space • Separate areas for learning • Lecture-style seating • Display area

1987), architecture and design (Moore, 1987; Sanoff, 1995), and environmental psychology (Evans, 2006; Gump, 1987; Wohlwill & Heft, 1987). The ideal environment is intriguing; rich; and challenging to young children's physical, socio-emotional, and cognitive development. Visual, aural, and tactile experiences should be complex, yet not overstimulating. Consideration must be given to noise control, physical barriers, and traffic patterns when separating the activity areas within the space. Generally, desirable child development centers reflect a homelike environment and offer children variety and balance of categories of activities and spaces. The following section provides a summary of general research findings for the design of the classrooms in child development centers.

The Open Setting

The majority of early childhood education curriculum models, those emphasizing constructivist or project teaching, employ a large, open setting in the classroom. The open space must simultaneously accommodate several smaller activity and learning areas. The challenge can be daunting for the designer who must integrate, in one large space, activity spaces for art, reading, movement, nature, music, and symbolic play, along with spaces for eating and napping. The advantages of an open setting are (1) the ability to see and hear children and staff throughout the space and (2) the flexibility of the space, allowing activity center locations to be moved, based on needs of curriculum expectations and staff recommendations. Additionally, natural light is an advantage because it can be transmitted through the space by windows on the perimeter or through skylights that will filter light into the activity areas at varying degrees, depending on the location. The disadvantages of the open setting are (1) the noise levels within the setting are often high, (2) areas for privacy for staff and children are limited or nonexistent, and (3) circulation, boundaries, adjacencies, and traffic patterns throughout the space may be confusing. Sensory overstimulation may also be of concern because the interior space has several activity areas that provide visual and aural sensory input.

Arrangement and Layout

The plan layout of the preschool classroom influences several aspects of the open plan. Clearly defined areas help children focus on the activity materials, thereby promoting interactions with peers and complex play (Dempsy & Frost, 1993). Irregular shapes are preferred over square shapes for classrooms because they offer children spatial variation with alcoves, nooks, recesses, and angles (Moore et al., 1979). Somewhat enclosed areas tend to reduce aggression and withdrawal behaviors (Neill & Denham, 1982). Campos-de-Carvalho and Rossetti-Ferreira (1993) found that young children show a preferential use of circumscribed zones, areas created to be smaller activity areas within a larger space. Legendre (1999) found that a visually restricted arrangement had a negative impact on the percentage of time spent in peer interactions. The open arrangement with low dividers is visually and spatially supportive of young children's development for constructivist and project-oriented education.

The design of the activity spaces is determined by the square footage and materials requirements for the activity. Materials for each activity area should be displayed on low shelves and easily accessible to children. The learning centers should also provide flexibility for staff to easily change materials on a routine basis. Kantrowitz and Evans (2004) found that the ratio of children to the total number of activity areas in the space is positively correlated with off-task time. Withdrawal behavior occurs because of overstimulation. Petrakos and Howe (1996) found that children's play was less imaginative when the dramatic-play center was designed with a theme. It is suggested that less defined dramatic-play areas provide space for children to be more imaginative in their symbolic play.

In addition, young children need privacy in the room. Retreat spaces are very important; therefore, learning and activity centers should be spatially separated (Moore, 1994; Prescott, 1987; Sanoff, 1995). The space is most favorable for creating areas for privacy when it is subdivided with furniture, partitions, and varying floor levels. In one study, younger preschoolers, three-year-olds, identified special places of their own for privacy in the child care setting more often than older preschoolers, four-plus-year-olds (Zeegers, Readdick, & Hansen-Gandy, 1994).

The National Association for the Education of Young Children recommends at least 35 square feet per child of indoor space; however, this square footage requirement is too small because children need at least 40 to 60 square feet per child of indoor space for free movement. Additional space is needed for setting up cots for naptime for full-day programs (Decker & Decker, 2001). Legendre (2003) found that children ages 18 to 24 months had higher levels of the hormone cortisol, meaning increased stress levels, when there was less available space per child in the classroom. In another study, children in high-density classrooms were found to have more behavior problems and scored lower on a test measuring cognitive style than children who were in low-density classrooms (Maxwell, 1996). Children will benefit most when the classroom is spacious with clearly defined activity areas or learning centers.

Noise

The task of controlling noise within the open classroom is difficult. Interior and exterior noise can be reduced by adding absorbent surfaces and varying furniture and ceiling heights. Lower ceiling heights (5.5 feet) that accommodate only young children's movements have been found to encourage cooperative play behavior (Read et al., 1999). Additionally, lower ceilings (7.5 to 9 feet) are desirable in quiet areas and higher ceilings (9 to 11 feet) in more active areas (Olds, 2001). These heights would be appropriate in a small area of the center. For example, a lowered soffit reading area that extends from the wall between 4 and 6 feet would create a quieter area for reading. Controlling the noise in a space can be achieved from the sound-absorbing properties of the finish materials by incorporating sound-absorbent materials, such as carpets, upholstery, ceiling banners, and ceiling acoustic panels and tiles to dampen undesirable sound transfer within the space.

Enclosed Plans

A representative floor plan for the Behavior Analysis Model divides the classroom with high or full partitions. There may be two separate lesson areas, one individual work area, one group area, and additional space for tables, books, and games (Decker & Decker, 2001). All areas are smaller and more enclosed than those spaces in the constructivist and project approaches. Floor plans for the Montessori curriculum characteristically provide children with a spacious area that typically separates rooms, one room for intellectual work using the didactic materials, another room for social interactions, and a room with accessible cupboards for dining (Decker & Decker, 2001). Additionally, there should be direct access to an exterior garden. As with the open-plan classrooms, the enclosed plan spaces vary along a continuum by degree of enclosure.

Plan Layout Recommendations for Inclusive Environments

Inclusive environments are preschool programs designed for typical and special needs children. Across the United States, the inclusive classroom is found utilizing all types of curricular approaches. The classroom is structured to serve a wide range of children; the environment is flexible and organized to meet the unique needs of all the children. Inclusive classrooms should have larger areas for maneuvering wheelchairs or walkers for activity areas. Additionally, materials and activities that have multiple objectives and several modes of instruction allow for the inclusion of students with different levels of skill. Adaptations occur in materials and cues, sequences and rules, and levels of support. It is important to allow square-footage space for clearance, transfer, height, width, reach range, and maneuverability of adaptive equipment for children with disabilities. Children using crutches, braces, or wheelchairs require wide, clear transit pathways thorough the classroom and at the entry to activity areas. Doctoroff (2001) suggests reducing noisy environments with drapes, carpets, and corkboards and providing well-lit, reduced-glare areas for children with hearing and vision impairments.

Furniture and Equipment

Children become independent and competent when they can master their environment. Child-scaled furniture is important for children's physical, cognitive, and social development. It is ergonomically designed for the 3- to 5-year-old's body size and shape. Children are able to complete tasks by themselves without an adult's assistance when they can maneuver the chairs and tables around on their own (Greenman, 1998; Ruth, 2000). Young children spend approximately one-third of their time seated in chairs in the preschool classroom. Consequently, they need furnishings that are designed for their size and developmental abilities.

Display

Providing display areas for children's project work is a particularly important component in the design of the classroom space. The Reggio Emilia approach considers display areas to be central to the design of the environment (Fleet & Robertson, 1998). Display areas should be located at the child's eye level. There is a delicate balance between appropriate display areas and those that create visual overstimulation. Many teachers use too much wall space for display, thus creating a confusing appearance to the space. The overstimulation that is created by the display can negatively affect wayfinding abilities for the children. Additionally, project work attached to the ceiling throughout the classroom can negatively influence children's wayfinding abilities and concentration levels. This method of display occurs frequently. It is not ideal for children or adults because it detracts from focal points around the classroom and can make movement through the space frustrating when the person must avoid colliding with the art projects.

Natural and Artificial Lighting

Küller and Lindsten conducted a study of 90 elementary school students in Sweden. They tracked their behavior, health, and cortisol levels in four different classrooms with different combinations of daylighting and fluorescent lighting conditions. The researchers found that the seasonal and daily rhythms were typical in children in classrooms with daylight, whereas children in the classroom with only warm white fluorescent light exhibited abnormal patterns of both behavior and cortisol production (Küller & Lindsten, 1992). The classroom should have maximum natural lighting on two sides of the space to balance the light and reduce glare. Some windows should be child-scaled so that children have views to the outside. Artificial lighting, whether general ambient or task-specific, should be warm, natural, and homelike. The types of lighting should vary throughout the space depending on the desired level of activity in an area and the traffic patterns. Appropriate lighting can be achieved through a combination of direct and indirect lighting.

Color

Color in children's classroom environments should be used in relation to the light and materials within the space. Read, Sugawara, and Brandt (1999) found in an experimental design study that children playing in a room with one red wall and three white walls exhibited higher levels of cooperative play than children playing in a space with four white walls. A varied hue in a center may promote cooperative play behavior in young children. The use of color as a wayfinding tool in exterior and interior design of child development centers was investigated by Read (2003). Findings indicated that designers of centers could use more creative methods of applying color to the exterior to define the entry to the center. Additionally, color was evidenced on the exterior of the centers at just over half of the sample. The interior environments of the child care facilities had warm colors and bright accents in the setting; however, the majority of centers used only white, off-white, or gray on the walls.

Camgoz et al. (2003) found that high-chroma or bright colors on any color background draw an individual's attention. Ou et al. (2004 a, b, c) suggest that there is no difference in color preference between females and males. The presence of too much bright color in an environment can have deleterious effects. Children may become agitated and exhausted because of visual overstimulation in the center.

Natural Elements

Studies show that children respond positively to natural elements (Faber Taylor & Kuo, 2006). Children with a strong bond to their pets scored higher on a measure of empathy than those who did not have a pet (Poresky, 1990). Exposure to animals in a classroom is ideal for preschool-age children as they develop their understanding of different types of animals and their needs. Caution must be taken, however, when placing animals in the space because of hygiene and safety issues associated with animals. Animals that require extensive care are burdensome to staff at the facilities. Nontoxic plants in the classroom and views of green space from the interior are also essential elements. Wells (2000) found that children whose homes had more green elements following a move tended to have the highest levels of cognitive functioning. A study by Faber Taylor et al. (2002) examined concentration and view in children. They found that the greener a girl's view was from her home, the higher the score on measures of self-discipline. Kirkby (1989) found that children observed in a school yard engaged in more creative forms of play in green play spaces than in built play spaces. Incorporating nontoxic plants, views of green space, and exterior green space are quite significant for enhancing a variety of children's developmental needs.

Informed Design Example

Child Development Center Project

Students were asked to complete a child development center design project for course credit in a four-year interior design program. They selected the curriculum program of interest to them. The drawings included the following:

- Concept drawings, sketches, rendered perspective sketches
- Floor plan depicting furnishings, fixtures, and equipment layout
- Lighting plan
- Sample materials on one to two boards, depicting color, texture, and form
- Elevations or a section

The program included the following:

- Exterior transition space
- Vestibule
- Main entrance
- Reception area

- Two preschool classrooms for 16 children each with child-sized toilets; two per 10 to 14 children; child-sized sinks: two per 10 to 14 children
- One commercial kitchen/food storage
- One laundry room
- One janitor's closet
- One director's office
- One teacher's office for 2 teachers
- Restrooms
- One electrical/mechanical equipment space
- One conference room for 8 people
- Storage for supplies within spaces
- Additional storage
- Detail access to the exterior playground
- Outline exterior playground.

Activities in the classroom include book looking, rocking, playing, building, listening, eating, and napping. Spaces for arts and crafts, symbolic play, food preparation, sand and water play, and music must be incorporated in the design.

The design of the classroom must incorporate an entrance; cubby storage; small diaper-changing area; classroom and teacher storage; children's toilets and sinks (one sink at toilet exit preferable to avoid congestion, and separate toilets for male and female for ages four-plus); eating/table area; art sink; water play area; drinking fountain; loft area; area with level change (three risers minimum); open, unrestricted activity area; and block area, located away from main circulation.

Students were given copies of the author's research publications for review. In addition, they were shown examples of effective designs of facilities. For example, Figure 7.5 illustrates successful use of color on the floor to enhance children's wayfinding abilities in a long corridor. Multi-hued tiles are used to define the main entrance to the classroom. Another ex-

Figure 7.5.
Corridor showing indirect
lighting and color definition
on floor for wayfinding.

ample depicts the use of colored fabric to lower the ceiling in a particular
area. This technique creates an attractive variation to the ceiling (Read, et
al., 1999) while reducing the noise in the open space (see Figure 7.2).

Examples of student project work are shown in Figures 7.6 through
7.11. Figure 7.6 illustrates a schematic plan that includes effective use
of a display area at the entry and spaces successfully defined, primarily by alcoves and bay windows. Wayfinding is defined in the space by
separation of hues. Natural light and views are central to the design of
the plan. Based on the research from Faber Taylor (2002) and Küller
and Lindsten (1992), the student incorporated views of green space and
significant natural lighting in the space. Figure 7.7 depicts the final perspective drawing developed from the concept plan. Colors vary on the
walls and flooring to define spaces and activities. The ceiling is lowered
in the large-circle section (Read, et al., 1999). Circumscribed zones are

seen in the concept plan for space definition (Campos-de-Carvalho & Rossetti-Ferreira, 1993) reinforcing the researchers' findings that children enjoy playing in a defined activity space within a larger area rather than playing in a larger, undefined area. The loft area offers both spatial variety and retreat spaces for children. These two drawings reflect a curriculum that is a constructivist approach to early childhood education. Figures 7.6 and 7.7 show the project designed by Reade Northup.

Figures 7.8 and 7.9 depict J. Davis Harte's concept drawing and final plan of a center that utilizes an eclectic approach to early childhood education curriculum. The classrooms are semi-divided by offsets within the space and low shelving units. The constructivist and project approaches

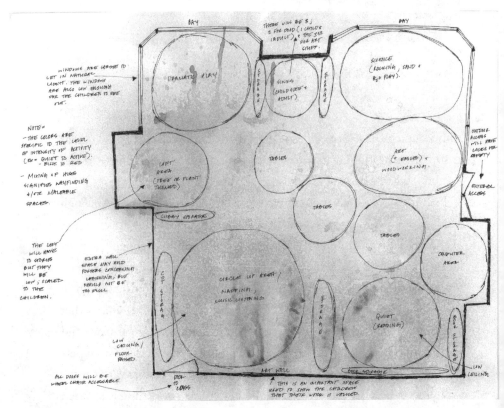

Figure 7.6. Concept drawing of classroom by R. Northup, 2007.

Figure 7.7. Perspective of classroom by R. Northup, 2007.

are suggested in the plan layout with defined areas and open spaces for group work. The influence of the Reggio Emilia approach is seen in the large, wide-open area at the entry. The concept sketch shows the entry with clear views of the exterior windows, allowing natural light in the space. Children can see into the space through the circular windows in the doors prior to entry, as suggested by Moore and others (1979) and Sanoff (1995), who found that children preferred irregular shapes to square shapes. Subdued hues are used on the walls, and vivid colors are chosen for the stained glass. One of the student's goals is for the classroom to reflect beauty in the space with variation of color, form, and texture.

Figure 7.10 is the final plan of a space designed by Robin Freeburn depicting a center using a constructivist approach. The loft between the reading area and the dramatic-play area provides spatial variety (Moore, et al., 1979). The plan layout defines the various areas with low dividers and cabinetry. The dramatic-play area shows the change in levels with

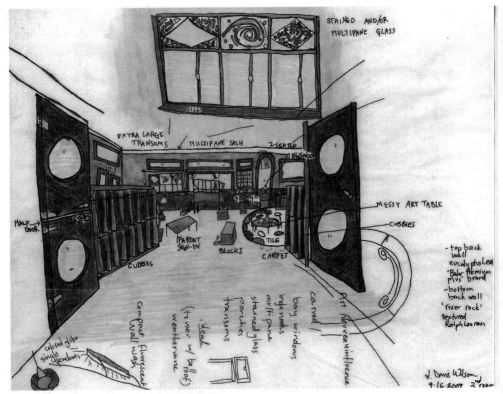

Figure 7.8. Concept sketch with window detail by J. D. Harte, 2007.

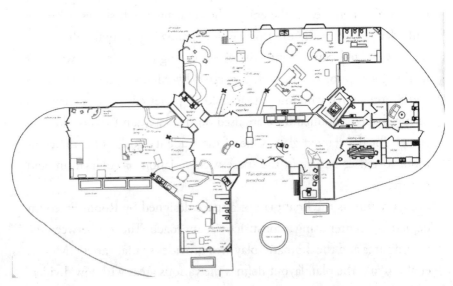

Figure 7.9. Concept plan of child development center by J. D. Harte, 2007.

a small stage. While the plan is rectilinear, the interior forms integrate a variety of angles and curvilinear structures to balance the linearity of the plan.

Figure 7.11 by Ellen Anderson is a unique plan with a cluster of cylindrical areas radiating from a central space for large-circle time. The active area with a loft is where the change in levels occurs. The lighting reflects the central area in a circular pattern. In the quiet area, the ceiling is lowered to promote quiet behavior (Moore et al., 1979). The loft area is built along the wall with a curvilinear form.

Figures 7.12 and 7.13 were executed by Justine Dawson. Figure 7.12 is a concept painting of three activity areas showing different forms for definition. The dramatic play area is located within a small-scale façade of a home. The loft is a turret with a slide on the perimeter and an open space on the floor. The reading area has a lowered ceiling to promote cooperative play behavior. This design is based on the research study by Read and others (1999), who found that a lowered ceiling height promotes cooperation among young children. This student designed the space with an emphasis on spatial definition and variety. Figure 7.13 is a concept materials board showing textures, colors, and finishes for the classroom.

These student projects reflect the scope and variety of curriculum approaches of child development centers. The designs support the research in physical environments of child development centers by creating multiple learning spaces in one larger space, integrating natural lighting, and offering children variety and complexity in the design of the space. As described in the introduction of this chapter, the designs of centers are as varied as the teachers and children who inhabit them. The most important accomplishments of the professional designer are the function and the beauty of the child development center.

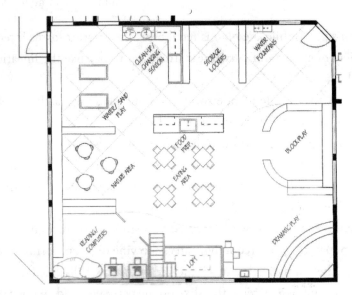

Figure 7.10. Concept plan of classroom by R. Freeburn, 2007.

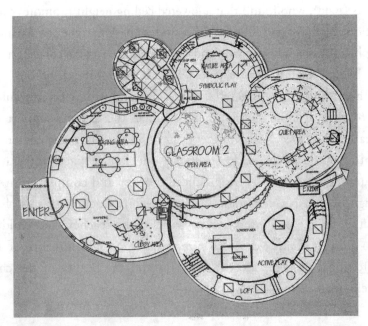

Figure 7.11. Concept plan of classroom by E. Anderson, 2007.

Figure 7.12. Sketch of activity areas by J. Dawson, 2007.

Figure 7.13. Finish board by J. Dawson, 2007.

BIBLIOGRAPHY

Campos-de-Carvalho, M., & Rossetti-Ferreira, M. C. (1993). Importance of spatial arrangements for young children in day care centers. *Children's Environments, 10*(1), 23–41.

Camgoz, N., Yener, C., & Guvenc, D. (2003). Effects of hue, saturation, and brightness: Part 2: Attention. *Color Research and Application 29*(1), 20–28.

Committee on Family and Work Policies (2003). *Working families and growing kids: Caring for children and adolescents.* Washington, DC: The National Academic Press.

Cooper Marcus, C. (1995). *House as a mirror of self.* Berkeley, CA: Conari Press.

Cryer, D. (1999, May). Defining and assessing early childhood program quality. *The Annals of the American Academy of Political and Social Science, 563,* 39–55.

Cryer, D. (2003). Defining program quality. In D. Cryer, & R. M. Clifford, (Eds.), *Early childhood education and care in the USA* (pp. 31–46). Baltimore: Paul H. Brookes.

Cuffaro, H. K., Nager, N., & Shapiro, E. K. (2005). The developmental-interaction approach at Bank Street College of Education. In J. L. Roopnarine & J. E. Johnson, (Eds.), *Approaches to Early Childhood Education* (5th ed.), (pp. 280–295). Upper Saddle River, NJ: Pearson Prentice Hall.

Day, C. (1998). *A haven for childhood: The building of a Steiner Kindergarten.* Glanrhydwilym, UK: Starborn.

Decker, C. A., & Decker, J. R. (2001). *Planning and administering early childhood programs* (7th ed.). Upper Saddle River, NJ: Prentice Hall.

Dempsey, J. D., & Frost, J. L. (1993). Play environments in early childhood education. In B. Spodek (Ed.), *Handbook of research on the education of young children* (pp. 306–321). New York: Macmillan.

Doctoroff, S. (2001). Adapting the physical environment to meet the needs of all young children for play. *Early Childhood Education Journal, 29*(2), 105–109.

Dudek, M. (2000). *Kindergarten architecture: Spaces for the imagination.* 2nd ed. London: Spon Press.

Dudek, M. (Ed.). (2005). *Children's spaces.* London: Architectural Press.

Evans, G. (2006). Child development and the physical environment. *Annual Review of Psychology, 57,* 423–451.

Faber Taylor, A., & Kuo, F. E. (2006). Is contact with nature important for healthy child development? State of the evidence. In C. Spencer & M. Blades (Eds.), *Children and their environments: Learning, using, and designingspaces* (pp. 124–140). Cambridge: Cambridge University Press.

Faber Taylor, A., Kuo, F. E., & Sullivan, W. C. (2002). Views of nature and self-discipline: Evidence from inner city children. *Journal of Environmental Psychology, 22*, 49–63.

Fleet, A., & Robertson, J. (1998). (Eds.). Unpacking educational environments: Visions from Reggio Emilia, Australia, Sweden, Denmark and the United States. Conference Papers from the Unpacking Educational Environments Conference at Macquarie University, May 16, 1998.

Greenman, J. (1988). *Caring spaces, learning places: Children's environments that work.* Redmond, WA: Exchange Press.

Guilfoyle, U. (Producer), & Pollack, S. (Director). (2006). *Sketches of Frank Gehry* [Motion picture]. United States: Sony Pictures Classic.

Gump, P. V. (1987). School and classroom environments. In D. Stokols, & I. Altman, (Eds.). *Handbook of environmental psychology,* Vol. I, (pp. 691–732). New York: John Wiley & Sons.

Harms, T., Clifford, R. M., & Cryer, D. (1998). *Early Childhood Environment Rating Scale* (Revised Ed.) (ECERS-R). New York: Teachers College Press, Columbia University.

Katz, L. G., & Chard, S. C. (2005). The project approach: An overview. In J. L. Roopnarine & J. E. Johnson, (Eds.), *Approaches to Early Childhood Education* (5th ed.), (pp. 296–310). Upper Saddle River, NJ: Pearson Prentice Hall.

Kantrowitz, E. J., & Evans, G. W. (2004). The relationship between the ratio or children per activity area and off-task behavior and type of play in day care centers. *Environment and Behavior, 36*(4), 541–557.

Kirkby, M. (1989). Nature as a refuge in children's environments. *Children's Environments Quarterly, 6,* 1–12.

Kritchevsky, S., Prescott, E., & Walling, L. (1969). *Planning environments for young children: Physical space.* Washington, DC: NAEYC.

Küller, R., & Lindsten, C. (1992). Health and behavior of children in classrooms with and without windows. *Journal of Environmental Psychology, 12,* 305–317.

Legendre, A. (1999). Interindividual relationships in groups of young children and susceptibility to an environmental constraint. *Environment and Behavior, 31*(4), 463–486.

Legendre, A. (2003). Environmental features influencing toddlers' bioemotional reactions in day care centers. *Environment and Behavior, 35*(4), 523–549.

Lin, M. Y. (2000). *Boundaries.* New York: Simon & Schuster.

Maxwell, L. E. (1996). Multiple effects of home and day care crowding. *Environment and Behavior, 28*(4), 494–511.

Maxwell, L. E. (2007). Competency in child care settings: The role of the physical environment. *Environment and Behavior, 39*(2), 229–245.

Montessori, M. (1965). *Dr. Montessori's own handbook: A short guide to her ideas and materials.* New York: Shocken Books.

Montessori, M. M., Polk, L. (Ed.). (1976). *Education for human development: Understanding Montessori.* New York: Shocken Books.

Moore, G. T. (1987). The physical environment and cognitive development in child-care centers. In C. S. Weinstein & T. G. David (Eds.), *Spaces for children: The built environment and child development* (pp. 41–72). New York: Plenum.

Moore, G. T. (1994). *Early childhood physical environment observation schedules and rating scales: Preliminary scales for the measurement of the physical environment of child care centers and related environments.* Milwaukee: University of Wisconsin–Milwaukee, Center for Architecture and Urban Planning Research.

Moore, G. T., Lane, C. G., Hill, A. B., Cohen, U., & McGinty, T. (1979). *Recommendations for child care centers.* University of Wisconsin–Milwaukee: Center for Architecture and Urban Planning.

National Association for the Education of Young Children (2007). Accreditation Criteria for the Physical Environment, Standard 9. Retrieved May 15, 2007, from the NAEYC Web site at http://www.naeyc.org/academy/standards/standard9/standard9C.asp

Neill, S. R. St. J. & Denham, E. J. M. (1982). The effects of preschool building design. *Educational Research, 24*(2), 107–111.

Neisworth, J. T., & Buggey, T. J. (2005). Behavior analysis and principles in early childhood education. In J. L. Roopnarine & J. E. Johnson, (Eds.), *Approaches to Early Childhood Education* (5th ed.), (pp. 186–210). Upper Saddle River, NJ: Pearson Prentice Hall.

Olds, A. R. (2001). *Child care design guide.* New York: McGraw-Hill.

Ou, L. C., Ronnier Luo, M., Woodcock, A., & Wright, A. (2004a). A study of color emotion and color preference. Part I: Color emotions for single colors. *Color Research and Application, 29*(3), 232–240.

Ou, L. C., Ronnier Luo, M., Woodcock, A., & Wright, A. (2004b). A study of color emotion and color preference. Part II: Color emotions for two-color combinations. *Color Research and Application, 29*(4), 292–298.

Ou, L. C., Ronnier Luo, M., Woodcock, A., & Wright, A. (2004c). A study of emotion and color preference. Part III: Color preference modeling. *Color Research and Application, 29*(5), 381–389.

Petrakos, H., & Howe, N. (1996). The influence of the physical design of the dramatic play center on children's play. *Early Childhood Research Quarterly, 11,* 63–77.

Poresky, R. H. (1990). The young children's empathy measure: Reliability, validity, and effects of companion animal bonding. *Psychological Reports, 66,* 931–936.

Piaget, J. (1954). *The construction of reality in the child.* New York: Ballantine.

Prescott, E. (1987). The environment as organizer of intent in child-care settings. In C. S. Weinstein & T. G. David (Eds.), *Spaces for children: The built environment and child development* (pp. 73–88), New York: Plenum.

Read, M. A. (2003). Use of color in child care environments: Application of color for wayfinding and space definition in Alabama child care centers. *Early Childhood Education Journal, 30*(4), 233–239.

Read, M. A., Sugawara, A. I., & Brandt, J. A. (1999). Impact of space and color in the physical environment on preschool children's cooperative behavior. *Environment and Behavior, 31*(3), 413–428.

Rivlin, L. G., & Wolfe, M. (1985). *Institutional settings in children's lives.* New York: John Wiley & Sons.

Ruth, L. C. (2000). *Design standards for children's environments.* New York: McGraw-Hill.

Sanoff, H. (1995). *Creating environments for young children.* Raleigh, NC: North Carolina State University School of Design.

Sugiyama, T., & Moore, G. T. (2005). Content and construct validity of the early childhood physical environment rating scale (ECPERS). Paper in H. Chaudhury (Ed.), *Proceedings of the 36th annual Environmental Design Research Association Conference.* Norman, OK: Environmental Design Research Association, pp. 32–37.

Thornton, L., & Brunton, P. (2005). Understanding the Reggio approach. London: David Fulton. University of Newcastle, The Centre for Learning and Teaching, School of Education, Communication and Language Science. (2005, February). The impact of school environments: A literature review. Retrieved from the Design Council Web site at http://www.design-council.org.uk/en/Design-Council/3/Publications/

Weinstein, C. S. (1987). Designing preschool classrooms to support development: Research and reflection. In C. S. Weinstein & T. G. David (Eds.), *Spaces for children: The built environment and child development* (pp. 41–72). New York: Plenum.

Weikart, D. P., & Schweinhart, L. J. (2005). The High/Scope curriculum for early childhood care and education. In J. L. Roopnarine & J. E. Johnson, (Eds.), *Approaches to Early Childhood Education* (5th ed.), (pp. 235-250). Upper Saddle River, NJ: Pearson Prentice Hall.

Wells, N. M. (2000). At home with nature: Effects of "greenness" on children's cognitive functioning. *Environment and Behavior, 32*(6), 775–779.

Wohlwill, J. F., & Heft, H. (1987). The physical environment and the development of the child. In D. Stokols, & I. Altman, (Eds.), *Handbook of Environmental Psychology*, Vol. I, (pp. 281–328). New York: John Wiley & Sons.

Zeegers, S. K., Readdick, C. A., & Hansen-Gandy, S. (1994). Daycare children's establishment of territory to experience privacy. *Children's Environments*, *11*(4), 265–271.

8   Environments for Individuals with Dementia and Frail Elders: Students as Consumers of Research

Joan Dickinson

> It is often said that the value and meaning of a civilization can be determined from the record it leaves in the form of architecture and that the true measure of the compassion and civility of a society lies in how well it treats its frail older people.
>
> (Regnier, 2002, p.1)

Abstract

This chapter examines environments for older individuals. The first part of the chapter reviews demographics on aging and illustrates how important facilities for our oldest seniors will become in the future. Next, senior housing alternatives are described, and the models of care are explained so that readers can better understand how these theories have influenced the design of spaces for older adults. In the last part of the chapter, informed design examples are provided for memory care units and for aging-in-place issues. This chapter illustrates how students and practitioners can become consumers of research to better inform their design solutions.

Introduction

The population of older individuals has been on the rise since the 1900s. Between 1900 and 1990, the senior population increased by 88 percent compared to a 34 percent increase in individuals under the age of 65 (U.S. Department of Commerce, 2002). These trends will continue, and by the year 2030 there will be approximately 70 million older persons, more than twice the number in 2000 (Administration on Aging [AOA], 2003).

The average life expectancy in 1950 was 68 years. Today that life expectancy is 78 years (Novelli, 2004; U.N. Business Council Luncheon, 2003). More important is the growth of elders who are 85 and over. A person who reaches the age of 62 can expect to live an additional 25 years (Hobbs, 2001; U.S. Department of Commerce, 2002). These increases in life expectancies have changed the structure within the older population, and individuals who are 85 years and older are the fastest-growing segment among senior citizens (Hobbs, 2001). This group of oldest seniors often has chronic health problems that greatly influence their ability to age in place (U.S. Department of Commerce, 2002).

The growing population of older adults over the next 30 years will affect almost all sectors of life including healthcare, politics, transportation, retirement, the economy, and housing (Novelli, 2004; U.N. Business Council Luncheon, 2003). Furthermore, people who are over the age of 50 in the United States control 75 percent of the nation's disposable income (Novelli, 2004). The purchasing and voting power of this group of individuals will command more attention over the next decade when the population of senior citizens will outnumber the population of young children (U.S. Department of Commerce, 2002).

In this chapter, we examine environments for older individuals. The demographic information above illustrates the influence this segment of the population will have on built environments of the future. We begin this chapter with an overview of housing options available to older adults and discuss the models of care that have affected the design of these facilities. Next, we examine areas of research that have a direct impact on nursing homes and aging-in-place issues. Most importantly, we explore how these research studies can aid in the problem-solving process of design.

Housing Options for Older Individuals

As individuals age, one area of concern is where they will live. Fortunately, the majority of older people are healthy, independent, and mobile and do not require institutional care. As a result, 75 percent of older adults have remained in their single family homes, and 86 percent want to stay in their present home and never move (American Association of Retired Persons [AARP], 1992; Kochera & Bright, 2005–2006). Yet the housing occupied by seniors is generally older and less adequate than the balance of the nation's housing (Golant & LaGreca, 1995; McFadden & Brandt, 1993). More troubling, however, is the lack of housing policy and supportive services that allow frailer, less independent elders to age in place (Kochera & Bright, 2005–2006; Maddox, 1995; McFadden & Brandt, 1993; VanVliet, 1992). Although institutionalization affects only 5 percent of older persons, as individuals continue to live longer (e.g., 80 and over), 30 percent will require long-term care (Schwarz & Brent, 1999). When older adults are forced to move, nursing home care or assisted living is often the only alternative (Regnier, 2002). In fact, the long-term care industry has grown tremendously, and estimates are that the number of elderly needing long-term care will double to 14 million over the next two decades (U.S. Congress General Accounting Office [U.S. GAO], 1999). The most dramatic response to the long-term care sector has been the emergence and growth of facilities known as assisted living (American Seniors Association [ASHA], 1998; Citro & Hermanson, 1999; Marsden, 2005; Regnier, 2002).

Long-Term Care Facilities

In examining the long-term care industry, it is first important to understand the various options that are available to the aging senior.

Assisted Living

Assisted living is an industry term for multifamily housing that provides personal and healthcare services in a group setting that claims to be residential in character and appearance (Assisted Living Federation of America [ALFA], 2000; Kochera, Straight, & Guterbock, 2005; Regnier, 1999; Regnier, 2002). The services provided in these facilities vary but frequently include meals, housekeeping, transportation, and often assistance with laundry, grooming, medication, and other functions of daily living (Utz, 2003).

Congregate Housing

Typically an apartment building for people living independently who require hospitality services such as meals and housekeeping are said to live in *congregate housing*. Usually no healthcare or personal care services are provided (Kochera et al., 2005).

Nursing Homes

Nursing homes, by definition, provide long-term care services in skilled and/or intermediate care settings (Kane, 1994). The majority of nursing homes across the United States provide both types of care within the same facility (Pieper, 1989).

Intermediate Care

In an *intermediate care setting*, individuals may have problems associated with memory loss, increased frailty and dependency, or some form of dementia, and typically a minimal amount of medical care is required (Pieper, 1989).

Skilled Care

Skilled care facilities, on the other hand, provide medical care for individuals who are seriously impaired, for instance, individuals who are recuperating from surgery or who require round-the-clock medical attention (Pieper, 1989).

Continuing Care Retirement Communities (CCRC)

Facilities that provide care across a continuum of needs are called *continuing care retirement communities*. In a campus setting, typically private apartments, assisted living, and nursing home care are available. Thus, older individuals may move through differing levels of care on an as need basis (Kochera et al., 2005).

Selection of an Appropriate Facility

Which type of facility is appropriate for an older individual at a particular time may be dictated in part by that person's ability to engage in *activities of daily living* (ADLs), which include personal care activities such as dressing, grooming, using the toilet, bathing, feeding oneself, getting in and out of bed, and navigating around one's own home (Lawton & Brody, 1969; Marsden, 2005).

Instrumental activities of daily living involve the ability to manage everyday chores and include use of the telephone, meal preparation, housework, money management, taking medications, and food or clothes shopping (Lawton & Brody, 1969; Marsden, 2005). Individuals who live in an assisted-living facility or nursing home environment typically need some level of assistance with these types of activities. In fact, 40 percent of individuals over the age of 85 have difficulty with at least two or more ADLs (Gibson et al., 2003; Marsden, 2005). Individuals who live in a nursing home may need help with four or more ADLs (Brawley, 2006).

Despite the choices of long-term care available to the older adult, many of these facilities do not meet the needs of an aging population. Nursing homes are an inappropriate housing option for many people because they do not need the 24-hour skilled care provided. Not only is the care more extensive than what is required, but nursing homes are expensive and have caused a huge economic burden on society. In addition, the majority of nursing homes have been designed to emulate small hospitals and have a sterile, medical imagery that is inappropriate for senior citizens (Biley, 1996; Calkins & Hoglund, 1999; Kane, 1994; Regnier, 1999; Reinardy & Kane, 1999; Schwarz, 1999). Although the major goal of assisted living is to create a supportive social setting that elders can call home, the majority of residents do not feel comfortable in these facilities despite efforts to create a residential ambience (Frank, 1999). More importantly, these forms of long-term care are not desirable to many senior citizens. Older adults are protective of their independence and have a strong desire to remain in their single-family homes for as long as possible (Kochera & Bright, 2005).

There are numerous reasons why older individuals choose to age in place. First, a dwelling is much more than a physical shelter or financial investment (Golant, 1992; Golant, 1999). Many seniors have lived in the same home for 20 to 30 years (Golant, 1992), and a sentimental attachment to their homes has developed. Home provides people with a sense of security, privacy, organization, comfort, and independence and facilitates social interactions with family and friends (Wacker, Roberto, & Piper, 1998). As part of the experience of a dwelling, home holds for its residents a great many memories and a sense of continuity in life. More importantly, many older adults spend 85 to 90 percent of their time in the immediate home environment. As a result, home is a major variable physically, socially, and psychologically in the lives of older persons (Atchley, 1994), and their well-being may depend on the kind of place in which they live.

Second, the majority of senior citizens are satisfied with their living conditions, and 83 percent think the quality of their housing is either good or excellent (AARP, 1992). Yet many of these individuals are living in homes that were built before 1950 and have not relocated in over three decades. These older homes may have a variety of physical conditions that could affect safety.

Despite efforts to remain independent and at home, the effects of normal and pathological aging cause many individuals to seek long-term care services (Marsden, 2005). For the past several years, assisted-living facilities have dominated new construction of housing for seniors (ASHA, 1998). Indeed, one-third of facilities that call themselves, "assisted living" have been in business for five or fewer years, and 60 percent have been in operation for ten or fewer years (Hawes, Rose, & Phillips, 1999). In 1995, assisted-living facilities (ALFs) were estimated to be between 30,000 and 40,000 in number, serving 600,000 to 1 million residents (Wood, 1995). More recently, the National Center for Assisted Living (NCAL) reported that the number of ALFs is rising in the United States, and there are approximately 1.15 million people living in these residences (National Center for Assisted Living [NCAL], 1998). The assisted-living target population is expected to increase sixfold over the next 25 years, when a large portion of the baby boomer generation enters their seventies (NCAL, 1998).

Nursing homes have also remained a provider of long-term and healthcare services (Kane, 1994; Kuzbek, 2001; Rantz & Zwygart-Stauffacher, 1997). There are over 27,000 nursing home facilities across the United States, and 1.4 million people (43 percent of those over the age of 65) will reside in a nursing home at any given point in time (Kane, 1994; Rantz & Zwygart-Stauffacher, 1997; Schwarz & Brent, 1999; Wilson, 1995).

Both of these long-term care options have shown steady growth over the past few decades, and growth will continue because of several factors including (1) an increase in the overall age of the population, (2) an increase in geographic mobility (i.e., many extended families no longer live in the same vicinity, making informal care giving to the older adult difficult), (3) an increase in working women who are the primary caregivers of elders, and (4) an increase in the population of individuals who are over the age of 85 who are typically frailer and need help with activities of daily living (Administration on Aging, 2003; Foner, 1994; Freedman, 1996; Marsden, 2005; Moore, 2000; Pyke & Bengston, 1996; Regnier, 2002; Schwarz, 1996; Tinsley & Warren, 1999; Wilson, 1995).

Models of Design and Care

Because of the growth in long-term care, it is important to examine the models of design that have permeated the aesthetic, form, and function of these facilities. These are the medical, hospitality, residential, green house, and planetree models.

The *medical model* is characterized as follows:

- Model of care with a focus on treatment of the disease or condition (Biley, 1996; Calkins & Hoglund, 1999; Joseph, 2006).
- Focus on curing the illness ("We are going to make you well.").
- Facilities that emulate small hospitals in their design imagery.
- Institutional, sterile, and featureless aesthetics (Joseph, 2006).
- Design attributes that enhance disease treatment such as large, centralized nurses station, double-loaded corridors, shared resident bedrooms, and bathing facilities (Joseph, 2006; Kane, 1994; Rhode, 1999; Schwarz, 1996). See Figures 8.1, 8.2, and 8.3.
- Regimented staff routines and focus on the schedule of the day rather then on resident feelings or well-being.

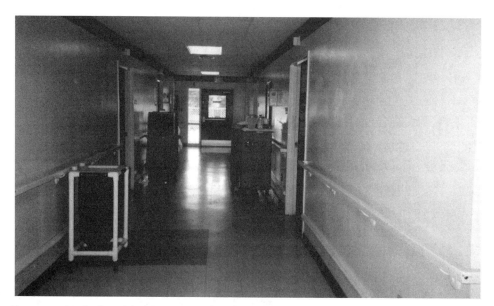

Figure 8.1. Medical model of design in a nursing home. White walls, 2-by-4 acoustical ceiling tiles, vinyl composition tile floors, and double-loaded corridor design create a featureless environment. The focus in the facility is to cure the illness, yet most individuals in nursing homes cannot be cured. Leads to a hospital image that is inappropriate for nursing homes where most residents are there for extended stays.

Figure 8.2. Resident rooms in a nursing home. Shared resident room with little to no personalization. Sterile white walls and white ceiling. Focus on cleanliness, medical issues, and cure of the disease. Follows the hospital model of care.

Following are characteristics of the *hospitality model*:

- Facilities are designed to emulate an upscale hotel ambience particularly in the shared, public spaces such as lobbies, dining rooms, or living areas (Zavotka & Teaford, 1997).
- The design is characterized by formality and lack of personalization and familiarization (Zavotka & Teaford, 1997). See Figure 8.4.

The residential model is based on the following ideas:

- The model advocates using design elements to create an environment that simulates a residential, single-family home (Brawley, 2006; Perkins, Hoglund, King, & Cohen, 2004; Calkins & Hoglund, 1999).
- Homelike attributes such as privacy, independence, resident control, personalization, security, dignity, and familiarity are used to simulate a home setting with the freedoms associated with domestic living (Bone, 1998; Brawley, 1999; Brawley, 2006; Davidson, 1995; Malkin, 1994; Regnier, 2002).
- Design features could include smaller-scaled facilities (human scale) (Regnier, 2002), increased personal space, informality, familiarity, and comfort (Brawley, 2006; Perkins et al., 2004).

The *green house model* is based on the work by Dr. William Thomas and is characterized by a move toward the residential paradigm where residents are treated in an increasingly humane way (Brawley, 2006). This model is portrayed by the following:

- Smaller-scaled facilities that house eight to ten elders (Joseph, 2006).

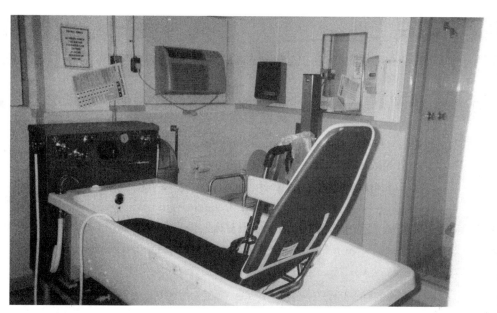

Figure 8.3. Shared bathing facility in a nursing home. Cold, institutional materials and finishes are apparent in this bathing area. Dignity is compromised due to the lack of privacy.

Figure 8.4. Seating area in assisted living facility. Formality of finishes and furnishings, lack of personalization or person-centered items such as family photos, heirlooms, or personal collections contributes to a hotel setting. Use of symmetry and "matched" accessories creates the upscale hotel look. Lacks the individual uniqueness of home (Eshelman & Evans, 2002).

- No nurses' stations. Instead of the large, centralized nurses station found in the medical model, the nurses visit each room to dispense medications to residents (Brawley, 2006; Joseph, 2006).
- No scheduled or regimented day. Residents have the freedom and autonomy seen in community living. Thus, residents can decide on when to eat their meals, when to take a nap, what activities to participate in, their preferences in bathing, or when to have a snack (Alliance for Health Reform, 2008). The bureaucracy found in institutional living is eliminated as the residents control menus and planned activities.
- Residents have complete access to the kitchen areas and may help in meal preparation.
- A change to a consumer-driven, person-centered model of care instead of focusing on acute or medical issues so prevalent in the medical model (Alliance for Health Reform, 2008; Joseph, 2006). The care of elders comes first instead of the demands of the institution (PBS, 2008).
- Private resident rooms and bathrooms (Brawley, 2006). Residents are encouraged to bring furnishings and personal mementos from home.
- Centralized dining and living area for community meals (Brawley, 2006).
- Connection to nature through the use of indoor plants and landscaping and outside access to courtyards (PBS, 2008).

The *planetree model* was founded in 1978 by Angelica Thieriot after her experiences as a patient in a hospital. Despite the advanced care and high technology she received during her treatment, she experienced a lack of personalized care throughout her stay (Brawley, 2006). The planetree concept is based on the following:

- Patient involvement and patient-centered care. A more holistic approach to care based on the physical, mental, spiritual, social, and emotional needs of the patient (Brawley, 2006; Planetree, 2007).

- A healing environment that provides compassionate caregiving. Patients are informed about their care options and fully involved in the decision making for their care and treatment (Brawley, 2006). Libraries and resource centers are located in the facility for patient and family member education (PBS, 2008).

- The creation of secure and non-threatening interior spaces (Brawley, 2006) such as smaller nurses stations located outside of patient or resident rooms. Stations that are accessible and open in nature.

- Recognizing the importance of family and friends in the care of the resident or patient. Providing space for family and social support and space for privacy.

- Views to nature. Design that creates a healing environment through the use of softer finishes, materials, and textiles (Brawley, 2006). The use of artwork to provide positive distractions (Planetree, 2007).

- The importance and nutrition values of food. Kitchens that are accessible to family members and patients that can serve as gathering areas for informal social support (Planetree, 2007).

- The creation of spaces that promote spirituality or reflection such as gardens, meditation rooms, or chapels. The use of complementary medicine such as massage or therapeutic art (Brawley, 2006).

These five models influence the design and type of care that is administered in the facility. To illustrate, nurses who work in a setting that espouses the medical model are often rewarded for how fast they dress, feed, and medicate their "patients." An environment that is designed to simulate a hospital in its imagery only reinforces how staff will react and ultimately how residents will be treated. In examining these models, it is clear that many of these long-term care facilities are not meeting the needs of the older consumer. Nursing homes that adopt a medically oriented environment are inappropriate for the senior citizen who is typically not in need of acute care (Joseph, 2006).

Assisted-living facilities that advertise their residential appeal are often designed to emulate upscale, formal hotels rather than the unique attributes found in the home (Eshelman & Evans, 2002). A hotel may be initially appealing, but over the long run, the formality does not suit the long-term needs of older individuals (Zavotka & Teaford, 1997). To illustrate, Zavotka and Teaford examined 11 different assisted-living facilities with shared social spaces. In conducting interviews with the residents, the investigators found that the traditional, formal furnishings, use of red and green color scheme, and coordinated accessories did not match the resident's previous home experiences. Although the design imagery was closely aligned with the hospitality model, the residents did not find the shared social spaces to be private, homelike, or personal. This research study clearly makes designers question the use of the hospitality model for the design of environments for older adults.

Eshelman and Evans (2002) surveyed 92 individuals living in a continuing care retirement community in upstate New York to determine the environmental predictors of place attachment and self-esteem (see Chapter 2 for a description of this study as an example of a correlation research strategy). The overall theme throughout their research study was personalization. The most important predictors of self-esteem and place attachment included that the home could easily accommodate possessions, that it has satisfactory display spaces, that the home appearance reflects the personality and character of the resident, and that the home appears lived in. As summarized in the research article,

"What residents truly want is their own quirky, individually unique setting: their home" (p. 6).

Research has supported the residential model for individuals with dementia as well. Residents who live in noninstitutional settings are less aggressive, have less anxiety, use less medication, have increased food intake, and have improved motor functions (Annerstedt, 1997; Cohen-Mansfield & Werner, 1998; Evans & Crogan, 2001; Reed, Zimmerman, Sloane, Williams, & Boustani, 2005).

Kane, Lum, Cutler, Degenhultz, and Yu (2007) examined the effects of the green house model on resident's quality of life. The two-year longitudinal study compared four 10-person green houses (40 residents at the time of the study) to two traditional, institutional nursing homes (40 residents selected randomly from the two nursing homes for a total of 80 residents). Quality of life domains included physical comfort, functional competence, privacy, dignity, meaningful activity, relationships, autonomy, food enjoyment, spiritual well-being, security, and individuality. In general, the residents at the green house (GH) reported a better quality of life than those living in the traditional nursing homes. In particular, privacy, dignity, autonomy, and food enjoyment were rated higher in the GH than in the two nursing homes.

This research provides justification to designers for using the residentially oriented paradigm found in the green house and planetree models. In this next section, we examine several areas of research that are important to long-term care and aging in place. First, we explore investigations that have studied exit-seeking behavior and wandering in nursing home environments and present design solutions that not only reflect the findings from these studies but that also represent a residentially oriented, green house model of design. This is an emerging area of research in the field of aging, as many healthcare environments have advocated creating more homelike spaces for their residents. Last, we consider the topic of falls and how this common injury among older individuals can influence their ability to stay in their single-family home.

Informed Design Examples

Facilities for Individuals with Dementia

Although nursing homes are not the desired place to live among older adults, because of pathological aging, many seniors have no other housing options. In the past, nursing homes were one of the few places for individuals with advanced forms of dementia. In fact, half of all nursing home residents suffer from Alzheimer's disease or a related disorder (Alzheimer's Association, 2006), and 60 percent of all individuals who are over the age of 85 will develop some form of dementia (Brawley, 2006; Kincaid & Peacock, 2003). Therefore, facilities that house individuals with advanced forms of dementia will become an important building type for aging adults in the future. Alzheimer's disease leads to a number of symptoms including memory loss; disorientation; and wandering, which involves aimless walking throughout the facility (Alzheimer's Association, 2006; Brawley, 2006; Kincaid & Peacock, 2003). Some 60 percent of residents with Alzheimer's disease wander, and in many facilities, this type of behavior leads to attempted exits (Alzheimer's Association, 2006; Kincaid & Peacock, 2003).

As illustrated in Figure 8.5, the nursing home in our study has a double-loaded corridor design, where the rooms are arranged around a central hallway reminiscent of the medical model mentioned previously. The residents walk out of their rooms, wander in this hallway, and inevitably reach the exit door. To make matters worse, the exit door has a window, which provides the only view and source of natural light to the wandering path. The residents are clearly attracted to the view and natural light (Leibrock, 2000). Once wandering residents reach the exit door, they often try to leave the facility. This type of attempted exiting behavior is not uncommon in nursing homes and other types of facilities and, if successful, is dangerous (Kincaid & Peacock, 2003; Leibrock, 2000; Lucero, 2002). Residents who do exit can get lost or injured, and

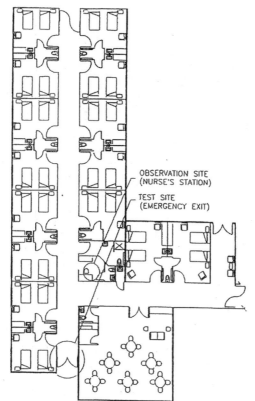

OBSERVATION SITE
(NURSE'S STATION)

TEST SITE
(EMERGENCY EXIT)

Figure 8.5.
Plan of a double-
loaded corridor design
in a nursing home.

unfortunately, some have been found dead (Alzheimer's Association, 2006; Lucero, 2002). In Figure 8.5, the door at the end of the hallway is a means of egress and cannot be locked. Therefore, the staff installed an alarm system on the door. Whenever a resident touched the panic bar of the door, the alarm would go off. Once the alarm went off, the lock on the door was released. Here is a typical scenario: (1) the resident would wander to the door; (2) the resident would touch the panic bar of the door; (3) the alarm would go off, which would release the lock on the door; (4) a nurse on duty would escort the resident away from the door; and (5) the nurse would reset the alarm on the door. These attempted exits were a serious problem in the nursing home. The alarm could go

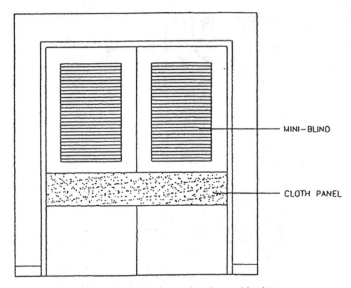

Figure 8.6. Exit door with the cloth panel and mini-blinds.

off 42 times in one hour, and in each case, a nurse would have to escort the resident away from the door. Sometimes the nursing staff would forget to reset the alarm. This allowed two residents to escape the facility.

Clearly a design problem is evident in this nursing home, and in this next section we will describe a research study in which the door was altered in an attempt to reduce exiting from this facility.

The central corridor with resident rooms on either side created the only wandering path in the nursing home. Residents would ultimately wander to the exit door located at the bottom of the plan. The door at the top and right of the plan lead to other areas of the nursing home (see Figure 8.5). Three test conditions were observed:

- In test condition one, we put mini-blinds on the window of the door. Our thought here was to eliminate the view and natural light. Residents who wandered to the exit door because they were attracted by the natural light might not try to exit the facility or may not wander to the door (see Figure 8.6).

- In test condition two, we covered the panic bar with a cloth panel that matched the color of the door. In this test condition, we eliminated the shiny panic bar. Our observations and literature review revealed that many residents are attracted to shiny objects because of the symptoms of Alzheimer's disease. Covering the panic bar eliminated this shiny protrusion (see Figure 8.6).
- In the last test condition, we combined the previous two, so the residents were exposed to the mini-blind and the cloth panel (see Dickinson, McLain-Kark, & Marshall-Baker, 1995, for a detailed description of the methodology).

During our data collection, we recorded the number of attempted exits from the facility. We counted an exit only when the alarm was triggered. In this research study, we discovered that all three test conditions reduced exiting behavior. Yet the cloth panel seemed to be the most effective. In fact, exiting attempts were reduced from 115 times in a one-week period during baseline conditions to 5 times when the cloth panel was installed (Dickinson, McLain-Kark, & Marshall-Baker, 1995). Camouflaging the panic bar or doorknob may be a low-cost solution for many nursing homes that have exiting problems (see Figure 8.7). It is critical, however, to discuss these alternatives with the local code officials. In a fire situation, residents and staff could easily push through the cloth panel, and this test condition was approved by the code official prior to installation.

In designing new facilities that house residents who have Alzheimer's disease, careful consideration should be given to the exit doors (Joseph, 2006). Clearly the plan in Figure 8.5 was not conducive to safe wandering. This is an excellent example of how a building design based on the medical model (i.e., a double-loaded corridor) has shaped resident behavior. In this plan, there was nowhere to wander, and the residents were attracted to the exit door by the natural light and shininess of the panic bar.

How do the findings from this research study aid in the problem-solving process? First, the results allow designers of facilities for individuals with dementia to better place exit doors and provide evidence for why the location is important. Second, the findings illustrate that exiting behavior is problematic (Leibrock, 2000) and give designers credence on designing wandering paths that encourage safe and beneficial wandering. Third, the findings illustrate to designers that camouflaging doors in existing nursing home facilities reduces exiting attempts.

The project in Figure 8.8, completed by a student, nicely illustrates the value of research in creating informed design solutions (Guerin & Thompson, 2004) as follows:

- The plan provides safe wandering paths. Residents never encounter a door directly at the end of the wandering corridor (Leibrock, 2000; Regnier, 2002). Instead, the student placed living areas close to the resident rooms, and the exit adjacent to the soiled and clean linen rooms enters an enclosed garden and outdoor courtyard area.

- The residents have free access to an indoor courtyard as well. As suggested by Namazi and Johnson (1992) and Mooney and Nicell (1992), providing access to outdoor spaces can reduce agitation among individuals with dementia.

- The plan provides a diversion from aimless wandering that often leads to negative behaviors such as attempted exiting. The beauty salon, theater, billiards room, and café (shown toward the bottom of the plan adjacent to the indoor courtyard) give the residents autonomy and freedom of choice as illustrated in the green house model. These areas also provide for more meaningful use of time and may distract the resident from incessant wandering. As suggested by Hoglund and Ledewitz (1999), movement can be made more purposeful to provide quality experiences (Regnier, 2002).

Figure 8.7. Example of camouflaged door.

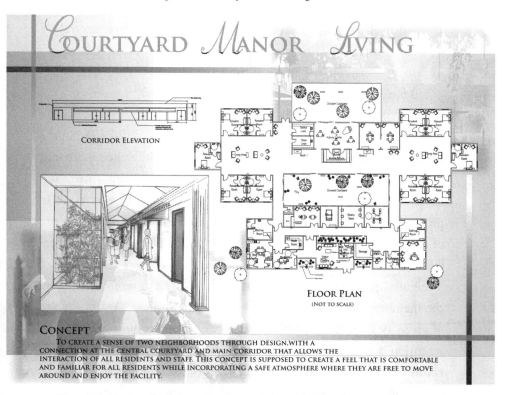

COURTYARD MANOR LIVING

CORRIDOR ELEVATION

FLOOR PLAN
(NOT TO SCALE)

CONCEPT

TO CREATE A SENSE OF TWO NEIGHBORHOODS THROUGH DESIGN,WITH A CONNECTION AT THE CENTRAL COURTYARD AND MAIN CORRIDOR THAT ALLOWS THE INTERACTION OF ALL RESIDENTS AND STAFF. THIS CONCEPT IS SUPPOSED TO CREATE A FEEL THAT IS COMFORTABLE AND FAMILIAR FOR ALL RESIDENTS WHILE INCORPORATING A SAFE ATMOSPHERE WHERE THEY ARE FREE TO MOVE AROUND AND ENJOY THE FACILITY.

Figure 8.8. Student floor plan with safe wandering paths that illustrates the residential and green house models designed by MaryAnn Wilmot.

- The plan also appears more residential in character. The plan in Figure 8.5 illustrates the medical model of design. The walls are pale blue, the floors are vinyl composition tile, and the ceiling is acoustical tile with fluorescent light fixtures. The only design interest in this home was the shiny panic bar and view to the outside. The institutional, featureless space led to inappropriate and unsafe wandering. Yet the plan in Figure 8.8 illustrates the residential and green house model of care with private resident rooms and baths; centrally located, small-scaled dining features; connection to nature; and meaningful activities (Brawley, 2006). There is interest and hominess with this plan through smaller scaled design that houses 10 residents (Regnier, 2002). The nurse's station also doubles as a residential kitchen to convey a homelike, familiar imagery that eliminates the large, centralized, institutional nurses' stations often found in hospitals and so prevalent in the medical model of design (Brawley, 2006; Marsden, 2005).

This facility also accommodates family members, as discussed in the planetree model. At the bottom of the plan is a conference room and library that allows family members to stay educated, informed, and involved in the care of their loved one. A connection to nature is also provided in this facility. The perspective in Figure 8.8 shows the use of landscaping and how skylights on the ceiling plane provide natural light in this town-center, neighborhood hallway (PBS, 2008).

Figure 8.9 shows a perspective of the entryway and reception desk of the memory care unit completed by the same student. Again, the use of greenery provides a familiar imagery and connection to nature. The reception desk uses materials such as stone and wood that are indigenous to the region, and the smaller-scaled desk demonstrates an open, welcoming, accessible greeting area. Skylights in the ceiling infuse the space with natural light.

Figure 8.9. Student perspective of entry to memory care unit designed by MaryAnn Wilmot.

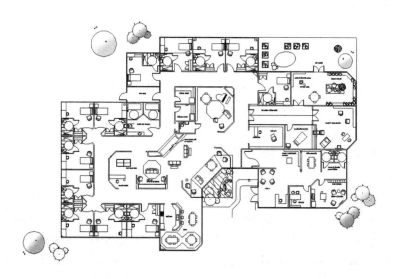

Figure 8.10. Student furniture plan illustrating the residential, green house, and planetree models and wandering paths designed by Katie Griffith.

Figure 8.10 shows another student example of a memory care unit. Smaller-scaled design is apparent in this plan, as the facility accommodates 11 residents (Brawley, 2006; Perkins et al., 2004; Regnier, 2002). The central part of the plan provides various activities such as living spaces, a Ping-Pong table, fish tanks, and a piano. These areas placed along the wandering path may influence residents to stop and engage in other activities (Hoglund & Ledewitz, 1999; Regnier 2002), and, as promoted by the green house model, gives residents the independence of homelike living.

Views to the outdoors help in orientation with time, place, and context. This plan also provides alternative therapies through a massage room, art and gardening therapy area, and a hair and nail salon (located on the right-hand side of the plan shown in Figure 8.11). These spaces give residents the opportunities for reflection and meditation. Complementary medicinal value may also be achieved through these types of areas as suggested by the planetree model of design.

This student also provided a centralized dining area adjacent to an open kitchen that allows residents to be involved in meal preparation. The large centralized nurses' stations are eliminated and become small desks scattered in the central living areas.

The perspective in Figure 8.12 strongly reflects the residential model through the creation of homelike façades on individual resident rooms (Brawley, 2006; Perkins et al., 2004). These unique elements produce spatial variety and aid in resident wayfinding (Bone, 1999; Calkins & Hoglund, 1999; Child, 1999; Steed, 2000). More importantly, these personalized façades could help to alleviate the boredom often associated with aimless wandering and exit-seeking behavior. A shelf placed outside of each resident room allows for the placement of personal mementos to aid in wayfinding and creates a more personalized, unique setting (Eshelman & Evans, 2002). This perspective also shows familiar finishes such as natural wood, residential doors, and sconces. The art

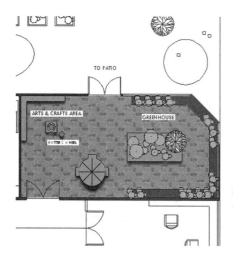

Figure 8.11.
Enlarged floor plan of
gardening and art therapy
area designed by
Katie Griffith.

Figure 8.12. Resident hallway illustrating personalized
room façades by Theresa Gilfrich.

on the wall provides accessories that might be seen in a domestic setting and illustrates an example of a positive distraction, as suggested by the planetree model.

The results from the research studies and models of design and care helped these students create solutions that were based on published investigations instead of using personal preference as a rationale for design decisions. All of the students could easily explain to a more sophisticated clientele the "why" behind their design decisions by referring to (1) the numerous research studies that have documented exiting behavior among residents with some form of dementia and have tested various design solutions to the door (e.g., Chafetz, 1990; Dickinson, 2004; Dickinson & McLain-Kark, 1998; Dickinson, McLain-Kark, & Marshall-Baker, 1995; Hamilton, 1993; Hussian & Brown, 1987; Lucero, 2002; Kincaid & Peacock, 2003; Namazi, Rosner, & Calkins, 1989), and (2) the residential, green house, and planetree models and the research investigations that support these future directions in the design of living spaces for senior citizens (e.g., Annerstedt, 1997; Cohen-Mansfield & Werner, 1998; Eshelman & Evans, 2002; Evans & Crogan, 2001; Joseph, 2006; Kane et al., 2007; Reed et al., 2005; Zavotka & Teaford, 1997). The results from these research studies are valuable to the design process and aid in justifying design solutions (Guerin & Thompson, 2004).

In addition to providing research evidence for design solutions related to exiting attempts and wandering, the study cited earlier follows the research process as outlined in Chapter 1. First, the problem is clearly defined, and it is a design-oriented problem. Remember that the definition of a problem can come from reading the literature or casually observing. Next, data are collected in a careful, patient, and systematic way. Note that an exit was clearly defined (the resident had to touch the panic bar, and the alarm had to go off). Third, the data are analyzed. Next, the results are interpreted and disseminated through publication. Last, the findings lead to discovery of new information that moves the field forward.

The study of exit-seeking behavior continues and illustrates the cyclical nature of research. Kincaid and Peacock (2003) examined camouflaging the means of egress through the use of a wall mural (see Figure 8.7 for an example). In their study of 12 residents, attempted exits were dramatically reduced. Thus, the findings from this study could substantiate the cost, effort, and time in painting a wall mural to conceal exit doors. Designers could point to investigations not only to rationalize design solutions but also to illustrate their knowledge of the literature and research.

Falls among Older Individuals

In this part of the chapter, we examine falling among the elderly. One-third of individuals 65 years and older fall each year, and falls are the leading cause of injury among older adults (National Center for Injury Prevention and Control [CDC], 2004; Pynoos, Rose, Rubenstein, Choi, & Sabata, 2006). The risk of falling not only increases with age but also reaches a prevalence of 50 percent in persons 85 years and older (Jensen, Lundin-Olsson, Nyberg, & Gustafson, 2002). The most common injuries due to falls are bone fractures, sprains, and dislocations. Yet physical injury is only part of the problem. Falls can result in decreased functioning, disability, and a reduced quality of life and account for one-third of all nursing home admissions (Hignett & Masud, 2006). Decreased confidence and fear of falling can lead to depression, feelings of helplessness, and social isolation (Yardley & Smith, 2002).

Despite the concern, falling is not considered an inevitable part of aging, and there are many controllable factors that can reduce the risk of a fall. The design of the interior environment, for example, is cited in the literature as a cause of falling among older individuals (Pynoos et al., 2006; Tse, 2005). In fact, 50 percent of all falls are attributed to interior design hazards within the home (Kochera, 2002). One environmental hazard frequently cited is tripping over uneven floor surfaces (Dickinson, Shroyer, Elias, Hutton, & Gentry, 2001; Wells & Evans, 1996, 2001). Examples of uneven floor surfaces include (1) high thresholds, (2) transitions between different floor materials, (3) high-pile carpet, (4) torn carpet, and (5) raised edges from carpet seaming and installation (Connell & Wolf, 1997; Gibson, 1998). In particular, soft carpet surfaces may cause a loss of balance when walking, and walkers, canes, and shoes can catch on high-pile carpet, causing a fall. As of 1998, flooring materials were estimated to cause 549,600 fall injuries per year (Gibson, 1998). Despite these problems, carpeting is often recommended in the home of the older adult because it decreases injury when a fall occurs (Tse, 2005), provides a warmer surface, reduces glare, and provides comfort.

Although carpet on pad is the most common residential floor covering used in the home, there are no recommendations or design guidelines for carpet selection specific to different age groups. In fact, most fall-prevention advice is considered by older individuals to be patronizing, not personally relevant, and common sense. To illustrate, older individuals are often told that eliminating throw rugs, using low-pile carpets, and tacking down carpet edges or seams will reduce the hazard of falling (Dickinson, Shroyer, Elias, Curry, & Cook, 2004). Yet the evidence is lacking. Moreover, some of the suggestions are vague and general. What exactly is a low-pile carpet?

We conducted several studies to test various carpets in order to provide seniors with carpet selections based on evidence and safety as opposed to aesthetic issues alone (see Dickinson, Shroyer, & Elias, 2002; Dickinson et al., 2001; and Dickinson, Shroyer, & Elias, 2000, which is also cited in Chapter 2). Specifically, we tested a common residential carpet (36 ounce, 1/8-inch gauge, 100 percent nylon, solid gray, 1/2-inch pile height, cut-pile carpet) with pad on 25 healthy older adults versus a commercial-grade carpet (28 ounce, 1/10-inch gauge, 100 percent nylon, solid gray, 3/16-inch pile height, level-loop carpet) on 45 healthy older adults. Our two studies along with a study conducted by Redfern, Moore, and Yarsky (1997) suggest that the compliancy of the carpet (i.e., the give or compressibility of the floor material) affects the gait and balance of older individuals. In all three studies, more compliant carpets that are installed with a pad caused the subjects to sway more. This finding is important because increases in postural sway are linked to falling. Thus, as carpet becomes more compliant, the risk of potential falls seems to rise.

Practicing designers can use this type of information when specifying carpet for an older population. Instead of recommending the use of a low-pile carpet, designers can examine the pile heights used in these three studies to determine that below 1/2 inch could be defined as low compliancy. This helps to eliminate the guesswork approach to one design solution: carpet selection. Moreover, a practicing designer could base a design solution that enhances safety on empirical, scientifically tested research.

BIBLIOGRAPHY

Administration on Aging [AOA]. (2003). A statistical profile of older Americans aged 65+. *U.S. Department of Health and Human Services.* Retrieved from http://www.aoa.gov

Alliance for Health Reform. (2008, March). *Changing the nursing home culture,* 1–4.

Alzheimer's Association (2006). Statistics about Alzheimer's disease. *Alzheimer's Association.* Retrieved from http://www.alz.org

American Association of Retired Persons. (1992). *Understanding senior housing for the 1990s: An American Association of Retired Persons survey of consumer preferences, concerns, and needs.* Washington, DC: AARP.

American Seniors Housing Association. (1998). *Seniors housing construction report—1998.* Washington, DC: ASHA.

Annerstadt, L. (1997). Group living care: An alternative for the demented elderly. *Dementia and Geriatric Cognitive Disorders, 8,* 136–142.

Assisted Living Federation of America [ALFA]. (2000). *ALFA's overview of the assisted living industry.* Fairfax, VA: PricewaterhouseCoopers and the National Investment Center.

Atchley, R. C. (1994). *Social forces and aging: An introduction to social gerontology* (7th ed.). Belmont, CA: Wadsworth Publishing.

Biley, F. C. (1996). Hospital: healing environments? *Complementary Therapies in Nursing & Midwifery, 2,* 110–115.

Bone, E. (1998). Aging in Eden. *Metropolis, 18*(4), 62–63, 93.

Brawley, E. C. (1999, September). Let's talk about better design for aging and Alzheimer's. *Proceedings of the Symposium on Healthcare Design,* 286–297.

Brawley, E. C. (2006). *Design innovations for aging and Alzheimer's creating caring environments.* Hoboken, NJ: John Wiley & Sons.

Calkins, M., & Hoglund, D. (1999, September). Bringing together research and design: Alzheimer's. *Proceedings of the Symposium on Healthcare Design,* 117–139.

Chafetz, P. K. (1990). Two-dimensional grid is ineffective against demented patients' exiting through glass doors. *Psychology and Aging, 5*(1), 146–147.

Child, M. (1999). Comfort is key. *Nursing Homes, 48*(9), 61–62.

Citro, J., & Hermanson, S. (1999). *Assisted living in the United States.* AARP working paper, unpublished. Washington, DC: American Association of Retired Persons, Public Policy Institute.

Cohen-Mansfield, J., & Werner, P. (1998). The effects of an enhanced environment on nursing home residents who pace. *The Gerontologist, 38*(2), 199.

Connell, B. R., & Wolf, S. L. (1997). Environmental and behavioral circumstances associated with falls at home among healthy elderly individuals. *Archives of Physical Medicine Rehabilitation, 78*(2), 179–186.

Davidson, A. W. (1995). Enhanced design strategies: Using the environment to promote human well-being. *Journal of Healthcare Design, 7,* 109–121.

Denmark, F. L. (2002). Myths of aging. *Eye on Psi Chi, 7*(7), 14–21.

Dickinson, J. I. (2004). Nursing home design: A student challenge and call for change. *The Journal of Interior Design, 30*(1), 31–55.

Dickinson, J. I., & McLain-Kark, J. (1998). Wandering behavior and attempted exits among residents diagnosed with dementia-related illnesses: A qualitative approach. *Journal of Women & Aging, 10*(2), 23–34.

Dickinson, J. I., McLain-Kark, J., & Marshall-Baker, A. (1995). The effects of visual barriers on exiting behavior in a dementia care unit. *The Gerontologist, 35*(1), 127–130.

Dickinson, J. I., Shroyer, J. L., & Elias, J. W. (2000). The effect of residential carpeting on the gait of healthy, community-dwelling older adults. *Housing and Society, 27*(2), 1–18.

Dickinson, J. I., Shroyer, J. L., & Elias, J. W. (2002). The influence of commercial-grade carpet on postural sway and balance strategy among older adults. *The Gerontologist, 42*(4), 552–559.

Dickinson, J. I., Shroyer, J. L., Elias, J. W., Curry, Z., & Cook, C. (2004). Preventing falls with interior design. *Journal of Family and Consumer Sciences, 96*(2), 13–21.

Dickinson, J. I., Shroyer, J. L., Elias, J. W., Hutton, J. T., & Gentry, G. M. (2001). The effect of selected residential carpet and pad on the balance of healthy older adults. *Environment and Behavior, 33*(2), 279–295.

Eshelman, P. E., & Evans, G. W. (2002). Home again: Environmental predictors of place attachment and self-esteem for new retirement community residents. *Journal of Interior Design, 28*(1), 3–9.

Evans, B. C., & Crogan, N. L. (2001). Quality improvement practices: Enhancing quality of life during mealtimes. *Journal for Nurses in Staff Development, 17*(3), 131–136.

Foner, N. (1994). *The caregiving dilemma: Work in an American nursing home.* Los Angeles: University of California Press.

Freedman, V. (1996). Family structure and the risk of nursing home admission. *The Journal of Gerontology: Social Sciences, 51B*, S61–S69.

Frank, J. (1999). I live here, but it's not my home: Residents' experiences in assisted living. In B. Schwarz & R. Brent (Eds.), *Aging, autonomy and architecture advances in assisted living* (pp. 166–182). Baltimore: Johns Hopkins University Press.

Gibson, L. (1998). How safe are your houses? *Professional Builder, 63*(3), 71–74.

Gibson, M. J., Freiman, M., Gregory, S., Kassner, E., Kochera, A., Mullen, F., Pandya, S., Redfoot, D., Straight, A., & Wright, B. (2003). *Beyond 50.03: A report to the nation on independent living and disability.* Washington, DC: AARP.

Golant, S. M. (1992). *Housing America's elderly: Many possibilities/few choices.* Newbury Park, CA: Sage Publications.

Golant, S. M. (1999). The promise of assisted living as shelter and care alternative for frail American elders: A cautionary essay. In B. Schwarz & R. Brent (Eds.), *Aging, autonomy and architecture advances in assisted living* (pp. 32–62). Baltimore: Johns Hopkins University Press.

Golant, S. M., & LaGreca, A. J. (1995). The relative deprivation of U.S. elderly households as judged by their housing problems. *Journal of Gerontology, 50B*, S13–S23.

Guerin, D. A., & Thompson, J. A. (2004). Interior design education in the 21st century: An educational transformation. *Journal of Interior Design, 30*(1), 1–12.

Hamilton, C. (1993). *The use of tape patterns as an alternative method for controlling wanderers' exiting behavior in a dementia care unit.* Unpublished master's thesis, Virginia Polytechnic Institute and State University, Blacksburg.

Hawes, C., Rose, M., & Phillips, C. (1999). *A national study for assisted living for the frail elderly, executive summary: Results of a national survey of facilities.* [Executive Summary and Full Report]. Beachwood, OH: Myers Research Institute

Hignett, S., & Masud, T. (2006). A review of environmental hazards associated with in-patient falls. *Ergonomics, 49*(5–6), 605–616.

Hobbs, F. B. (2001). The elderly population. *U.S. Census Bureau.* Retrieved from http://www.census.gov

Hoglund, D., & Ledewitz, S. (1999). Designing to meet the needs of people with Alzheimer's disease. In B. Schwarz & R. Brent (Eds.), *Aging, autonomy and architecture advances in assisted living* (pp. 229–261). Baltimore: Johns Hopkins University Press.

Hussian, R., & Brown, D. (1987). Use of two-dimensional grid patterns to limit hazardous ambulation in demented patients. *Journal of Gerontology, 47,* 558–560.

Jensen, J., Lundin-Olsson, L., Nyberg, L., & Gustafson, Y. (2002). Falls among frail older people in residential care. *Scandinavian Journal of Public Health, 30* (1), 54–61.

Joseph, A. (2006, August). Health promotion by design in long-term care settings. *The Center for Healthcare Design.* Retrieved from www.healthdesign.org

Kane, R. L. (1994). The American nursing home: An institution for all reasons. In E. J. Hollingsworth & J. R. Hollingsworth (Eds.) *Care of the chronically ill* (pp. 23–46). New York: Walter de Gruyter.

Kane, R. A., Lum, T. Y., Cutler, L. J., Degenholtz, H.B., & Yu, T. (2007). Resident outcomes in small-house nursing homes: A longitudinal evaluation of the initial green house program. *Journal of American Geriatrics Society, 55*(6), 832–839.

Kincaid, C., & Peacock, J. R. (2003). The effect of a wall mural on decreasing four types of door-testing behaviors. *The Journal of Applied Gerontology, 22*(1), 76–88.

Kochera, A. (2002, March). Falls among older persons and the role of home: An analysis of cost, incidence, and potential savings from home modification. Issue Brief *Public Policy Institute American Association of Retired Persons, IB56,* 1–14.

Kochera, A., & Bright, K. (2005–2006, Winter). Livable communities for older people. *Generations, 29*(4), 32–26.

Kochera, A., Straight, A. K., & Guterbock, T. M. (2005) *Beyond 50.05: A report to the nation on livable communities: Creating environments.* Washington DC: AARP.

Kuzbek, B. (2001, Spring). Trends in healthcare design 2001. *Perspective,* 29–31.

Lawton, M. P., & Brody, E. M. (1969). Assessment of older people: Self-maintaining and instrumental activities of daily living. *The Gerontologist, 9*(3), 179–186.

Leibrock, C. (2000). *Design details for health making the most of interior design's healing potential.* New York: John Wiley & Sons.

Lucero, M. (2002). Intervention strategies for exit-seeking wandering behavior in dementia residents. *American Journal of Alzheimer's Disease and Other Dementias, 17*(5), 277–280.

Maddox, G. (1995, July/August). Housing choices for older persons. *Journal of Housing and Community Development,* 15–28.

Malkin, J. (1994). Design technology: The design of healing and prosthetic environments. *Journal of Healthcare Design, 6,* 141–152.

Marsden, J. P. (2005). *Humanistic design of assisted living.* Baltimore: Johns Hopkins University Press.

McFadden, J. R., & Brandt, J. A. (1993). Aging in place: Pre-retirees' view of environmental adaptation in maintaining independence. *Housing and Society, 20*(1), 1–9.

Mooney, P., & Nicell, P. (1992). The importance of exterior environments for Alzheimer's residents: Effective care and risk management. *Healthcare Management Forum, 5,* 377–385.

Moore, J. (2000). Assisted living views market niche options. *Provider, 26*(9), 45–51.

Namazi, K., & Johnson, B. (1992). Pertinent autonomy for residents with dementias: Modification of the physical environment to enhance independence. *American Journal of Alzheimer's Disease and Related Disorders & Research, 7,* 16–21.

Namazi, K., Rosner, T., & Calkins, M. (1989). Visual barriers to prevent Alzheimer's patients from exiting through an emergency door. *The Gerontologist, 29,* 699–702.

National Center for Assisted Living (NCAL). (1998). *Assisted living facility profile.* Washington, DC: AHCA.

National Center for Injury Prevention and Control (CDC). (2004). *Falls among older adults: Summary of research findings.* Retrieved from http://www.cdc.gov

Novelli, W. D. (2004, June). Why America should be concerned about global aging. *AARP Policy & Research.* Retrieved from http://www.aarp.org

PBS. (2008). *Green house nursing homes expand as communities reinvent elder care.* Retrieved from http://www.pbs.org/newshour/bb/health

Perkins, B., Hoglund, J. D., King, D., & Cohen, E. (2004). *Building type basics for senior living.* Hoboken, NJ: John Wiley & Sons.

Pieper, H. G. (1989). *The nursing home primer.* Crozet, VA: Betterway Publications.

Planetree (2007). *Planetree components.* Retrieved from http://www.planetree.org

Pyke, K., & Bengtson, V. (1996). Caring more or less: Individualist and collectivist systems of family eldercare. *The Journal of Marriage and Family, 58,* 379–392.

Pynoos, J., Rose, D., Rubenstein, L., Choi, I. H., & Sabata, D. (2006). Evidence based interventions in fall prevention. *Home Health Care Services Quarterly, 25*(1/2), 55–73.

Rantz, M. J., & Zwygart-Stauffacher, M. (1997). Nursing homes and the chronically ill resident: Policy and issues. In E. A. Swanson & T. Tripp-Reimer (Eds.), *Chronic illness and the older adult* (pp. 179–195). New York: Springer Publishing.

Redfern, M. S., Moore, P. L., & Yarsky, C. M. (1997). The influence of flooring on standing balance among older persons. *Human Factors, 39*(3), 445–455.

Reed, P. S., Zimmerman, S., Sloane, P. D., Williams, C. S., & Boustani, M. (2005). Characteristics associated with low food and fluid intake in long-term care residents with dementia. *The Gerontologist, 45*(1), 74.

Regnier, V. (1999). The definition and evolution of assisted living within a changing system of long-term care. In B. Schwarz & R. Brent (Eds.), *Aging, autonomy and architecture advances in assisted living* (pp. 3–21). Baltimore: Johns Hopkins University Press.

Regnier, V. (2002). *Design for assisted living guidelines for housing the physically and mentally frail.* New York: John Wiley & Sons.

Reinardy, J., & Kane, R. A. (1999). Choosing an adult foster home or a nursing home: Residents' perceptions about decision making and control. *Social Work, 44,* 571–581.

Rhode, J. (1999, September). The impact of design on the older person. *Proceedings of the Symposium on Healthcare Design,* 151–244.

Schwarz, B. (1996). *Nursing home design consequences of employing a medical model.* New York: Garland Publishing.

Schwarz, B. (1999). Assisted living: An evolving place type. In B. Schwarz & R. Brent (Eds.), *Aging, autonomy and architecture advances in assisted living* (pp. 185-207). Baltimore: Johns Hopkins University Press.

Schwarz, B., & Brent, R. (Eds.). (1999). *Aging, autonomy and architecture advances in assisted living.* Baltimore: Johns Hopkins University Press.

Steed, B. (2000, March). Assisted living emerging concepts. *Design An Annual Publication of Nursing Homes Long Term Care Management,* 36–39.

Tinsley, R. K., & Warren, K. E. (1999). Assisted living: The current state of affairs. In B. Schwarz & R. Brent (Eds.), *Aging, autonomy, and architecture advances in assisted living* (pp. 21–32). Baltimore: Johns Hopkins University Press.

Tse, T. (2005). The environment and falls prevention: Do environmental modifications make a difference? *Australian Occupational Therapy Journal, 52,* 271–281.

U.N. Business Council Luncheon. (2003, June). A paradigm shift: From the challenges to the opportunities of aging populations. *AARP Policy & Research.* Retrieved from http://www.aarp.org

U.S. Congress General Accounting Office [U.S. GAO]. (1999). *Assisted living: Quality of care and consumer protection issues in four states.* Report to Congressional Requestors.

U.S. Department of Commerce. (2002, March). *An Aging World 2001.* U.N. Department of Public Information, DP/2264.

Utz, L. R. (2003). Assisted living: The philosophical challenges of everyday practice. *Journal of Applied Gerontology, 22*(3), 379–404.

VanVliet, W. (1992). Housing for the elderly in comparative perspective: The United States and the Netherlands. *Housing and Society, 19*(3), 63–71.

Wacker, R. R., Roberto, K. A., & Piper, L. E. (1998). *Community resources for older adults: Programs and services in an era of change.* Thousand Oaks, CA: Pine Forge Press.

Wells, N. M., & Evans, G. W. (1996). Home injuries of people over the age of 65: Risk perceptions of the elderly and of those who design for them. *Journal of Environmental Psychology, 16,* 247–257.

Wells, N. M., & Evans, G. W. (2001). *Home safety guidelines for older adults.* Retrieved from http://www.human.cornell.edu/extension

Wilson, N. L. (1995). Long-term care in the United States: An overview of the current system. In L. B. McCullough & N. L. Wilson (Eds.), *Long-term care decisions ethical and conceptual dimensions* (pp. 35–59). Baltimore: Johns Hopkins University Press.

Wood, M. (1995, September). Seniors housing, the unconventional real estate investment. *Real Estate Forum, 73.*

Yardley, L., & Smith, H. (2002). Prospective study of the relationship between feared consequences of falling and avoidance of activity in community-living older people. *The Gerontologist, 42* (1), 17–23.

Zavotka, S. O., & Teaford, M. H. (1997). The design of shared social spaces in assisted living residences for older adults. *Journal of Interior Design, 23*(2), 2–16.

9 The Design of Hotels:
Students as Conductors of Research

Lori A. Anthony

Abstract

The first part of this chapter provides a synopsis of the evolution of the hotel, discusses the various classifications typically allocated to hotel type, and examines the various needs of the hotel client. The chapter also stresses that most design decision making in the hotel industry is based on market research rather than human behavior research. In the second part of the chapter, three examples of undergraduate student work are presented. In the first example, the student conducted a small empirical study with practitioners to determine what age-related changes should be incorporated in hotel design. Sustainable rating systems were content analyzed to develop a list of design criteria for a boutique hotel in the second example. The third example illustrates how a student conducted an empirical study to inform her design project. Although the findings were used for a specific project, the study could help advance the field if disseminated.

Introduction

Tourism is the nation's largest service industry, with approximately 2.8 million hotel rooms sold daily in the United States. However, with national concerns of terrorism, war, and a lagging economy at the forefront of American decision making, domestic and international travel have experienced adverse affects following the events of September 11, 2001 (http://www.tia.org). During 2005 and 2006, domestic leisure travel noted an upturn and despite negative 2008 economic projections, industry trends suggest that travel will continue to increase but at a slower pace than in previous years (Beck, J.A., 2006; http://www.tia.org).

Revenues in the hospitality industry have not returned to levels enjoyed in the early 1990s, but steady increases have been noted since 2001, which in turn, have sparked renewed interest from the architecture and design professions. These increases are evidenced by an analysis conducted in 2006 by *Interior Design* magazine, in which reported annual revenue figures revealed an increasing number of design firms specializing in hospitality design. The number of leading hospitality design firms listed by this publication increased from 65 firms in 2005 to 75 firms specializing in this area in 2006 (Davidsen, Girmscheid, & Lee, 2006). Indicating an increase in annual earnings of more than 33 percent, these firms reported that hotels (including luxury) were the most profitable (Davidsen et al., 2006).

This chapter focuses on informed design decision making for the hospitality industry, namely in hotel design. Several models formulating hotel design are presented, and the use of information and research is illustrated through several examples of student work completed at the undergraduate level.

Evolution of the Hospitality Industry

The hospitality design industry has grown with the evolution of the hotel. Historically, the first inns that dated as far back as before the 1000s are vastly different from the hotels seen today (Rutes, Penner, & Adams, 2001). The Hoshi Ryokan in Komatsu, Japan, opened in 718

and is recorded as the oldest inn still in operation today (http://www
.hoshi.co.jp/jiten/Houshi_E/home.htm). The earliest European inn is
the Three King Inn in Basle, Switzerland. Established in 1026, this inn
is currently the oldest government-rated five-star hotel in Europe (Rutes
et al., 2001). From the 1660s to the early 1800s, the number of inns increased, in large part because of the European grand tour, a time when
young European men traveled after schooling and before inheriting the
family wealth. These tours could last anywhere from one month to several years and were a rite of passage for these young men into aristocratic
society (McDonough, Hill, Glazier, Lindsay & Sykes, 2001).

Originating from a French word denoting *mansion*, the term *hotel*
was adopted by Americans to describe the multifaceted inns that began to appear in the states after the American Revolution, and in the
1790s, the first downtown hotels (the City Hotel and the Corre's Hotel) opened in New York (Rutes et al., 2001). During the mid- to late
1800s, stagecoach travel increased as travelers headed west in search of
jobs and gold. As coach travel eventually gave way to the railroads, inns
and hotels became popular along the travel routes. Sometimes referred
to as the golden age of hotels, the 1920s brought the opening of well-
known hotels such as the St. Regis and the Plaza Hotel in New York
(McDonough et al., 2001).

Four notable surges in the hotel industry can be noted from 1920
to today. The first was in the 1920s, when economic prosperity marked
the introduction of prominent hotels such as the Flamingo in Miami
Beach, the Ritz-Carlton in Boston, the Stevens Hotel in Chicago, and
the Cloister in Georgia (Rutes et al., 2001). In the 1950s, the second
boom to the hotel industry was due largely to expanded education and
mass transit (Rutes et al., 2001). These conditions brought casino hotels
to Las Vegas, Nevada, and resort hotels to the Caribbean. The third
noteworthy time in the evolution of the hotel was in the 1980s, when
marketing and innovation brought large-scale commercial complexes
such as the Marriott Marquis in Atlanta and the Hyatt and Marriott

mega-hotels in Orlando, Florida (Rutes et al., 2001). The late 1990s marked the fourth resurgence in the hotel industry, largely due to advanced technology and successful mass marketing (Rutes et al., 2001). It was during this time that spa resorts and boutique hotels were marketed to baby boomers as essential to their health and well-being.

As the timeline of the hotel industry continues to expand, new types of hotels will emerge and older hotels will continue to redefine themselves. Categorizing hotels into classifications may become very complex and ambiguous over the next few decades.

Hotel Classifications

Once regarded as a dwelling intended only to provide temporary housing with basic food and shelter for a traveler, hotels were forced by competition to establish an identity enabling them to distinguish themselves in terms of service and amenities. This led to many different types of hotels—many of which are now seen as extravagant destinations, suggesting enhanced experiences and unique amenities. This evolution of the hotel has led to a highly specialized industry, and today, *hospitality design* is an overarching term used interchangeably when describing hotels and dining and drinking facilities (Piotrowski & Rogers, 1999).

Hotel types are numerous and ever-changing. In the past 20 years, hotels have shifted from merely describing their function to highlighting and promoting interiors and architecture (Curtis, 2001). Typically, hotels are classified by their geographic location, specific function, and special characteristics. It is important to note, however, that many hotels cannot be neatly categorized or labeled as one type—often they have characteristics of several hotel types (Rutes et al., 2001). Categorizing hotel types is important for research and marketing, and three broad categories have been established for most hotel types of today: (1) hotel, (2) interrelated, and (3) resort (Rutes et al., 2001).

Table 9.1. Hotel Categories and Examples of Types within each Category

Hotel	Interrelated	Resort
Airport Hotel	Condo	Mega-Hotel
Convention Hotel	Bed and Breakfast	Resort Theme Park
Boutique Hotel	All Villa Resort Community	Casino Resort
Adaptive Reuse	Vacation Ownership	Ecotourist Resort
Extended Stay	Residential Hotel	
Downtown Hotel		

Adapted from Rutes, Penner & Adams, 2001.

The *hotel* category encompasses a variety of subtypes and includes hotels that do not fall into either of the other two categories. *Interrelated hotels* serve a residential need; they often provide additional rooms beyond the standard bedroom and bathroom, such as kitchens, dining, and living rooms. These types of hotels offer limited food service but normally provide customers with fully equipped kitchens for food preparation in the rooms or suites. Interrelated hotels market to those travelers who are seeking a "home away from home," while *resort* hotels are designed to provide the traveler with an *experience*. These types of hotels can be large in scale, may be thematic, and offer opportunities for customers to be transformed to another place or time. Table 9.1 lists several well-known hotel types and groups them into these three main categories.

Client Needs

Similar to restaurant and retail design, hotel designs are as unique and varied as the customer each hopes to serve. The challenge is to define the customer first and then provide the product (in this case hotel environment) that best satisfies the needs and expectations of the patron. Categorizing consumer needs and preferences can be difficult in that often a hotel serves as a temporary home, taking a very personal role in the guest's expectations.

To foster clarity in classifying the needs of a hotel client, Daniela Freund de Klumbis, hospitality professor and lecturer at Sant Ignasi-Sarria in Barcelona, established three tiers of assessment for hotel selection (2004): (1) basic amenities; (2) elevated amenities; and (3) reward, identity, and refreshment. These classifications of client needs are integrated in varying degrees into the hotel types discussed in the previous section. For example, clients seeking elevated amenities may find them in a downtown hotel (hotel category), a condo (interrelated category), or an ecotourist resort (resort category). By first identifying the target client, hotels can focus on how to best satisfy client needs. Hotels that address basic amenities are typically chain hotels with standardized rooms and restaurants that appeal to the business traveler. Hotels that offer elevated amenities are ones in which the level of service is elevated; rooms may provide connectivity to the Internet, in-room refreshments, refined bedding, a gym, a pool, and an upscale restaurant. The last tier—reward, identity, and refreshment—encompasses a growing trend in hotels: the boutique, five-star deluxe, design, and lifestyle hotels. Appealing to a unique demographic that is well-educated, well-informed, environmentally conscious, and seeking downtime and reward, these hotels provide opportunities for patrons to experience luxury, service, and experiences unlike those found in a typical hotel environment. Trading palatial lobbies for intimate cafes, and tapas bars for highly rated restaurants, clients seek a connection to the local culture and community as they strive for a physical and spiritual life balance (Freund de Klumbis, 2004).

Models of Hospitality

Hotel providers seek to establish identities customers can remember, and they rely on market research to provide answers and give direction. Today's hotel customer shows a lack of brand loyalty (Freund de Klumbis, 2004). With each travel experience offering a multitude of choices, consumers seek to match their lifestyles with their choice of hotels. Each trip provides a new opportunity to make decisions based on experiential expectations. During the 1990s, hotels attracted patrons based on design, but in the twenty-first century, design appears to have taken a backseat to the expectations of the knowledge-based customer (Freund de Klumbis, 2004). For hotel providers to have a competitive advantage, they need to continually assess and transform themselves to provide the unique and memorable experience expected by today's travelers (Olsen & Connolly, 2000).

Experiential Model

A memorable and positive experience will encourage repeat business and therefore lead to a profitable and successful property. In an ever-increasing competitive environment, hotel owners seek to control customer loyalty through innovation, change, and experience (Pullman & Gross, 2004). The design of a hotel must incorporate these ideals, and it is important for designers, architects, and particularly hotel owners to understand the role of *experience* in consumer decision making.

The experiential model works from the premise that environments can create emotional connections with consumers, thereby eliciting a positive response and a desire to return and frequent a facility (Diller, Shedroff, & Rhea, 2006). Drawing from a multitude of disciplines including environmental design, psychology, and ethnography, experience design influences products, environments, and services that address the human experience (Diller et al., 2006). This design model considers the consumers' knowledge, beliefs, desires, and experiences as a basis for identifying design criteria. Several hotel types utilize the experiential model in attracting customers. These include the downtown, resort, super-luxury, mega, adaptive reuse, mixed use, and casino types. Note that these hotel types span the three categories (hotel, interrelated, and resort) previously mentioned, as they all strive to provide a unique experience that the client will remember.

This concept or model is best illustrated by the themed casino megahotels in Las Vegas, Nevada. These hotels transform the customer to another time, place, or socioeconomic status. Customers seek refuge, escape, and wonderment in these elaborate and extravagant environments. Capitalizing on these experiences has differentiated these hotels from one another and provided opportunities that focus on customer experiences (Schmitt, 1997).

Residential Model

Contrary to the escapist objectives of the experiential model, the residential model of hotel design aims to address the humanist needs of the customer. Typically targeting the business traveler, hotel designs centered on the residential model include creature comforts and amenities that are familiar to the customer and elicit internal feelings of comfort and security. Extended-stay facilities, vacation ownership, and bed-and-breakfast accommodations are designed around the residential model and incorporate design elements such as fireplaces, equipped kitchens, living rooms, and porches associated with the single-family house that dominates American housing.

Market Research and Design Research

Regardless of tier or category, hotels strive for the perfect balance between hard components (physical elements) and soft components (ambience) (Freund de Klumbis, 2004). Guests interact with their environment so personally and individually that finding this sense of symmetry can provide challenges. Incorrect decisions in any category can affect the balance and ultimately a guest's experience. Understanding the intricacies of soft and hard components warrants further study.

Design professionals tend to rely on market research rather than on human behavior research to drive the practical design decisions of hard and soft elements in hotel design. Beginning with site selection and influencing furniture, finishes, and the overall appearance of a hotel, market research gathers information that leads to forecasting, economic models, and strategic planning for the hospitality industry (http://www.pwc.com). Primarily relying on focus groups and surveys, with a concentration on service and customer satisfaction, marketing firms specialize in this data collection. Customer satisfaction and repeat business are the benchmarks of a successful hotel business, and hotel owners use the market reports to make decisions on site, type, and brand, thereby directing architects, interior designers, and developers to incorporate this information in their designs.

Limited human behavior research related to the design of hotels exists in the interior design, hospitality, or hotel management fields. Design decisions are based on market research, themes, demographics, industry standards, and branding, and yet rarely are research findings applied to the design process—mainly because they are difficult to find. In fact, designers in the field admit that their information primarily comes from the market. According to Rutes, Penner, and Adams (2001), "while supported by socioeconomic research, as in all growing industries, the hotel industry thrives on the market research of prevailing trends to shape future development" (p. 1).

Some empirical studies have been conducted to try to refine and understand market research. Once such study published in 2005 by Ugar Yavas and Emin Babkus, both professors of marketing, identified and rated important hotel attributes by distributing 342 questionnaires to residents of a metro area in the Southeast United States (2005). Respondents were to rate the importance of 28 attributes using a seven-point scale (Yavas & Babakus, 2005). Among those found to be most important were as follows: bathroom cleanliness, all amenities in good working condition, security and safety, bedroom comfort, courteousness of personnel, quietness of heating and air conditioning, and location. Those attributes deemed less important included dry cleaning services, meeting facilities, and computer and Internet connectivity (Yavas & Babakus, 2005).

With so little empirical data available in disciplines other than marketing, opportunities exist to explore this growing industry and apply the findings to viable design projects. Research and application seem to be overlooked in the hotel industry. Yet because hotels temporarily house patrons, they therefore affect the patrons' well-being. The risk of operating without a standardized body of knowledge is that critical decisions regarding the health, safety, and welfare may fall to those less qualified than an interior design professional.

For example, among the various health concerns affected by the design profession, one of the most prevalent in hotel environments is air quality. The origins of poor indoor air quality are easily identified as mold (found on shower curtains and tile), volatile organic compounds (VOCs) (found in carpet off-gassing and paint), radon, dust reservoirs, carbon monoxide, polybrominated diphenylethers (PBDEs), tobacco smoke, and formaldehyde (Laliberte, 2005; Chao, 2000).

While minor irritants can be problematic, poor hotel air quality proved fatal when, in 1976, approximately 200 American Legion convention attendees contracted a strain of bacterial pneumonia at the Bellevue-Stratford Hotel in Philadelphia. Often linked to cooling towers and evaporative condensers of large air-conditioning systems, cases of this pneumonia (now named Legionnaire's disease) have been reported worldwide (NIEHS, 1997).

To illustrate further, when housing a large number of patrons, hotel owners have the responsibility of providing a safe environment, and design is critical to ensuring the protection of a hotel patron. Notably, in 1980, the MGM Grand Hotel and Casino in Las Vegas, Nevada, experienced the second deadliest hotel fire in the United States (Clark County Department of Development Services, Building Division, 2005). Interior finishes not commercially rated or intended for public use exacerbated the fire, resulting in 87 fatalities and injuries to 785 people (Alin, 2007).

Empirical research in the areas of health, safety, welfare, aesthetics, trends, patron preferences, and design methodologies equips designers with knowledge that ultimately leads to informed design. This knowledge base is enhanced when students, faculty, and practitioners contribute to, use, and/or conduct research in the hotel field. Application of the findings enriches design, provides a safe and healthy environment, and ultimately provides a foundation for marketing and management decisions.

Informed Design Examples

The following section of this chapter details the use of research and its application to self-designed projects assigned for a capstone undergraduate senior studio project. Timely topics including green design, aging, and design trends were investigated in the following projects in relation to hotel design.

Hotel Design: Understanding the Aging Population
(Author/Designer: Cheryl McLaughlin)

With the aging of the baby boom generation, more and more hotels will be serving an older guest population. This study examined the perceived need to address the design of hotels to accommodate the older traveler. The design project for this study incorporated elements identified in the research findings into the creation of a boutique hotel.

Purpose

The purpose of this study was to investigate whether interior designers are considering the needs of an aging population in designing hotel environments.

Background

In 1946, a baby boom began as World War II veterans returned to their home and lives. This boom continued for nearly 20 years until 1964, with 76 million Americans born during this time (an average of approximately 4 million babies per year) (Baucom, 1996). At the time of this design project, baby boomers ranged in age from 43 to 61 and represented one-third of the overall population (Baucom, 1996). These adults have disposable income and a great impact on the tourism and hospitality industry. As this group ages, they will begin to feel the effects of limited mobility, changes in visual acuity, and impaired hearing. The baby boomers are a very influential group, and as they age, they will have a significant role in transforming culture's view on aging.

Method

This student researcher determined that the best method for integrating research into the design process was to distribute an e-mail questionnaire with open-ended questions to interior designers specializing in hotel design. Internet searches using key words such as *hospitality design firms* and *hotel design firms* identified potential candidates. Additionally, *Interior Design* magazine's list of Top Hospitality Giants from 2003 was used to compile a list of 25 firms specializing in hotel design. Because of time constraints, only the first 25 firms from the list of 50 were used for this study. These firms were located throughout the United States, with a majority of them located in large metropolitan areas. Of the 25 firms, eight designers agreed to participate.

An e-mail questionnaire was developed to assess the designers' positions on designing for an aging population in relation to hotel design, as well as their influence over design decisions pertaining to universal design.

Findings

Although such a small number of designers responded to the survey, some overarching conclusions can be drawn from the results. Of those designers who responded, a majority (five of the eight), were not creating specific design solutions for the aging population beyond those required by the Americans with Disabilities Act (ADA). The three who reported that they are designing purposely for the aging group included addressing vision, hearing, mobility, accessibility, and safety needs in their client proposals. These designers identified five key factors that should be incorporated into the design: color, light, accessibility, weight, and security. Visual issues related to aging should be addressed by employing color contrasts that provide clarity for the aging eye. Careful planning of light fixtures can control visual concerns such as glare. Keeping walkways open and clear makes circulation around furniture and fixtures accessible, and items that might require movement should be light in weight or on casters. The older population is more vulnerable to crime, and providing security measures within a hotel environment will provide the older guest with a sense of security.

It was clear from the responses that some designers and hotel chains are making design decisions for a growing older population. Marketing to this group of potential clients includes programs offering seniors discounts and rewards based on frequency of use. "When the pendulum swings from marketing to implementation, as the facility usage by this population increases, it is reasonable to expect the client/owners will begin to drive execution of design considerations beyond those required by the ADA" (McLaughlin, 2004, p. 20).

Project Overview

Based on the findings from the research project, the designer strived to incorporate the five key elements of color, accessibility, light, security, and weight into the design of a boutique hotel located in the Cultural District of Pittsburgh, Pennsylvania. The building for this project was an existing office building currently used by multiple tenants. The building was selected because of its location, architectural features, and footprint.

Application of Research Findings

The design solution focused extensively on the first floor and the guest rooms with the intent of incorporating the five key factors identified during the interviews with designers into the design of the space plan, and furniture and finish selections.

Color.   Figure 9.1 shows the first and second floor plans of the boutique hotel. The designer used color as a wayfinding tool by varying hues, values, and floor patterns in the public spaces. This helps orient the user and provides definable contrast between the different spaces on the floor. Differentiating between hue, value, and pattern, the designer successfully distinguishes the delineation of various spaces and areas.

Accessibility.   All public aisles in this boutique hotel were larger than those required by ADA, providing open and accessible circulation between furniture groupings. Guest rooms included attractive grab bars in tubs, shower stalls, and toilet areas. Large roll-in showers and generous clearances between furniture and fixtures provided ease of movement

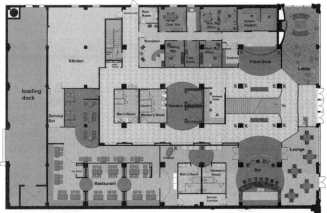

First Floor Plan

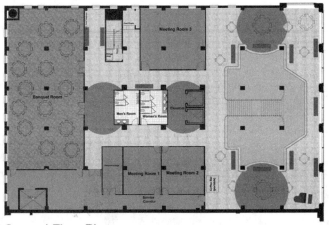

Second Floor Plan

Figure 9.1. First- and second-floor plans,
from final design project by C. McLaughlin, 2004.

for guests in the private rooms. The designer addressed the needs of an aging client who may need the assistance of a walker, cane, or wheelchair by keeping the transitions between soft and hard flooring surfaces in public and private spaces in compliance with ADA requirements. In addition, varying the hues and values of different floor material distinguished various areas within the guest rooms (Figure 9.2).

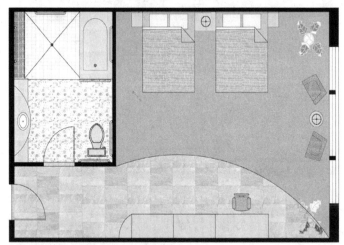

Queen Guestroom Floor Plan (N.T.S.)

King Guestroom Floor Plan (N.T.S.)

Figure 9.2. Guest rooms, from final design project by C. McLaughlin, 2004.

As strength and dexterity diminish with age, gripping a doorknob can be problematic for an aging adult. In the design of this boutique hotel, all door handles were levers instead of knobs.

Light. Windows with translucent shades to overcome glare line the front of the building, allowing natural light to filter into the lobby and public spaces. The designer selected indirect hanging pendant light fixtures and overall general fluorescent lighting to assist in visual acuity. In the guest rooms, the designer took advantage of large picture windows in each room for natural day lighting (Figure 9.3). In addition, task lighting over bedside tables and in the restrooms addressed the visual needs of an aging client.

Security. Signage, secure lockable door fixtures, and eyeholes in the doors of the guest rooms demonstrate that the designer incorporated design elements for guest security (Figure 9.3).

Weight. All of the furniture that required movement by guests was on casters. Dining chairs in the restaurant as well as desk chairs in the guest rooms were mobile and easy to roll, thereby making the furniture more adaptable and usable for the hotel guest.

Project Summary

In conclusion, the design of this boutique hotel addressed the needs of an aging population. Although many of the design elements incorporated into the project were directly related to requirements of ADA, this project went beyond merely satisfying the law by demonstrating a sensitivity to spatial relationships, awareness of security, application of color to define areas and elements within the design, and utilization of natural light to assist the aging eye. Because of the empirical research findings conducted prior to this project, the design solution addresses user needs, provides an inviting atmosphere, and satisfies the designer's project goals.

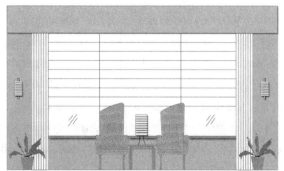

Queen Guestroom South Elevation (N.T.S.)

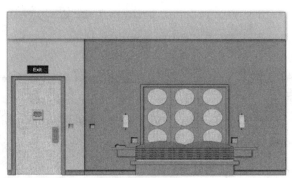

King Guest Room North Elevation (N.T.S.)

Figure 9.3. Guest room elevation, from final design project by C. McLaughlin, 2004.

Green Rating Systems for the Hotel Industry
(Author/Designer: Terri Hill)

This student's study focused was on indoor air quality. Sustainable rating systems developed by five different organizations were compared and contrasted based on their inclusion or exclusion of indoor air quality standards. Derived from the findings, a list of design criteria compiled by the designer was incorporated into the design of a boutique hotel.

Purpose

This research compared and contrasted the various rating systems commonly used in the hotel industry with a focus on indoor air quality.

Background

There are documented cases of hotel guests becoming seriously ill or dying from poor indoor air quality. The physical environment directly affects the health of hotel guests, and selections of paint, carpet, fabric, and furniture can directly affect indoor air quality.

Organizations have been established to set standards for creating and maintaining greener, healthier environments. One such voluntary organization is the United States Green Building Council (USGBC). This group developed a national standard rating system with the intent of reducing the impact of building on the environment (USGBC, 2005). Its rating system, Leadership in Energy and Environmental Design (LEED), is used on commercial buildings.

Rating systems created specifically for the hotel industry are Green Globe 21, The Hotel Association of Canada's Green Leaf Eco Rating Program, ECOTEL, and Green Hotels Association

Green Globe 21 is a "green" association whose rating system "is the worldwide benchmarking and certification program that facilitates sustainable travel and tourism for consumers, companies and communities" (Green Globe 21, 2005; Hill, 2005, p. 8).

The Green Leaf Eco-Rating Program was started by Terra Choice Environmental Services (TerraChoice, 2005). Hotels wanting to participate in this environmental rating system are awarded "Green Leafs" if they meet the criterion that is set by Terra Choice (TerraChoice), (Hill, 2005).

ECOTEL certification promotes environmentally friendly hotels. The certification utilizes a rating system that is based on five areas of inspection: "environment commitment, solid waste management, energy efficiency, water conservation, and employee environmental education and community involvement" (ECOTEL, 2005).

Green Hotels Association is an environmental organization that disseminates information to the hotel industry. Although it is not based on a certification system, Green Hotels Association encourages, promotes, and supports the "greening" of the lodging industry through educating its members (Green Hotels, 2005).

Method

During the preliminary stages of this research, it was determined that five rating systems would be analyzed. Four of the systems were selected because they were directly used by the hotel industry: Green Globe 21, The Hotel Association of Canada's Green Leaf Eco Rating Program, ECOTEL, and Green Hotels Association The fifth system, LEED, was included because it was an industry standard within the commercial building community.

Each rating system was analyzed based on information gathered from each organization. A chart was devised to compare and contrast the criteria of each rating system as they pertained to indoor air quality. The chart was sectioned into three categories, and the designer classified information from documentation on each rating system into the following categories:

- HVAC systems
- Low-emitting materials
- Indoor chemical and pollutant control

The completed chart was then analyzed to determine which rating system had the most comprehensive indoor air quality standards per category.

Findings

Designing a green hotel requires a tool that is recognized within the environmental community. While all of the five systems analyzed were respected instruments, each one addressed indoor air quality differently. The following summarizes the findings:

- ECOTEL (a widely recognized rating system for hotels) is dedicated to environmental stewardship but does not include a specific category emphasizing on indoor air quality.
- Green Globe 21's system includes a section devoted to CO_2 emissions but lacks a clear stand on indoor air quality.
- The Hotel Association of Canada's Green Leaf Eco Rating Program provided limited factual data on indoor air quality, making it difficult to make an accurate comparison for this research project.
- Green Hotels Association's methodology toward providing better indoor air quality was respectable with regard to this research project. It was an approach that addressed many of the requirements set forth in this study.
- Leadership in Energy and Environmental Design (LEED) has systematically developed a detailed rating system. According to this research project, it exceeded the other systems in addressing indoor air quality standards (Hill, 2005, pp. 25–26).

Many of the recommendations concerning indoor air quality found in the rating systems were non-design-related. Those that could be influenced by an interior designer included the following:

From the LEED standards:

- Select low-emitting materials to reduce VOCs and toxins for the following:
  - Adhesives/sealants
  - Paints and coatings
  - Carpet
  - Composite wood/laminate adhesives
  - Furniture and furnishings

From the Green Hotels Association:

- Install ceiling fans promoting airflow
- Include live potted plants in the design to keep air healthier

Project Overview

This student's design project incorporated the knowledge gained from the research of green rating systems used by the hotel industry to create a space that provided good indoor air quality. A number of components were included in the design of this boutique hotel. The building selected was a vacant bank built in the 1800s in East Liberty, Pennsylvania.

The research found that both LEED's rating system and the Green Hotels Association's rating system addressed a number of components regarding indoor air quality.

Application of Research Findings

A design specification notebook accompanied this design project. Details regarding the sustainable nature—particularly pertaining to indoor air quality—of the furniture, finishes, and materials selected for this project were recorded. These finishes and materials were recycled, emitted low to no VOCs, and contributed to a higher level of indoor air quality.

Figure 9.4. Hotel lobby, from final design project by T. Hill, 2005.

Other design elements incorporated into the design of this hotel were operable windows and ceiling fans to promote air circulation, and the inclusion of potted plants in public spaces to assist in the removal of toxins from air in the indoor environment (Figure 9.4).

Furniture Trends in Destination Hotel Lobbies
(Author/Designer: Emily Lisek)

The aesthetics of a hotel play an important role in branding, marketing, and customer satisfaction. Although many design elements contribute to the success of a hotel, furniture plays a critical role in a guest's first impression. This research study investigated the style of furniture used in the lobbies of top destination hotels. The findings from this research were then incorporated into the design of a destination boutique hotel.

Purpose

Although subtle, the appearance of a hotel lobby is critical in communicating image, vision, and service. Often the use and selection of furniture play a key role in contributing to the ambience and style of a hotel lobby. Is there a tendency among leading hotels to rely on traditional furniture styles over contemporary ones? This research study examined the use of furniture styles and details and systematically compared the interiors of destination hotel lobbies.

Background

As is found in experiential theory, first impressions are most important when deciding to stay at a hotel. Often they lead to memorable experiences and return stays—especially at a destination hotel. A destination hotel is one in which the hotel itself is as much the vacation destination as the hotel location. Often rated as four or five star, these hotels are known for their level of service, amenities, and luxuriously and refined interiors.

"Furniture is intrinsic to the way a hotel guest will experience the lobby—walking around it, sitting in it, touching it, and having it within one's personal space" (Lisek, 2005, p. 27).

Method

Photographs of the lobbies from the top ten destination hotels as rated by *Travel and Leisure* magazine's World's Best Hotels for 2005 were used for this study. These lobby photographs were collected from *Travel and Leisure* magazine, on the *Travel and Leisure* Web site, or on the hotels' Web sites and were used to analyze trends in the design of the interior space. Two images from each hotel lobby were examined for similarities and differences in furniture details (i.e., fabrics, finishes, and decorative elements), historical references, and thematic or demographic links. Information was recorded on a chart devised to categorically analyze the variables (Table 9.2).

Findings

In analyzing the photographs, the designer determined that there was a dominant preference for traditional styles. The findings suggested a trend toward traditional styles with a mixture of reproductions and pieces that utilized a combination of various stylistic elements. The student concluded that perhaps patrons preferred the familiarity that traditional styles afforded or that they appealed to a broad range of guests. Hotel management may have decided to utilize traditional pieces because they are timeless and do not tend to go out of style. Regardless of the current design trends, top destination hotels used traditional furniture pieces in their lobbies.

Project Overview

This project utilized an existing bank building in downtown Pittsburgh. The building was erected in 1906 and is currently on the Register of Historic Places. This 21-story structure has traditional architectural elements that complemented the objectives of this boutique hotel.

Application of Research Findings

While applying the research findings to this project was not difficult, the designer's decision to forego the impulse to design a hip, contemporary hotel lobby now popular in boutique hotels was justified by the completed research. Furniture pieces selected were adaptations of traditional styles (Figure 9.5). This complemented not only the architectural style of the building but the many original elements of the interior.

Table 9.2. Furniture Analysis Chart

| Hotel | Location | Date Built, Renovated | Design Style | | | | | | | Theme |
			Furniture Piece	Structural Material	Fabric	Stain/ Color	Feet	Arms	
Rusty Parrot Lodge & Spa	Jackson Hole, WY		Seating						
			Tables						
			Accents						
Blackberry Farm	Walland, TX		Seating						
			Tables						
			Accents						
The Point	Saranac Lake, NY		Seating						
			Tables						
			Accents						
The Peninsula	Beverly Hills, CA		Seating						
			Tables						
			Accents						
Post Ranch Inn	Big Sur, CA		Seating						
			Tables						
			Accents						
Tu Tu'Tun Lodge	Gold Beach, OR		Seating						
			Tables						
			Accents						
Marquesa Hotel	Key West, FL		Seating						
			Tables						
			Accents						
Monmouth Plantation	Natchez, MS		Seating						
			Tables						
			Accents						
Windsor Court Hotel	New Orleans, LA		Seating						
			Tables						
			Accents						
The Peninsula	Chicago, IL		Seating						
			Tables						
			Accents						

Note: This table is for explanation only. It illustrates the type of information researched regarding the furniture styles.

Figure 9.5. Hotel lobby, from final design project by E. Becker, 2004.

Summary

Hotel design continues to rely heavily on market research to influence design decisions. Tight deadlines and limited budgets seem to be the major deterrent in enabling interior designers the opportunity to conduct and employ empirical research in this specialty area. While limited studies have contributed to what is known about hotel design, additional research in the areas of trends, behavior, aging, and environmental conditions will not only assist the designer in making educated decisions but will ultimately benefit the hotel guest by improving the quality of his or her environment and contributing to the overall experience.

BIBLIOGRAPHY

Alin, M.C. (2007, March 29). A profession of substance. *The Washington Post*, p. A18.

Baucom, Alfred H. (1996). *Hospitality Design for the Graying Generation.* New York: John Wiley & Sons.

Beck, J. A. (2006). The importance of sales manager's activities and time allocation toward job success in lodging properties. *Journal of Human Resources in Hospitality and Tourism, 5*(2), 1–1.2

Chao, C. (2000, April). *Indoor Air Quality Issues for Hotels.* Presentation at the Hotel Ezra Conference, Cornell University, Ithaca, NY.

Clark County Department of Development Services, Building Division. (2005). *Large building fires and subsequent code changes.* Las Vegas, NV: Jim Arnold, Associate Engineer.

Curtis, E. (2001). *Hotel: Interior structures.* West Sussex, England: John Wiley & Sons.

Davidsen, J., Girmscheid, L., & Lee, C. (2006, October 1). Suite success: Hotel work leads a surge in business at 75 top firms. *Interior Design,* 216.

Department of Justice. (1994). *Nondiscrimination on the basis of disability by public accommodations and in commercial facilities* (28 CFR Part 36). Washington, DC: U.S. Government Printing Office.

Diller, S., Shedroff, N., & Rhea, D. (2006). *Making meaning: How successful businesses deliver meaningful customer experiences.* Berkeley, CA: New Riders.

ECOTEL. (n.d.) Retrieved from http://www.http://ecotel.com

Freund de Klumbis, D. (2004, June). *Seeing the ultimate hotel experience.* Lecture presented at the Workshop with Piero Lissoini – Hotel Design 2004, Milano, Italy.

Green Hotels. (n.d.) Retrieved from http://greenhotels.com

Green Globe 21. (n.d.) Retrieved September 25, 2005, from http://www.greenglobe21.com

Hill, T. (2005). *Green rating systems for the hotel industry.* [Bachelor's thesis]. Pittsburgh, PA: La Roche College, Interior Design Department.

Houshi Inn. (n.d.) Retrieved from http://www.ho-shi.co.jp/jiten/Houshi_E/home.htm

Laliberte, R. (2005, September). How to Clear the Air: 30 ways to breathe easier at home. *Organic Style.* pp. 104–109, 127.

Lisek, E. (2005). *Furniture trends in destination hotel lobbies.* [Bachelor's thesis]. Pittsburgh, PA: La Roche College, Interior Design Department.

McDonough, B., Hill, J., Glazier, R., Lindsay, W.B., & Sykes, T. (2001). *Building Type Basics for Hospitality Facilities*. New York: John Wiley & Sons.

McLaughlin, C. (2004). *Hotel design: Understanding the aging population*. [Bachelors thesis]. Pittsburgh, PA: La Roche College, Interior Design Department.

National Institute of Environmental Health Sciences (1997, January). Legionnaire's disease. Retrieved from http://www.niehs.nih.gov/external/faq/legion.htm

Olsen, M. D. & Connolly, D. J. (2000). Experience-based travel. *Cornell Hotel and Restaurant Administration Quarterly, 41*, 30–40.

Piotrowski, C. M., & Rogers, E. A. (1999). *Designing commercial interiors*. New York: John Wiley & Sons.

Pullman, M. E., & Gross, M. A. (2004). Ability of experience design elements to elicit emotions and loyalty behaviors. *Decision Sciences, 35*, 551.

Rutes, W. A., Penner, R. H., & Adams, L. (2001). *Hotel design planning and development*. New York: W. W. Norton.

Schmitt, B. (1997, September). *Visual Identity in the International Luxury Hotel Industry*. Report presented to the Center for Hospitality Research School of Hotel Administration, Cornell University, Ithaca, NY.

TerraChoice. (n. d.) *Green Leaf Eco-Rating Program*. Retrieved from http://www.terrachoice.ca/hotelwebsite/main.htm

USGBC. (n. d.). Retrieved September 25, 2005, from http://www.usgbc.org

Yavas, U., Babakus, E., (2005). Competing for guests: An application of extended quandrant analysis. *Journal of Hospitality and Leisure Marketing, 12*(3), 29–44

10 The Design of Hospitals and Neonatal Intensive Care Units: Students and Practitioners as Conductors of Research

Debra D. Harris

Abstract

This chapter is dedicated to the exploration of hospitals and evidence-based design. General background information is provided about hospital construction and design and about models and the concept of evidence-based medicine and design. The examples of informed design discuss real-world research and how it is used in practice. The chapter then goes on to show how research in the classroom investigates a research question and reaches conclusions that inform design and contribute to the quality of education in interior design.

Introduction

Hospital construction is a growing $17 billion industry that increased 15 percent from 2005 to 2006 (Haughey, 2006) and is projected to increase to $30 billion by 2010 (Medical Construction & Design, 2007). Projected demographics suggest that there will be a continuing demand for hospital construction long into the future. Owing to changes in technology, the hospital industry is in a construction boom attempting to support changes in patient intake, diagnosis, procedures, and recovery. In 2003, Turner Construction surveyed 219 healthcare executives; 89 percent of those who were at institutions with capital budgets of $5 million or more stated that they were planning to undertake a major capital program within the next three years (Turner, 2004). For the first time in 30 years, there is an increase in the number of general acute-care beds in the United States. The growing population and the need for new and enhanced hospital buildings have created a growth trend that is likely to continue for years to come (Turner, 2004).

Reasons cited for the boom in hospital construction include the following:

- Building obsolescence
- The increased number of older Americans
- The need for flexibility for facilities to accommodate rapidly changing technologies
- Consumer expectations for privacy and family-centered care

Hospital administrators want to meet or exceed consumer expectations. Understanding the patient experience; providing services typically found in hospitality environments; and focusing design and facility maintenance to minimize risk of infection falls, and errors are topics of great interest to the healthcare establishment (Carpenter, 2007).

Ultimately, the objective of great healthcare design is to provide the infrastructure and support to enable healthcare providers to offer excellent medical interventions. The mirrored version is also true—a poorly planned facility can compromise the delivery of quality healthcare. Evidence-based design is a process for the design and construction of healthcare facilities that fosters an environment of care that supports excellence in medicine.

Models of Evidence-Based Design

According to the Centre for Evidence-Based Medicine, "Evidence-based medicine is the conscientious, explicit and judicious use of current best evidence in making decisions about the care of individual patients." The practice of *evidence-based medicine* requires the integration of individual clinical expertise with the best available external clinical evidence from systematic research. The theory behind evidence-based medicine is that one without the other is not enough; the practice of medicine without current research threatens to become obsolete, while without clinical expertise, the practice of medicine controlled by external evidence may be inappropriate for an individual patient. It is the symbiotic relationship that produces the benefit of intelligent practice (CEBM, 2007).

Evidence-based design for healthcare facilities parallels evidence-based medicine in that it combines the best practices from professional experience and project evaluations with the knowledge from research. Professionals involved in the planning, design, and construction of healthcare facilities use the process to develop design solutions that have measurable outcomes. Critical analysis of these outcomes enables them to evaluate the effectiveness of their designs. Social science focuses on strategies to reduce stress by measuring environmental impacts on the patients, families, and staff, including social dynamics; control of the environment (privacy, sound, light, temperature, respite); positive distractions, including art, music, and entertainment; and the influence of nature (plants, water, natural sounds, pet therapy). The medical and scientific literature focuses on models of care quality and safety (hospital-acquired infections, medical errors, and falls) and rehabilitation. From the administrative viewpoint, organizational management focuses on financial performance measures; operational efficiency; and satisfaction of patients, healthcare staff, and visitors (Ulrich & Zimring, 2004).

A conceptual model of evidence-based design, posited by Associate Professor Kirk Hamilton at Texas A&M University College of Architecture, identifies four levels of integration of research into practice (Hamilton, 2004):

1. Practitioners who make a positive effort to design based on available evidence, through the use of design concepts based on reviews of other projects and the interpretations of published research.

2. Practitioners who, based on readings, hypothesize about the expected outcomes of design decisions and then follow through with measuring the results, for example, through the use of post- occupancy evaluations (the evaluation of the performance of a facility that includes the operational aspects of a building and its performance in regard to meeting the objectives of the building user—productivity, comfort, rate of healing, and the retention of employees, just to name a few).

3. Practitioners who employ the strategy from Level 2 but additionally report their findings publicly. The process of review extends the knowledge outside of the firm but also positions the practitioner to be subjected to review and criticism from others who may or may not agree with the findings.

4. Practitioners who follow the research design process—literature review, hypothesizing intended outcomes, measuring results, and reporting the findings. These designers publish their findings in peer-reviewed journals and may collaborate with academic researchers. Their work is subjected to the highest level of rigorous review.

The growing body of evidence shows that the design of the healthcare environment affects the users of the space—staff, patients, and visitors. In addition to measuring levels of satisfaction and preferences of the users, it is well accepted that patient health outcomes can be greatly improved by designing with the knowledge available (Lawson, 2005). The current state of the evidence suggests that design should provide patients with privacy, dignity, and access to loved ones; views to the outside of the building and access to nature; comfort, through control over lighting, noise, and temperature of the immediate environment; and an understanding of how to navigate the building and use methods of positive distraction such as art, nature, and performance (Lawson, 2005). Research focused on environmental impacts and certification programs like LEED (http://www.usgbc.org) and operational issues like life cycle costs and maintenance is a growing area that will lead to a better understanding of the benefits of integration of the building as a system and the model of care for the healthcare organization. While the body of knowledge for healthcare design research is growing, there are many opportunities and directions to pursue to participate in the development of evidence-based design solutions for future healthcare facilities.

Informed Design Examples

The benefit of history is that we can use prior examples to learn processes and evaluate the level of success of prior experiences in learning how to design by utilizing research during predesign and schematic design. The following informed design examples demonstrate how research is applied in practice.

Design Implications for Single-Family NICUs

Designing for healthcare facilities is complex; meeting the functional requirements while addressing the programmatic needs that support the

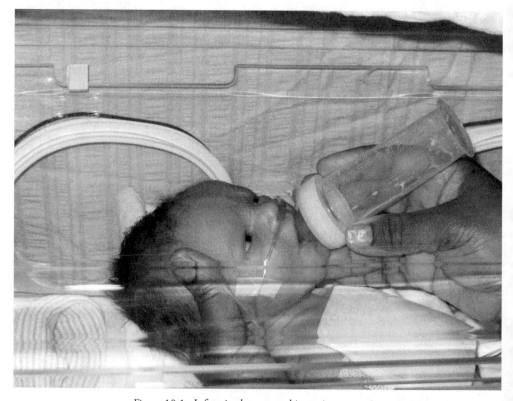

Figure 10.1. Infant in the neonatal intensive care unit.

model of care is complicated by consideration of how the environment affects the patients, healthcare staff, and visitors. This assertion rings most true in the neonatal intensive care unit (see Chapter 6 for another discussion of the design of NICUs). A design trend that is changing the model of care for neonates is the single-family room (SFR), a private patient room for neonates and their families.

Infants are affected directly by their immediate environment and indirectly by the influence the environment has on their caregivers (Harris, Shepley, White, Kolberg & Harrell, 2006). See Figure 10.1. Factors that have contributed to the interest in SFR rooms include the following:

- Increased understanding of the value of breastfeeding and kangaroo-care, the way of holding an infant so that there is skin-to-skin contact between the infant and the person holding him or her (Ferber & Makhoul, 2004)
- The positive impact of developmentally appropriate care on infant outcomes
- The need to reduce nosocomial (hospital-acquired) infections (Ulrich & Zimring, 2004)
- The trend toward all-private-room hospitals
- The documented success of innovative prototypes
- The need to provide patient privacy
- The implementation of the Health Insurance Portability and Accountability Act (HIPAA) (Mathur, 2004)

The Purpose and Methodology of the Study

In 2004, a research study was funded by the Coalition for Health Environments (CHER) to investigate the implications of the SFR NICU (Harris et al., 2006). Does the SFR model provide environmental conditions that support the medical interventions for the neonate? How does it affect healthcare staff? And finally, do the parents of the neonate prefer SFR or one of the more traditional configurations, the open unit?

Eleven hospitals across the United States participated in the study. The methodology included plan reviews, site visits, and post-occupancy evaluations to assess the physical environment and impacts on the users. Construction cost data were evaluated by cost per square foot and cost per infant station. Medical records provided aggregate patient data including average daily census, average length of stay, and other patient medical data. Furthermore, surveys focusing on the preferences and experiences of NICU medical staff and parents were collected from two of the participating facilities; one facility was an SFR NICU and the other was a combination unit with SFRs and open-bay infant stations.

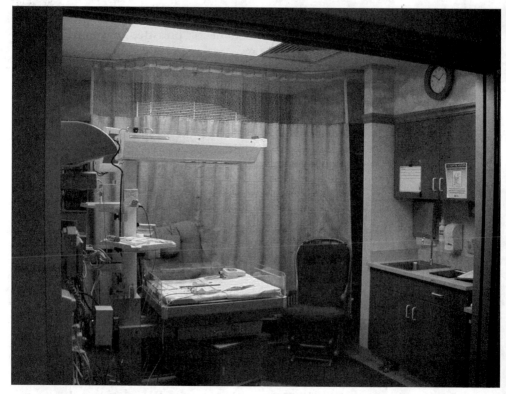

Figure 10.2. Single-family room (SFR) providing control of immediate environment and parent privacy.

Findings

The results of this initial study found that SFR NICU design provides solutions for increasing parent privacy and presence, supporting HIPAA compliance, and minimizing the number of "undesirable beds" (Figure 10.2). Moreover, healthcare staff and parent satisfaction was increased, while self-reported levels of stress of staff were reduced. In addition to these findings, limitations of the SFR design were defined. SFR units limited parent-to-parent social contact and created feelings of isolation of staff and parents. Interestingly, the increase in construction costs was minimal, averaging 3 percent higher for SFR units compared to open-bay units. In the end, the study recommended that SFR units be considered when developing an NICU. If the SFR unit design is not possible, the recommendation is to consider a unit combining infant stations in private rooms and open bay (Harris et al., 2006).

A criticism of design research is that it is often too far removed from practice to be useful to practitioners in applying the results to current and future projects. This research study provided the following guidelines for NICUs with specific guidelines for SFR NICUs (Harris, Shepley & White, 2005):

- Increase the usable space for patients, families, and nursing staff; minimize linear circulation, unless this space is necessary for the movement of equipment or to provide separation between babies to increase privacy.
- Provide both centralized nursing stations and charting areas at or near bedside; these dual options support staff members by providing opportunities for collegial interaction and making independent work areas available at or near bedside.
- Provide decentralized clean supply and support areas to minimize time and distance traveled by nursing staff.
- Increase the number of hand-washing sinks throughout the patient area; for SFR units, provide hand-washing sinks in each SFR and additional easily accessible sinks within the unit. Meeting minimum requirements by providing hand-washing stations within 20 feet of all infant stations may not meet the need for easy access; provide waterless hand cleaners and soaps, and institute an ongoing campaign to direct attention to the importance of hand washing as a part of an effective infection-control strategy.
- Provide natural light in family, patient, and staff areas; these light sources should be fitted with shading devices to control quantity of light.

- Provide a comprehensive patient monitoring and security system that has the flexibility to incorporate technology as needed; current solutions may include a staff locating system, call system, and infant monitoring system.
- Minimize exposure to noise (e.g., staff entry, pneumatic tube depository, equipment storage, door closures, and elevators) and traffic that are located in close proximity to nursing work areas.
- Address visual and auditory privacy within the patient area of the unit; provide partitions or moveable screens for manipulation of unit layout.
- Provide line of sight for nursing staff when possible; if possible, provide a remote camera system for patient observation.
- Minimize parents' and families' visual exposure to medical equipment.
- The provision of single family room units should be seriously considered when creating an NICU; if this is not possible, a combination of both SFR and open-bay units is recommended.
- Regardless of allocated space for family at bedside, design SFR units with family space within the unit for parent-to-parent socialization, education, dining, resting, and respite; additional amenities should include laundry and shower facilities.
- Provide individualized control of environmental conditions, including temperature, artificial light, and daylight.
- Provide enough space to accommodate families who want to stay with their infants by providing a work surface, sitting/sleeping furniture, storage for personal belongings, and additional seating solutions such as recliners and rockers.
- Provide meeting space to support organized activities for parent-to-parent and parent-staff interaction.

Another important source for NICU design is the Recommended Standards for Newborn ICU Design by the Consensus Committee to Establish Recommended Standards for Newborn ICU Design (2006).

Of the 800 or so NICUs in the United States, about 20 hospitals have built SFR NICUs and over 40 hospitals are planning or building SFRs for new or expanded facilities (Hauser, 2007). Healthcare administrators have used the results of the study to justify the decision to pursue SFR design instead of the traditional open-bay design. Architects and interior designers have used the guidelines from the study to implement design elements that exceed minimal recommendations set by the AIA Guidelines to create healthcare environments that support the programmatic function of the unit and the needs of neonates and their caregivers (Figure 10.3). For instance, the recommendation is to increase the number of hand-washing sinks throughout the patient area. While the AIA Guidelines state minimum requirements, the strategy for increasing the number of hand-washing sinks is to provide an environment that supports behaviors that may lessen nosocomial infections, which affect 20 percent of low-birth-weight infants. By reducing the number of nosocomial infections, the amount of time spent in the hospital, the mortality rate, and the cost of care may be reduced, affecting the patients' medical outcomes, the parents' stress and satisfaction, the healthcare staff's stress, and the hospital's bottom line.

Student Research—Spatial Needs for SFR NICU

As the CHER-funded SFR NICU study came to a close, it became apparent that the research really draws attention to the need for further inquiry into the topic of single-family-room NICUs. It has been estimated that SFR NICUs require approximately 650 square feet (SF) per licensed infant station to meet the programmatic needs for patient, staff, and families in the unit (R. D. White, personal communication, Janu-

Figure 10.3. Open-bay nurse work area with privacy partitions for one open station (above); single-family room nurse work area with SFR patient room, door open (below).

ary 26, 2006). Mathur (2004) stated that SFR design did not increase the total space needs of the NICU, suggesting that the SFR configuration may require less circulation than traditional open-bay designs and that there were certain economies of space such as eliminating the parent sleep rooms. The parents were able to stay in the single-family room, instead. The study by Harris and colleagues had indicated that there was about a 2 percent reduction in circulation space compared to open-bay units. In addition, the concern of isolation of staff and parents as well as the documented reduction of parent-to-parent contact had several of the SFR units in the original study questioning whether they should be adding space to provide NICU community programs. Finally, while Mathur's position may reflect a design based on new construction, many hospitals were renovating existing space and were hindered by conditions that inhibited efficient design of a SFR NICU.

Purposes of the Student Research Project

This design question provided an opportunity to bring active research to the classroom. In the fall of 2006, seven senior interior design students at the University of Florida and I proceeded to investigate this question through design, documentation, and program evaluation. The anticipated outcomes of the experience were that students would (1) gain knowledge specific to healthcare design, (2) learn about the value of research within the context of design, and (3) contribute to the growing body of research that translates to practical application. Involving students in healthcare design research contributes to the preparation of future designers to develop creative solutions based on evidence for environments that support family-centered care and healing.

The current literature on the subject of NICU design and, specifically, SFR NICU design was made available to the research team. This included the CHER NICU study, the Recommended Standards for Newborn ICU Design (2006), and the Guidelines for Design and Construction of Hospital and Health Care Facilities (AIA Guidelines, 2006).

The AIA Guidelines call for 120 SF of clear floor area per infant station, excluding sinks and aisles, and in the design of single-patient rooms, an adjacent aisle of not less than 8 linear feet in width to permit the passage of equipment and personnel. The Recommended Standards for Newborn ICU Design (Committee to Establish Recommended Standards for Newborn ICU Design, 2006) states that the configuration of the NICU should "individualize the care-giving environment and services for each infant and family." This recommended standard reconciles with the AIA Guidelines for minimum space, clearance, and privacy requirements for the NICU unit.

Methodology of the Students' Research

Four existing hospital non-SFR NICU units were utilized to test the assumption that SFR NICU design does not require increased area to accommodate the same number of infant stations and meet the programmatic needs of patients, families, and staff. Using the existing program, the research team redesigned the units as a single-family-room NICUs.

The plan analysis for each NICU involved measuring total square feet of the unit and categorizing every room into one of six general categories for allocation of space: patient, family, staff, public, systems, and unit circulation. A spreadsheet documented all measurements including total SF, individual room SF, circulation, and the net to gross factor (unusable SF). Diagrams were developed for each participating hospital, and aggregate data identified the circulation patterns and user zones for each setting (Figure 10.4). The data were then compared to the existing unit data to evaluate the differences in the unit space allocations and number of infant stations designed for the SFR NICU configuration. The diagrams show the space allocation and unit organization as well as circulation. Descriptive statistics are used to express the values of space allocation within each unit plan and across unit plans.

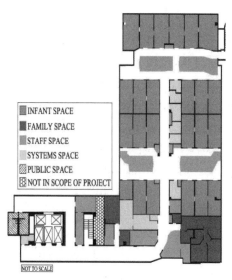

INFANT SPACE
FAMILY SPACE
STAFF SPACE
SYSTEMS SPACE
PUBLIC SPACE
NOT IN SCOPE OF PROJECT

NOT TO SCALE

NICU Double Occupancy
16,337 Total Square Feet
48 Licensed Beds

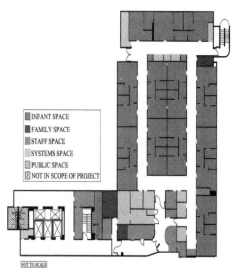

INFANT SPACE
FAMILY SPACE
STAFF SPACE
SYSTEMS SPACE
PUBLIC SPACE
NOT IN SCOPE OF PROJECT

NOT TO SCALE

NICU SFR Design Test
16,337 Total Square Feet
21 Licensed Beds

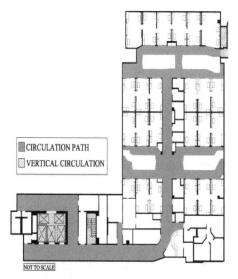

CIRCULATION PATH
VERTICAL CIRCULATION

NOT TO SCALE

NICU Double Occupancy
27% Unit Circulation

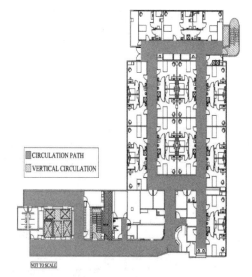

CIRCULATION PATH
VERTICAL CIRCULATION

NOT TO SCALE

NICU Double Occupancy
30% Unit Circulation

Figure 10.4. Example diagrams of NICU allocated space by defined category and unit circulation.

Findings of the Students' Research

Table 10.1 shows the total square feet for each NICU and the type of existing unit configuration, the number of licensed beds, average infant area, and the unit SF per licensed bed based on unit configuration. All unit SFR design test plans exceeded the estimated SF need of 650 SF per licensed infant station. The number of licensed beds per unit decreased in all four SFR design test sites. Table 10.2 focuses on comparing the existing space allocations for patient, family, and healthcare staff of the original NICU with the SFR design test. In addition to user group categories, the table shows unit circulation and net-to-gross factor for each unit.

NICU 1, an existing combination unit, had 35 licensed beds with an average infant area of 109 SF. The SFR design test layout accommodated 17 licensed beds with an average of 244 SF. Average unit SF per infant station increased 51 percent; space allocated to patients increased 2 percent while family and staff space decreased by 3 percent and 14 percent, respectively. Unit circulation increased 5 percent. Based on the estimated need for 200 SF, this unit may have accommodated up to 24 SFR patient rooms.

Table 10.1. Sizes and Unit Configurations of NICUs

Unit Code	Unit Square Feet (SF)	Unit Configuration	Unit SF per Licensed Bed	Avg. Infant Area	No. Licensed Beds
NICU 1	15,682	Combination	448	109	35
		SFR Design Test	922	244	17
NICU 2	16,337	Double Occupancy	340	111	48
		SFR Design Test	778	319	21
NICU 3	20,519	Open Bay	456	111	45
		SFR Design Test	977	309	21
NICU 4	10,871	Open Bay	544	115	20
		SFR Design Test	776	199	14

Table 10.2. Comparison of Current Unit Configurations and SFR Designs

Unit Code	Unit Configuration	Patient (%)	Family (%)	Staff (%)	Unit Circ. (%)	Net to Gross Factor (%)	Balance* (%)	Total (%)
NICU 1	Combination	24	7	38	21	7	3	100
	SFR Design Test	26	4	24	36	7	3	100
NICU 2	Double Occupancy	33	7	17	27	9	8	100
	SFR Design Test	40	2	8	30	12	8	100
NICU 3	Open Bay	24	10	19	30	10	7	100
	SFR Design Test	31	11	16	26	8	8	100
NICU 4	Open Bay	21	11	33	22	12	1	100
	SFR Design Test	26	8	25	24	9	8	100

* Balance includes public space, building and medical systems, and vertical circulation.

NICU 2, an existing double occupancy unit, had 48 licensed beds with an average infant area of 111 SF. The SFR test layout produced only 21 licensed beds with an average of 319 SF. Average unit SF per infant station increased 56 percent. Space allocated to patients increased 7 percent while family and staff space decreased 5 percent and 9 percent, respectively. Unit circulation increased 3 percent. Based on the estimated need for 200 SF, this unit may have accommodated up to 25 patient rooms.

NICU 3, an existing open-bay unit, had 45 licensed beds with an average of 111 SF. The SFR test layout provided for 21 licensed beds with an average of 309 SF for the patient room. Average unit SF per infant station increased 53 percent. Space allocated to patients increased by 7 percent; family space increased 1 percent; and healthcare staff space decreased 3 percent. Unit circulation decreased 4 percent. Based on the estimated need for 200 SF, this unit may have accommodated up to 32 patient rooms.

NICU 4 was also an existing open-bay unit with 20 licensed beds and an average patient area of 115 SF. The SFR test layout accommodated 14 beds with an average of 199 SF for the patient room. Average unit SF per infant station increased 30 percent. Space allocated to patients increased 5 percent while family and healthcare staff space decreased 3 percent and 8 percent, respectively. Unit circulation increased 2 percent. Based on the estimated need for 200 SF, this unit may have accommodated up to 17 patient rooms.

Each of the four NICU test plans presents a unique set of existing conditions that influences the design outcome for a SFR plan. Because of variability in the existing conditions and limitations of the building configuration, all four units were unable to sustain the original number of licensed beds, contradicting the premise that the design of single-family-room NICUs did not require more space than traditional units. Another assertion was that SFR NICU configuration requires less circulation than other types of unit configurations. This study shows that only 1 of the 4 SFR Design Tests managed to reduce circulation within the unit. The other 3 SFR Design Tests incurred an increase of unit circulation ranging from 2 percent to 15 percent. Nonusable square feet remained the same or decreased in three of the four unit designs, indicating that existing conditions of a hospital renovation site may influence the plan efficiency more than the perceived increase in nonusable square feet. This study utilized four NICU plans, limiting the potential to generalize the findings owing to small sample size. It is recommended that future studies compare new facility and existing facility design of SFR NICUs to compare space allocations and limitations of implementing the SFR NICU design.

The main research question for this investigation was whether more space was required to maintain the same number of licensed infant stations for SFR NICUs. None of the four unit designs were able to sustain the same number of licensed beds, indicating that limitations of the unit layout may limit the efficiency of the design. With further examination, through a comparison with new unit design, research may show that Mathur's theory that SFR design did not increase the total space needs of the NICU is correct when designing a new facility. How can this information be translated to practical application? Clearly, caution must be exercised when designing a SFR NICU in an existing facility with preexisting conditions. Perhaps, by utilizing the results from the CHER study, a design that provides a combination of open-bay and single-family rooms may provide the best overall environment of care. In the design of a new hospital, a design similar to other single patient room units may provide the outcomes in terms of space allocation and the number of square feet per infant station needed to justify the design.

Pedagogical Value of the Students' Research

In addition to the expectations for the student research team previously mentioned, the research project was successful as a teaching tool. Student researchers used existing research-based design guidelines to develop new designs of single-family-room NICUs, which were tested against the literature to evaluate space allocations in existing acute care facilities.

Evidence-based studio assignments and student research team investigations of design research are exciting for the students and the instructor. For the student preparing to enter the professional realm of design, the experience provides an opportunity to gain expertise in a specialty of design. Furthermore, the student researchers gained knowledge in the process of research and learned how to implement evidence-based design recommendations. Finally, through participation in critical evaluation—of the literature, the designs generated for the study, and the findings—the students became aware of the important role of research in practice. This student-driven research project was presented at the IDEC International Conference (2006) as a poster presentation and published in the conference proceedings.

Resources for Healthcare Design Research

Awareness of the relevant resources for healthcare design research is important, as it is the baseline level of knowledge expected by the industry. The following resources are used by the profession and are easily accessible to students interested in furthering their knowledge of healthcare design issues.

Additional Resources for NICU Design

The research related to healthcare design and, specifically, SFR NICU design is growing. It is important to note that relevant literature may be found in design, medicine, nursing, social science, and scientific journals. In addition to peer-review published literature, studies may be published by the funding organization. Besides research studies, guidelines and recommendations may be available through independent organizations. The AIA Guidelines (2006) is available through the American Institute of Architects and is generally adopted by municipalities, making it an addendum to the building code. The Recommended Standards for Newborn ICU Design (2006) is available online and is developed by a multidisciplinary committee focused solely on NICUs.

A small book that, in this author's opinion, contains a large amount of practical design information specific to healthcare design is Kliment's (2002) *Building Type Basics for Healthcare Facilities*. This text provides relevant healthcare design information on organizational theory and hospital programming showing diagrammatic relationships and specific functional needs by department. Another book that provides evidence-based design guidelines is *Healthcare Environments for Children and Their Families* (1998) by Shepley, Fournier, and McDougal.

Another important hospital topic involves medical errors. Medical errors encompass a variety of factors in addition to what one may consider a medical error. For instance, it includes hospital-acquired infections as well as falls. Finally, *The AIA Academy Journal* published an article on research-based environments for the NICU (Williams & Burger, 1998), a case study that uses post-occupancy data to tell the story of the process and outcomes of evidence-based design for the NICU.

In addition to journals and published guidelines for research and the design of healthcare facilities, Web-based resources such as the Center for Health Design (http://www.healthdesign.org) and InformeDesign (http://www.informedesign.umn.edu/) provide access to research studies, white papers, and a community of healthcare designers and researchers willing to provide insight and opinion based on their expertise. The Center for Health Design Pebble Project is a collaborative consisting of hospital partners, researchers, and design professionals who have joined together for the purpose of providing assistance and support for healthcare facilities as they develop and execute new construction projects focused on creating facilities utilizing research-based design strategies. Finally, a post-professional accrediting organization called the American Academy of Healthcare Interior Designers provide an exchange of information and would be happy to assist interested students with their interests in healthcare interior design. This organization also has a graduate research fellowship for those studying healthcare interior design.

Translating the Literature for Practical Application

In review of the literature, it is important to understand the research question or hypothesis, the methods employed for discovery, and how to apply the recommendations that come from the results. The research question or hypothesis explains the rationale for the study and provides indicators of valid methodologies for investigating the topic. The CHER-funded SFR NICU research study had multiple hypothesis, attempting to posit a comprehensive set of research questions based on the potential impacts of the physical environment. The methodology may be quantitative, qualitative, or multi-method. The CHER NICU study was a multi-method research design that focused on the hypotheses presented. The student research team study focusing on whether the redesign of a NICU is as efficient when designed as a single-family-room design had one primary research hypotheses and utilized a quantitative method of analyzing design criteria through plan reviews. The findings are straightforward, and the publication provides the reader with discussion of the findings that can be extended into design recommendations.

BIBLIOGRAPHY

The American Institute of Architects Academy of Architecture for Health. (2006). Guidelines for design and construction of hospital and healthcare facilities. Washington, DC: The Facilities Guidelines Institute, with assistance from the U.S. Department of Health and Human Services.

Carpenter, D. (2007). Behind the boom. Health Forum. Retrieved on September 16, 2007, from http://www.hfmmagazine.com

CEBM. (2007). Introduction to evidence-based medicine. Centre for Evidence-Based Medicine. Retrieved on September 16, 2007, from http://www.cebm.net

Committee to Establish Recommended standards for Newborn ICU Design. (2006). Recommended Standards for Newborn ICU Design. Report of the Sixth Consensus Conference on Newborn ICU Design. Retrieved on September 25, 2006, from http://www.nd.edu/~nicudes/

Ferber, S.G. & Makhoul, I.R. (2004). The effect of skin-to-skin contact (kangaroo care) shortly after birth on the neurobehavioral responses of the term newborn: A randomized controlled trial. *Pediatrics, 113*(4), 858–865.

Harris, D., Shepley, M., and White, R. (2005). *NICU environmental design research: The impact of single family rooms on patients, families, and healthcare workers.* The Coalition for Health Environments Research.

Harris, D., Shepley, M., White, R. Kolberg, K., & Harrell, J. (2006). The impact of single family room design on patients and caregivers: Executive summary. *J. of Perinatology* (in press), 1–11.

Haughey, J. (2006). Nonresidential construction growth continues in '07. Building Design and Construction. Retrieved from Reed Business Information Web site on September 16, 2007, from http://www.bdcnetwork.com

Hauser, C. (2007, May 29). For the tiniest babies, the closest thing to a cocoon. *The New York Times.* Retrieved June 15, 2007, from http://www.nytimes.com

Kliment, S. A. (2002). *Building type basics for healthcare facilities.* New York: John Wiley & Sons.

Lawson, B. (2005). Evidence-based design for healthcare. *Hospital Engineering & Facility Management, 2,* 25–27.

Mathur, N. S. (2004). A single-room NICU: The next generation evolution in the design of neonatal intensive care units. Retrieved from the AIA Web site on November l2, 2004, from http://www.aia.org/aah_a_jrnl_0401_article3

Medical Construction & Design. (2007). Retrieved February 29, 2008, from http://www.mcdmag.com/

Moon, S. (2005). Construction—and costs—Going up. *Modern Healthcare, 35*(10), 30–42.

Shepley, M. M., Fournier, M. A., & McDougal, K. W. (1998). *Healthcare Environments for Children and Their Families.* Dubuque, IO: Dendall/Hunt Publishing Company.

Turner. (2007). Retrieved from the Turner Construction Company Web site on September 14,2007, from http://www.turnerconstruction.com

Ulrich, R. & Zimring, C. (2004). *The role of the physical environment in the hospital of the 21st century: A once-in-a-lifetime opportunity.* San Francisco: The Center for Health Design.

Williams, S. T. & Burger, C. A. (1998). A research-based environment: A NICU that feels like home. *The Academy Journal.* Washington, DC: The American Institute of Architects.

About the Contributors

Lori A. Anthony, M.S.   *Author of Chapter 9*

Lori A. Anthony is currently director of the interior architecture programs at Chatham University in Pittsburgh. She joined Chatham after serving as department chair and assistant professor of interior design at La Roche College. She earned a Master of Science degree in interior design from Virginia Tech and a Bachelor of Science degree in interior design from Seton Hill University. She has 16 years' experience as an interior design practitioner specializing in corporate environments. Ms. Anthony is currently serving as a site visiting team chair for the Council of Interior Design Accreditation and is the ASID President for the PA West Chapter.

Joan Dickinson, Ph.D.   *Coeditor of the text*
Coauthor of Chapter 1
Author of Chapters 2 and 8

Joan Dickinson is an assistant professor of interior design at Radford University. Her research areas include design theory and research, environments for older individuals, nursing home design, and healthcare design. She received her bachelor's and master's degrees in interior design from Virginia Tech, where she specialized in gerontology during her advanced studies. She received her Ph.D. from Texas Tech University and focused on how the interior environment can influence falling among older individuals. Prior to receiving her advanced degrees, she worked as a practicing designer for over 10 years and passed the NCIDQ exam. Dr. Dickinson has published numerous articles in a variety of journals including *The Journal of Interior Design*, *The Gerontologist*, *Environment and Behavior*, and *Housing and Society*.

Debra D. Harris, Ph.D., AAHID   *Author of Chapter 10*

Debra D. Harris is a principal of RAD Consultants, a research and strategic firm located in Austin, Texas. She holds a Ph.D. from Texas A&M University in Architecture, a Master of Interior Architecture from the University of Oregon and a Bachelor of Science from Texas State University. She is a founding member and serves as the director of research for the American Association of Healthcare Interior Designers. Dr. Harris currently serves on the Center for Health Design Research Advisory Board, and the Greenguard Environmental Institute Advisory Board. She is a consultant with more than 20 years of practice, specializing in healthcare facility design, assimilating research into evidence-based strategies, and environmental forensics. Her publications focus on factors affecting patients, families, and healthcare workers including patient outcomes, infection control and transmission, healthcare staff retention, and cost implications of the physical environment.

Stephanie Heher, M.S.   *Coauthor of Chapter 5*

Stephanie Heher is an instructor in the Interior Design Department at Mercyhurst College located in Erie, Pennsylvania. Stephanie received a Bachelor of Science in Family and Consumer Science (Interior Design Concentration) from Mercyhurst and a Master of Science in Interior Architecture from Chatham University in Pittsburgh, Pennsylvania. Stephanie worked as a space planner/designer for National City Bank in Cleveland, Ohio prior to obtaining her graduate degree. Her master's thesis research was based in retail and specifically focused on design trends in the supermarket industry.

Erik Lucken   *Coauthor of Chapter 4*

Erik Lucken is the global communications manager for Gensler's work-place practice. In this role, he provides strategic and creative direction in support of Gensler's position as the world's leading designer of work environments. Mr. Lucken leads knowledge management efforts, including the capture and synthesis of ideas and experience generated across the firm's 32 offices worldwide. He holds a Master of Architecture degree from Iowa State University.

John P. Marsden, Ph.D.   *Coeditor of the text*
                                           Coauthor of Chapters 1 and 5

John P. Marsden is Provost and Vice President for Academic Affairs at Mount Mercy College in Cedar Rapids, IA. Prior to joining Mount Mercy College, he served as the Division Chair of Arts and Design and founding Director of the Interior Architecture program at Chatham University, was a faculty member at the University of Florida and Auburn University, and practiced in architecture firms. He holds a Ph.D. and Master of Science from the University of Michigan, a Master of Architecture and Graduate Certificate in Gerontology from the University of Arizona, and a Bachelor of Architecture from Carnegie Mellon University. He is the coauthor of two books on dementia care settings and is the author of *Humanistic Design of Assisted Living*, which was published by the Johns Hopkins University Press. In addition, he is on the review board for the *Journal of Housing for the Elderly* and the *Journal of Interior Design*.

Anna Marshall-Baker, Ph.D.   *Author of Chapter 6*

Anna Marshall-Baker teaches Interior Architecture at the University of North Carolina at Greensboro, focusing on sustainability and reciprocal effects of environments and human development. She is a former president of the Interior Design Educators Council and currently serves as the coordinator of the Center for Sustainability and co-chair of the

University Committee on Sustainability at UNCG and as a member of the Recommended Standards Consensus Committee for Newborn Intensive Care Unit Design. She received her bachelor's degree in art from Longwood University and her master's degree in interior design and Ph.D. in psychology from Virginia Tech. She regularly presents her work at design and medical conferences and has published in journals such as *The Gerontologist*, *Journal of Interior Design*, *Journal of Perinatal and Neonatal Nursing*, and *The Journal of Perinatology*.

Heather Modzelewski, LEED AP   *Coauthor of Chapter 4*

Heather Modzelewski is an analyst in the Washington, DC, Consulting Studio at Gensler, where she is primarily responsible for the facilitation of client visioning and working sessions and the communication of the resulting analyses. Ms. Modzelewski received a five-year professional degree in landscape architecture from Clemson University and her Master of Mass Communication/Journalism degree from the University of Georgia. Her current projects include site observation, visioning, and recommendations for the Crystal City Business Improvement District's revitalization efforts, and in-depth interviews and focus group discussions resulting in a best practices guide for the Administrative Office of the US Courts.

Marilyn Read, Ph.D.   *Author of Chapter 7*

Marilyn Read is an associate professor of interior design at Oregon State University. She was an associate professor and coordinator of the interior design program at Auburn University. She received her Ph.D. at Oregon State University in Human Behavior in the Near Environment. Her research is concerned with the relationship between the physical design of child development centers and children's behavior and perceptions. Her research has been published *in Environment and Behavior*, the *Early Childhood Education Journal*, and the *Journal of Interior Design*.

Elizabeth Riordan, LEED AP *Coauthor of Chapter 4*

Elizabeth Riordan is a senior associate at Gensler, a global design firm whose mission is to create design that empowers people and transforms organizations. Based in the Washington, DC, office, Ms. Riordan directs the Consulting Studio, where she is primarily responsible for developing workplace strategy engagements with a wide variety of public and private sector clients in the Southeast United States. Ms. Riordan received her bachelor's degree from the University of Virginia and her Master of Business Administration degree from the Darden School at the University of Virginia, where she concentrated on corporate strategy and organizational behavior. Her current projects include the development of Gensler's Workplace Performance Index, a proprietary pre- and post-occupancy assessment tool that provides clients with comparative internal data as well as industry and marketplace best practices as a diagnostic and educational tool.

Lisa Tucker, Ph.D. *Author of Chapter 3*

Lisa Tucker is an assistant professor of interior design at Virginia Tech. Her research is concerned with the intersections between sustainability and historic preservation. She earned her bachelor's degree in architecture, a Master of Architectural History degree from the University of Virginia, and has a Ph.D. in Architectural Studies from the University of Missouri. She holds a certificate of Historic Preservation from the University of Virginia and has done post-graduate work at the University of Missouri in the Department of Architectural Studies, where she is currently a doctoral candidate. Ms. Tucker is a licensed architect and certified interior designer in Virginia and is currently working on a book for designers about sustainable building systems.

Credits

Chapter 1

Figure 1.1:   © Bettmann/CORBIS

Figure 1.3:   © Bettmann/CORBIS

Chapter 2

Figure 2.1:   Drawn by Joan Dickinson.

Figure 2.2:   Drawn by Joan Dickinson.

Chapter 3

Figure 3.1:   Courtesy of Lisa Tucker.

Figure 3.2:   Courtesy of Lisa Tucker.

Figure 3.3:   Courtesy of Lisa Tucker.

Figure 3.4:   Courtesy of Lisa Tucker.

Figure 3.5:   Courtesy of Lisa Tucker.

Figure 3.6:   Courtesy of Lisa Tucker.

Figure 3.7:   Courtesy of Lisa Tucker.

Figure 3.8:   Courtesy of Lisa Tucker.

Figure 3.9:   Courtesy of Lisa Tucker.

Figure 3.10:   Courtesy of Lisa Tucker.

Figure 3.11:   Drawn by Lisa Tucker.

Figure 3.12:   Drawn by Lisa Tucker.

Chapter 4

Figure 4.1:   Courtesy of Gensler and Associates.
Figure 4.2:   Courtesy of Gensler and Associates.
Figure 4.3:   Courtesy of Gensler and Associates.
Figure 4.4:   Courtesy of Gensler and Associates.
Figure 4.5:   Courtesy of Gensler and Associates.
Figure 4.6:   Courtesy of Gensler and Associates.
Figure 4.7:   Courtesy of Gensler and Associates.
Figure 4.8:   Courtesy of Gensler and Associates.
Figure 4.9:   Courtesy of Gensler and Associates.
Figure 4.10:   Courtesy of Gensler and Associates.

Chapter 5

Figure 5.1:   Courtesy of The Kroger Company.
Figure 5.2:   Courtesy of The Kroger Company.
Figure 5.3:   Courtesy of The Kroger Company.
Figure 5.4:   Courtesy of The Kroger Company.
Figure 5.5:   Courtesy of The Kroger Company.
Figure 5.6:   Courtesy of The Kroger Company.
Figure 5.7:   Courtesy of The Kroger Company.
Figure 5.8:   Courtesy of The Kroger Company.
Figure 5.9:   Courtesy of The Kroger Company.

Chapter 6

Figure 6.1:   Courtesy of Lippencott Williams & Williams.
Figure 6.2:   Courtesy of the Journal of Pediatrics.
Figure 6.3:   Courtesy of the Journal of Perinatology.
Figure 6.4:   Courtesy of Robert D. White, MD.
Figure 6.5:   Courtesy of Robert D. White, MD.
Figure 6.6:   Courtesy of Anna Marshall-Baker.
Figures 6.7:   Courtesy of Kristi Ennis.
Figure 6.8:   Courtesy of Anna Marshall-Baker.
Figure 6.9:   Courtesy of Kristi Ennis.
Figure 6.10:   Courtesy of Lynne Wilson-Orr.
Figure 6.11:   Courtesy of Lynne Wilson-Orr.

Chapter 7

Figure 7.2:	Courtesy of Marilyn Read.
Figure 7.3:	Courtesy of Marilyn Read.
Figure 7.4:	Courtesy of Marilyn Read.
Figure 7.5:	Courtesy of Marilyn Read.
Figure 7.6:	Drawn by Reade Northup.
Figure 7.7:	Drawn by Reade Northup.
Figure 7.8:	Drawn by J. Davis Harte.
Figure 7.9:	Drawn by J. Davis Harte.
Figure 7.10:	Drawn by Robin Freeburn.
Figure 7.11:	Drawn by Ellen Anderson.
Figure 7.12:	Drawn by Justine Dawson.
Figure 7.13:	Courtesy of Justine Dawson.

Chapter 8

Figure 8.1:	Courtesy of Joan Dickinson.
Figure 8.2:	Courtesy of Joan Dickinson.
Figure 8.3:	Courtesy of Joan Dickinson.
Figure 8.4:	Michael Mahovlich/Masterfile www.masterfile.com
Figure 8.5:	Courtesy of *The Gerontologist*.
Figure 8.6:	Courtesy of *The Gerontologist*.
Figure 8.7:	Courtesy of Joan Dickinson.
Figure 8.8:	Courtesy of the *Journal of Interior Design*.
Figure 8.9:	Courtesy of the *Journal of Interior Design*.
Figure 8.10:	Courtesy of the *Journal of Interior Design*.
Figure 8.11:	Courtesy of the *Journal of Interior Design*.
Figure 8.12:	Courtesy of the *Journal of Interior Design*.

Chapter 9

Figure 9.1:	Drawn by C. McLaughlin.
Figure 9.2:	Drawn by C. McLaughlin.
Figure 9.3:	Drawn by C. McLaughlin.
Figure 9.4:	Drawn by T. Hill.
Figure 9.5:	Drawn by E. Becker.

Chapter 10

Index